PLAYING PRESIDENT

PLAYING PRESIDENT

*My Close Encounters with Nixon, Carter,
Bush I, Reagan, and Clinton—and How They
Did Not Prepare Me for George W. Bush*

by ROBERT SCHEER

WWW.TRUTHDIG.COM
LOS ANGELES

AKASHIC BOOKS
NEW YORK

Published by Akashic Books
A Truthdig Book
©2006 Robert Scheer

ISBN-13: 978-1-933354-01-9
ISBN-10: 1-933354-01-1
Library of Congress Control Number: 2005934821

First printing
Printed in Canada

Akashic Books
PO Box 1456
New York, NY 10009
Akashic7@aol.com
www.akashicbooks.com

Grateful acknowledgment is made to the following for permission to reprint previously published material:

Los Angeles Times: "Nixon: Scorn Yielding to New Respect" by Robert Scheer, March 8, 1984; "U.S.-Soviet 'Star War' Studies Urged by Nixon" by Robert Scheer, July 1, 1984; "Bush Assails Carter Defense Strategy" by Robert Scheer, January 24, 1980; "Clinton Sketches Scenarios for Easing Urban Problems" by Robert Scheer, May 31, 1992. Copyright ©1980, 1984, 1984, 1992 *Los Angeles Times.* Reprinted with permission.

Playboy magazine: interview with Jimmy Carter by Robert Scheer, November 1976; "Jimmy, We Hardly Know Y'all" by Robert Scheer, November 1976; photograph by Ken Hawkins of Robert Scheer and Jimmy Carter on the back cover and page 96. Copyright ©1976 *Playboy.* Reprinted by special permission.

To my wife Narda and sons
Christopher, Joshua, and Peter:
my best editors, critics, and friends

TABLE OF CONTENTS

Foreword by Gore Vidal   9
Author's Introduction   15

Richard Nixon's Frozen Smile   19
    LETTER FROM NIXON TO SCHEER   22
    NIXON RETROSPECTIVE   23
    INTERVIEW WITH RICHARD NIXON   37

Jimmy Carter's Lustful Heart   49
    INTERVIEW WITH JIMMY CARTER   56
    LETTER FROM CARTER TO SCHEER   57
    JIMMY, WE HARDLY KNOW Y'ALL   99

Ronald Reagan's Obscure Complexity   133
    LETTER FROM NANCY REAGAN TO SCHEER   138
    PROFILE AND INTERVIEW WITH RONALD REAGAN 139

George H.W. Bush's Entitlement Cool   173
    INTERVIEW WITH GEORGE H.W. BUSH   180

Bill Clinton's Rascal Component   197
    LETTER #1 FROM CLINTON TO SCHEER   203
    LETTER #2 FROM CLINTON TO SCHEER   205
    INTERVIEW WITH BILL CLINTON   209
    COLUMNS 1996–2000   224

George W. Bush's Perpetual Adolescence   233
    COLUMNS 2000–2006   238

FOREWORD
by Gore Vidal

T
HE TWENTIETH CENTURY PRODUCED A GREAT DEAL OF
writing about American politics, much of it bewil-
dered when new notions like *empire* started to sneak
into nervous texts whose authors were not quite certain if
"empire" could ever be an applicable word for the last best
hope of earth.

The bidding then changed dramatically after World War
Two, when Harry Truman armed us with nuclear weapons and
gave us an icy sort of permanent war against Godless Atheistic
communism, as personified by Joseph Stalin, standing in for
Hitler, whom we had got rid of with rather more help than we
liked to admit from the new world demon Stalin. How, why
did Truman lock us all into a national security state, armed to
the teeth? The simple story was dread of communism everywhere on the march, but those of us who had served in World
War Two knew as well as our political leaders that the Soviet
Union, as of 1950, was not going anywhere very soon: They
had lost twenty million people. They wanted, touchingly, to
be like us, with consumer goods and all the rest of it.

What actually happened was tragic for the Russian people and their buffer states: Truman, guided by that brilliant
lawyer Dean Acheson, was quite aware that by 1940 the
world Depression of the early '30s had returned. The New
Deal of Franklin Roosevelt had largely failed. What was to be

done? FDR took a crash course in Keynesian economics. As a result, he invested $8 billion into re-arming the United States, in order to hold our own against the Fascist axis of Germany, Japan, Italy. To the astonishment of Roosevelt's conservative political enemies, the U.S. suddenly had full employment for the work force and a military machine of the first rank with which we were able to defeat Fascism, and just about anyone else who defied us.

Truman and friends learned and never forgot an important lesson: It was through war and a militarized economy that we became prosperous with full employment. After victory in Europe and the Pacific, Truman himself began to play the war drums. Stalin was menacing Turkey and Greece (Acheson threw in nearby Italy, and why not France?). We must stop the rising Red tide, while acquiring that era's latest propaganda toy, a TV set. This wearisome background was well known to historians like William Appleman Williams, but hardly suspected by too many of the usual publicists of the American way of life.

Robert Scheer has had the good fortune to observe firsthand the last half-dozen Presidents, from Nixon to "W". He has also had the perseverance as a journalist to insist that he be able to conduct one-on-one conversations with the odd sort of men who were playing (or trying to play) President. This makes for a fascinating immediacy in the book at hand, particularly when he is giving his protagonists a harder time than they had expected. Scheer has always suspected that he would be one of the last journalists able to use the print medium fully in the electronic age that had dawned around 1960.

Scheer makes a telling analysis of Nixon and his "frozen smile," with the comment that "despite being unquestionably the best prepared of all modern Presidents before assuming office, it was his indelibly awkward and secretive style that did him in." Scheer is impressed by this President's mind despite himself, as was Walter Lippmann, whom I once teased for supporting Nixon. Walter was serene: "I only know," he said, "if I had a difficult lawsuit on my hands, I would go to him as a lawyer. He presents you an entire case before your eyes: He is simply brilliant, unique in public life."

Print journalism is a challenge to the writer's intelligence, as well as to that of his subject. Of course, few journalists and player Presidents are up to Scheer and Nixon. Yes, Nixon did much that was evil along the way (Cambodia, Watergate), but he usually managed to harm himself most— a form of good manners. He was primarily interested in foreign affairs and the opening up to China; *détente* with the Soviets; these were significant achievements, and he had no strong domestic policies, which should have been a great relief for Us the People. No wartime tax breaks for cronies is quite enough for us to applaud him in other roles.

Presidents are trapped in history as well as in their own DNA codes. After Watergate, Nixon starred as Coriolanus for a while, but when he saw that this got him nowhere, he realized he was so steeped in blood that he could not turn back, so he went on as Macbeth, to our benefit at times. Scheer is not the first of our journalists to recognize how like classical players the Presidents tend to be if they have the right war or disaster to contend with. Scheer is generally good-humored about them, though Bush I's implacable self-love seems to rub him the wrong way; also, Reagan's rambling does not get either of them very far, yet Scheer has grasped what few others have: Mrs. Reagan's importance not only to her somewhat listless husband but to our country, where she seems to have understood before other politicians that the Cold War was getting us nowhere.

Scheer had problems with Jimmy Carter and, perhaps, with Southern politicians in general. He struggled with the man's compulsive fibbing about himself and his place in an imaginary Plains, Georgia, which kept changing to fit his restless re-imagining of his career, recalling homely barbershop quartets as well as killer rabbits at large in catfish ponds. Scheer had an edgy time with Carter, but it was to Scheer that Carter confessed he had lusted in his heart for ladies, causing much of the nation to admire and smirk.

Scheer concedes Clinton's brilliance as a player but frets over (as many of us did) "the end of welfare as we know it." It is with this President that Scheer is most interesting, largely because Clinton is as intelligent as he, at least on the subjects they discuss. Clinton has dared occasionally to touch the third rail of American political discourse: the superiority of other nations' economies to that of America the Beautiful and the Earmarked.

SCHEER Some now blame the Europeans and Japanese for our problems and call for protectionism. Are you sympathetic to such calls?

CLINTON . . . But to be fair, the biggest problems we have in maintaining the manufacturing base are our failures to work together to achieve high levels of productivity, to control health care costs, to have a tax system which is pro-manufacturing. Our tax system now is anti-manufacturing. And it was during the Reagan/Bush years. I think, you know, it rewarded money making money and not production, not jobs, not goods, and not services.

SCHEER Well, that's what we say now. But when the last tax-reform package was passed, many Democrats supported it. It was supposed to help production.

CLINTON I never thought it would . . . You know, the elemental principle of taxation should be [that] people should pay according to their abilities to pay. And you should have incentives that do specific things. Those ought to be the two driving, in my view, principles of the tax system.

This is very grown-up stuff.

The final chapter, perhaps in every sense, deals with George W. Bush. Scheer confesses he was ill-prepared for someone who seems to have no idea of, or interest in, playing President, as opposed to playing "Wartime President," easily the trick of the week when Congress has modestly declined to declare war on anyone.

Certainly, with these observations on a section of our history, Scheer joins that small group of journalist-historians that includes Richard Rovere, Murray Kempton, and Walter Lippmann.

INTRODUCTION

P LAYING PRESIDENT IS NOT A BOOK TITLE SELECTED casually, but a distilled opinion gleaned over forty years of journalism, covering our most important democratic exercise. After decades spent interviewing dozens of leading presidential candidates, including those who ended up in the highest office, I came to the conclusion that the process endured in obtaining electoral power tends to be the controlling influence on the candidate's behavior once in office.

As sailors like to say, the journey is the destination, and for politicians with presidential aspirations, the experience of running for one office after another until they obtain the final prize informs as well as *de*forms their conduct. The problem is that in our system, as opposed to a parliamentary one, the presidential candidate's performance is a solo act. The basic test is not that of a leader emerging from a pack made up of peers; instead, it revolves around a performer and a largely untutored electorate that is his jury and his audience.

Whereas a parliamentary leader is pushed by the process of selection to grow in ways that are positive to governance, with policy substance stressed over rhetorical style, in the American presidential system, the electoral process stupefies rather than educates, undermining—indeed, *assaulting*—the capacity of the politician to consider public policy in ways that are truly thoughtful. In the uniquely grueling and essentially mindless process of our system, serious issues become little more than grist for the pollsters' mills, and substantive alternatives are reduced to slogans to be bandied about for electoral convenience and television sound-bite advertising.

I'm certain that this last sentiment will elicit a stridently defensive response from those who celebrate what they perceive as the rough-and-tumble of the American system, a robust and healthy exercise compared with the alternatives in other representative governments. Surely, those other systems have their problems, and I am not advocating that we change our constitutionally enshrined procedures for some idealized alternative. I am merely warning of the pitfalls in our presidential electoral process as I have observed them over and over again. It is a process that is intellectually dishonest and inevitably deleterious to the best interests of the voters.

All of the leading presidential candidates that I have interviewed, from Democratic Senator Gary Hart of Colorado to Republican Senator Bob Dole of Kansas, have been honorable individuals who sacrificed a great deal in their attempts to succeed at what is an extremely challenging ordeal. Whether it was John Anderson, the Republican Congressman-turned-Independent, or civil rights activist Jessie Jackson turned perennial Democratic Party candidate, these men for the most part struck me as basically well-intentioned in their eagerness to serve the nation. The fundamental hazards are in the process itself: that numbing effect of a modern mass media–observed campaign that requires such an incredible high-wire act—balancing fundraising with integrity, superficial sloganeering with profound commitment, and homogenizing the entire unwieldy package into a marketable commodity—that in the end, the candidate is transformed into a caricature who has difficulty remembering from whence he came.

That, of course, is the opposite of what the founders of the American system had in mind when they rooted our representative democracy in accountability, with even the smallest local village subject to the scrutiny of a media that was everyman, as personified by the proprietor of the penny press and the town crier.

Thomas Jefferson extolled the central importance of the media, declaring, "I would rather have free press and no government, than a government and no free press." Journalists were by no means presumed virtuous; they were often considered vile, intemperate, and cursory in their observations. Yet what defined the media in the infancy of the nation was variety, made possible by a press that thrived in conditions of undercapitalization. Famed media critic A.J. Liebling once wrote, "Freedom of the press is guaranteed only to those who own one," and in the time of Jefferson, that group included much of the electorate.

Today, the opposite is obviously the case, with media ownership enormously costly and concentrated in a very few centers of capital. Perhaps the Internet will change that; already there are signs that the blogosphere, when it is not merely mischievous noise, is revitalizing the democratic process. After all, money is often less important than spunk as the key ingredient to the success of a website. But the contrary tendency in the period of time during which I interviewed the presidential candidates in this book was increasingly toward larger and more suffocating media conglomeration. For this reason, there is something anachronistic about the interviews I conducted, as they were produced for print outlets even while the electronic media was beginning to fully assert its dominance. It is now extremely rare for a print journalist, accompanied only by pen and paper and a tape recorder, to be granted adequate time to assess a candidate's ability to reflect on the issues of the day.

In the introductions to each of the following sections, I attempt to provide some insight into how my exchanges with the men who served as President came to take place, and what was learned in the process. In the last section on President George W. Bush, I struggle to come to grips with the one recent President who was never subjected to such a test, from me or anyone else. While I did spend some time around him and the rest of the Bush family entourage while reporting on his father's campaigns, he is the one President here who I never interviewed on the public record. No matter, George W. Bush is, for better or worse, the first truly electronically projected President.

Robert Scheer
Los Angeles, California
March 2006

RICHARD NIXON'S
FROZEN SMILE

MOST OF THE TIME THAT I SPENT IN ONE-ON-ONE interviews with the Presidents in this book occurred while they were still trying out for the role, mostly in the rush of national campaigns for the presidency. As a print journalist, I was granted an access that—as the candidates' handlers would often remind—was unwarranted by the declining power of the news organizations I represented.

Difficult as it may be for younger generations to imagine, each of these Presidents could remember a time when print media was dominant and television was not to be taken so seriously. Some adjusted more fluidly to the evolving impact of the instantaneous and visual mass media, while others barely ever got it. Television entered the nation's life at different points in these men's political development, and they had varying degrees of familiarity with the medium while growing up.

Absent in the youth of Nixon, Carter, and Bush I, but increasingly dominant in the early years of Clinton and George W. Bush, television and its dramatic impact would prove decisive for all. Reagan is an exception in this regard, for while television was virtually nonexistent in the formative years of his life, his acting career made him superbly confident on any public stage.

The most reluctant to acknowledge the new television

age was Richard Nixon, who, despite being unquestionably the best prepared of all modern Presidents before assuming office, never fully adjusted to the media form, which requires mastering a casual, open, and confident demeanor. This was no small failing, for in the end, whatever one concludes about his performance as President, it was his indelibly awkward and secretive style that did him in. He became the most disgraced of our Presidents, not because of the substance of his performance, but because of its fatally flawed delivery before a national audience.

If not for that failure of style, Nixon would have been able to finesse the Watergate burglary with the ease that all these other Presidents handled crises of far greater international significance. For example, Jimmy Carter's overreaction to a pro-Soviet coup in Afghanistan, which ended up nurturing dangerous Muslim fundamentalists—most notably Osama bin Laden—represents a far greater betrayal of the public trust. So, too, Reagan's Iran Contra scandal and George W. Bush's cooking of the WMD smoke to justify occupying Iraq.

As much as I disagreed with some of Nixon's policies (and my anti–Vietnam War activities resulted in various forms of harassment from his Administration, including a tax audit), I came years later to acknowledge that I had underestimated the accomplishments of his tenure in the White House. That is what led me, in the following essay written for the *Los Angeles Times* a decade after Nixon was run out of office, to attempt to separate the man's often loathsome style from his at times quite impressive substance.

I didn't undertake this reporting assignment for the *Times* in an effort to rehabilitate Nixon, and certainly not to court the approval of the disgraced President then living in virtual exile in his own country. I knew in advance that my requests for an interview would be turned down, since I had established myself years earlier as one of his most vociferous critics.

It was much to my amazement, then, after sending my published article to Nixon's office as a matter of formality, that I received a letter from the man himself (see page 22). Given how most of us in this profession struggle so mightily to attain a degree of objectivity, I value Nixon's response to my article as professional praise.

My visit with Nixon after his kind offer to grant me an interview (reprinted here on page 37) proved to be every bit as awkward as I anticipated. What I recall most is a sort of box-step dance we did as I entered his office: A standing Nixon greeted me with that odd frozen smile of his, just like in all the pictures, appearing to be warmly welcoming me, while actually retreating—causing me to stumble forward with my hand extended.

But no sooner was he seated behind his desk than did the other Nixon appear, the old fox who had mastered world politics. Confident and resolute to a fault, he quickly ticked off facts and theories on any subject I brought up, as if he had a Wikipedia chip implanted in his brain.

I mean, the man was dazzling in his clarity, particularly as he dissected the Reagan Administration's obsession with a "Star Wars" missile-defense system. The overall effect was impressively different from what I had expected: In this arena, Nixon was truly at peace with himself.

As for my own view of the Nixon presidency, I stand by the first article reprinted here. My perspective was reinforced while working as a screenwriter (along with my son Christopher) on Oliver Stone's 1995 movie, *Nixon*, which I insisted place considerable emphasis on the former

RICHARD NIXON

March 26, 1984

26 FEDERAL PLAZA
NEW YORK CITY

Dear Mr. Scheer,

A number of people have written to me about
your article in the <u>Los Angeles Times</u> but I had not
had the opportunity of reading it until I received
it from you. I want you to know that I appreciated
your very objective and comprehensive coverage of
some of my activities since I left office.

Due to a number of commitments I have
previously made, my schedule for the next several
weeks is fully committed. If, however, you would
like to contact Mr. Ruwe in my office sometime
around the middle of May, I would like to arrange a
mutually convenient time when you are in the New
York area for a discussion of the origination of
some of my foreign policy initiatives as you
suggested in your letter.

Sincerely,

Richard Nixon

Mr. Robert Scheer
<u>Los Angeles Times</u>
Times Mirror Square
Los Angeles, California 90053

President's achievements—especially the opening to China—while of course visiting the all-too-evident dark side of his Administration. At that time, we had only minimal access to the Nixon White House tapes, but the thousands of hours of recordings made public since then support my earlier assessment of his presidency.

⌘

Following is a retrospective on Nixon's presidency that appeared on the front page of the Los Angeles Times *on Thursday, March 8, 1984, under the heading, "Deeds Re-Examined—Nixon: Scorn Yielding to New Respect."*

RICHARD NIXON IS COMING ON STRONG. AFTER A DECADE of ignominious forced retirement following the disgrace of the Watergate scandal, the old warrior is now back, writing books and articles, advising the President's advisers, meeting foreign heads of state, and granting carefully selected television and print interviews.

And what he has to say may confound the expectations of his many detractors. For in this incarnation, Richard Nixon reminds not of the vindictiveness of enemies lists, the obstruction of justice, or the break-in of a psychiatrist's office perpetrated by "plumbers" on his staff, but rather of the grander shifts of foreign policy in what he views as the pursuit of global peace.

The new Nixon is Nixon as he would prefer to be remembered. His latest book, *The Real Peace*, is a defense of his policy of *détente* with the Soviet Union and summit meetings between the superpower leaders.

What is more surprising, the Nixon Administration, scorned for so long, is also coming in for more favorable treatment by some commentators.

A small but growing number of historians, scholars, and even rival politicians are beginning to re-examine the Nixon era and to challenge the view commonly held of Nixon as a failed President, the most disgraced chief executive in American history.

Nixon in his reemergence remains totally unrepentant about his Administration, which he insists was a glorious one despite some excesses here and there. And even some victims of those excesses, such as former Senator George S. McGovern, his 1972 opponent for the presidency, acknowledge that the Nixon era looks better with the passage of time.

"In dealing with the two major Communist powers, Nixon probably had a better record than any President since World War Two," McGovern noted in a recent interview with the *Los Angeles Times*. "He put us on the course to practical working relationships with both the Russians and Chinese," an achievement which "stands in sharp contrast to the rigid, unyielding, backward-looking approach that Reagan takes toward all Communist regimes."

Reagan's foreign policy appears to be the major cause of the current reappraisal of Nixon. "Nixon is beginning to look better and more interesting after three years of Reagan," noted Jonathan M. Wiener, a historian at UC Irvine, "even among younger historians who were influenced by the anti–Vietnam War movement."

"History is all relative, and if you compare him to the current occupant of the White House, especially in his handling of foreign affairs, it's no wonder to me there's a nostalgia for Nixon at the helm," observed Robert Sam Anson, author of a forthcoming book about Nixon. Anson said his book "is not an apologia for the bad things he did," but he added that Nixon "did a number of undeniably good things that have been forgotten. He negotiated the first and only strategic arms limitation treaty, the opening to China. He ended the war, ended the draft; the eighteen-year-old vote came under his presidency. He did a lot of good things and they all got swept away by Watergate."

Author Harrison E. Salisbury, who has been critical of Nixon in the past, after reading an advance copy of *The Real Peace*, wrote to the former President and hailed his "vision" as "superb." Salisbury added, "As a primer for the country, and President Reagan, I cannot imagine a better [one]."

Nixon's foreign policy achievements are the focus of the current reappraisal, though some commentators also praise aspects of his domestic policy, especially his establishment of the Environmental Protection Agency and his efforts to reform the welfare system.

But other scholars and politicians still contend that however sound some aspects of Nixon's foreign policy were, they are not enough to brighten his tarnished image.

"To say that Nixon had the sensible and obvious view, shared by my thirteen-year-old daughter though unfortunately not by the incumbent President, that we must deal with the Soviets, is not sufficient to absolve him of the abuses of power represented by Watergate," John D. Anderson, the former Republican congressional leader and Independent presidential candidate, said in an interview.

That more critical view continues to dominate both journalistic and academic circles, where the memory of Watergate defines the man. In what remains one of the oddest chapters in American history, this President who had left his mark, as few have, on American foreign policy and who continues to be prolific in his pronouncements, has become, in some quarters, very much a non-person—more the perpetrator of a scandal to be forgotten than the architect of a policy to be studied.

Although without much honor in his own country, Nixon continues to be admired abroad. Georgy A. Arbatov, a member of the Soviet Communist Party's Central Committee and an expert on the United States, said in an interview last year that the Soviets consider Nixon to be the most effective post-war President.

Many Western Europeans share that view. "The Europeans always had a much higher opinion of Nixon than did the Americans, and looked upon Watergate more as a bagatelle than a crime," observed foreign policy expert Ronald Steel. "It's a difference of historical background. The Europeans are used to this sort of thing."

Since he left office, Nixon also has made several visits to China, each time receiving accolades for having opened the door to U.S.-China relations in 1972. The Chinese, who have never shown any interest in Watergate, explain their admiration for the former President by quoting an old Chinese proverb, "When drinking the water, don't forget those who dug the well."

Nixon's standing is also high in the Middle East. When Egyptian President Anwar Sadat was assassinated in October 1981, Nixon—along with former Presidents Jimmy Carter and Gerald R. Ford—represented the United States at his funeral. He then made an eight-day trip to Saudi Arabia, Jordan, Morocco, and Tunisia and, on his return, he issued a statement urging direct negotiations between the United

States and the Palestine Liberation Organization.

In Israel, however, Nixon is still fondly remembered as the first U.S. President to visit Jerusalem—a trip he made on the eve of his resignation. "Nixon was then a hated person on the verge of impeachment in Washington," Amir Shaviv, a leading Israeli journalist, recently recalled. "But when he came to visit Jerusalem, thousands cheered him on the streets and the government of Yitzhak Rabin received him as a great friend."

Yet in this country, despite the vast outpouring of books and articles devoted to his involvement in the burglary of the Democratic Party headquarters and related sordid events, there has been scant notice paid to the major shifts in policy brought about during the Nixon years.

"We haven't had an historical interpretation of him since Watergate, but we've had a number of hysterical ones," charged historian Joan Hoff-Wilson, a University of Indiana professor whose study of the Nixon years will be published this summer. "It's the worst body of literature I have read on anyone, presidential or otherwise. It's so skewed by Watergate that you can't get a picture of him."

Hoff-Wilson, executive secretary of the Organization of American Historians, has interviewed the former President and attributes much of this bias against him to the fact that "journalists have a vested interest in making sure that nothing good is ever said about him . . . Watergate is their major claim to fame and the whole investigatory syndrome that followed." By contrast, Hoff-Wilson argues that the Nixon Administration was the "most significant since [Franklin D.] Roosevelt's."

Whether or not one accepts that judgment, the abiding mystery of Richard Nixon is how a politician described by many as totally lacking in moral integrity and devoid of an intellectual and programmatic commitment could have achieved so much clarity of purpose in his presidency.

How is it that this man, who has been described in much of the Watergate literature as little more than a charlatan of the first order, accomplished so much as President? How can it be that Nixon, who for most of his life was derided by his liberal critics as a primitive and demagogic anti-Communist, who began political life in California by smearing his congressional opponent as a Red, now campaigns for "hard-headed *détente*" with the Soviets?

Some historians feel that such questions will inevitably compel a more complex assessment of the Nixon presidency. There are already some signs in the academic community of a perception that Watergate may be too narrow a window for viewing the Nixon legacy.

"Historians are trying out a Nixon revisionism in the classrooms," Stanford University historian Barton J. Bernstein said in a recent interview, "but so far a revised view of Nixon has not made its way into the literature."

Bernstein, who specializes in modern diplomatic history, is convinced, however, that "in another ten to fifteen years, I will be assigning literature that will argue the case for a reassessment of Nixon and for upgrading him because of some of his accomplishments in foreign policy."

Historian Hoff-Wilson is considerably less optimistic about the possibilities for a revisionist view of Nixon. "Until we die, I don't think there will be any significant change in the intellectual and published elite literature on Nixon," she said.

Hoff-Wilson, forty-four, considers herself part of that generation which opposed the war in Vietnam, but she chides her peers for not being able to transcend the "trauma" of that experience. "Most of my colleagues who are against him came out of the antiwar movement," she said.

One of her colleagues, Tufts University historian Martin Sherwin, has argued that his generation of historians is correct in making Nixon's role in Vietnam central to an evaluation of his Administration.

"Nixon is responsible for reaching a settlement of the Vietnam War in 1973 that he could have had in 1968, and this generation of historians remembers that and should," Sherwin said. He resists a revisionist view of Nixon "because there is no new body of documents or other information to warrant such a revisionism."

"I come down on the critical side," Sherwin said. "I think it's a mistake to believe that because the Reagan Administration has been such a disaster in the area of foreign policy, that that validates some of the worst policies that the Nixon Administration had pursued. After all, the U.S. bombing of Cambodia was an illegal, criminal act—a war against that country that was not approved by Congress."

UCLA historian Robert Dallek also disagrees with historians such as Hoff-Wilson who favor a major Nixon revisionism. "The history textbooks already give Nixon his due on *détente* and the opening to China and also hit him pretty hard on Vietnam and Watergate," Dallek said. "I don't think Hoff-Wilson's view of historians being blindly prejudiced toward Nixon is correct. The bulk of historians have made a more balanced assessment."

Hoff-Wilson conceded that "the negative things remain—Vietnam and the way that was handled, the secret war in Cambodia, and Watergate. I don't want to whitewash those things, but the problem is that that is all that's ever talked about. The problem is the imbalance with which we see him."

Hoff-Wilson has found that attempting to provide that balance is no easy chore: "I tell you, I have had the worst time in social gatherings, people just attack me. I don't think we will get beyond that in our time—we will constantly run into that."

Some tend to mistrust Nixon because of what historian Bernstein called "mud-slinging" in his first political races in California, and they "came to have that view confirmed by Watergate."

"One has difficulty liking Nixon," Bernstein said. "There is nothing winning about him; he's suspicious, he's covert, he's evasive, defensive, and lacks a sense of humor. There is an unwillingness on the part of historians and journalists to distinguish between the man and his policies, though obviously Watergate wedded the two."

But Bernstein added, "I think it is possible to dislike Nixon and to revile him for his brutal selective use of power as in the carpet bombing of Vietnam or the overthrow of the democratically elected, Marxist government of Salvador Allende in Chile, yet one should recognize that no American leader in the last forty years has been more calculatingly cautious about the use of American power in a setting of potential global conflict."

But for many, Nixon's Third World policies remain a sticking point.

"With the exception of the Soviet Union and the China card, which are admittedly very big issues, revisionists are going to have a hard row to hoe," said UC San Diego historian Michael Parrish. "We cannot ignore situations like Cambodia, Chile, and the way in which the war in Vietnam was prolonged much beyond what was a reasonable opportunity to end it. Those are pretty large black marks against him."

A similarly acerbic view was offered by Duke University political scientist James David Barber, who specializes in the presidency.

Any more favorable reassessment of Nixon is "puzzling," Barber said, because "he is the first President in all of history to have been tossed out. He is a demonstrated fabricator of history. His policies in Vietnam are responsible for a great many more persons being killed than needed to be. He would likely have been the first guy to have been convicted of a crime as a President if Ford had not pardoned him."

The public at large has proved as unforgiving of Nixon over Watergate as the journalists and historians. According to a *Washington Post*–ABC poll in June 1982, seventy-five percent of Americans said they thought Nixon was guilty of wrongdoing in the Watergate affair. By a margin of more than two-to-one, they felt he should be granted no future role in national affairs.

Since he resigned the presidency in August 1974, in the face of possible impeachment by the House of Representatives, Nixon has been given to long periods of seclusion, hiding behind the protection of the Secret Service to avoid encounters with the public or press.

But with increasing frequency he has, in the manner of a respected ex-President, ventured forth with speeches, interviews, articles, and books, and meetings with foreign and domestic dignitaries.

Nixon, who lives on a $1 million estate in New Jersey, commutes fifty minutes daily to the office quarters granted him as an ex-President in the New York Federal Building, where he maintains an arduous schedule of meetings. Over the last several months, for example, he met with representatives of Nepal and Japan, with the widow of Sadat, and with the Crown Prince of Jordan. King Hassan II of Morocco dined with Nixon at his New Jersey home.

Nixon has continued to travel widely over the last two years, visiting seventeen countries, where he has been welcomed for discussions with no fewer than sixteen heads of state. His five books have all sold well and indeed are often bestsellers abroad.

In *The Real Peace*, his latest book, Nixon has extended his campaign for what he calls "hard-headed *détente*," although that concept is not much in vogue in the United States any longer. Whereas Nixon favors a military buildup, he stresses the limits to the military option.

So obsessive is the former President about the urgency of the message of *The Real Peace* that he paid for its initial publication and sent 1,200 free copies to friends and business associates. One of those who received a copy was Samuel Summerlin, president of the *New York Times* Syndication Sales Corp., who bought the rights to the book and successfully marketed it to magazines and book publishers throughout the world. Little, Brown & Co. recently published an edition in this country.

The book's message is bold and simple: "The two superpowers cannot afford to go to war against each other at any time or under any circumstances. Each side's vast military power makes war obsolete as an instrument of national policy. In the age of nuclear warfare, to continue our political differences by means of war would be to discontinue civilization as we know it."

Nixon was not available to the *Los Angeles Times* to further delineate his views, saying through a spokesman that he wanted "his book to speak for itself."

While Nixon studiously avoids public criticism of Reagan, *The Real Peace* reiterates his earlier defense of *détente* in terms that challenge key tenets of the Reagan foreign policy.

And in an interview last month with the West German magazine *Stern*, which bought the serialization rights to his new book, Nixon took issue with those who are pushing for a reassertion of U.S. superiority and urged Reagan to accept the Soviets as equals.

He said, "I always accepted the Soviet Union, when I was President, as a superpower . . . It is very important for President Reagan to do exactly that, to recognize that they are . . . equal as a superpower, but it is very important also to recognize that they are different . . . The differences will never be resolved. We just have to live with it."

Nixon continues to deny that there is any contradiction between accommodation with the Communist giants and fighting communism in Vietnam or elsewhere. On the contrary, his "hard-headed *détente*" envisions the United States mounting militant opposition against any sign of Soviet expansionism.

Nixon's view of the Soviets is not simple. He frequently points with pride to his "hawkish" views and insists that he is not "soft" on the Soviets.

The complexity of his view was demonstrated this past May when he took issue with the pastoral letter adopted by the Roman Catholic bishops that questioned the morality of nuclear deterrence. In a letter to the *New York Times*, Nixon defended a policy of deterrence that includes "deliberate attacks on civilians," if necessary, as a counter to attacks by

Soviet conventional forces. And, as he is frequently wont to do, he blasted "well-intentioned idealists who cannot face up to the fact that we live in a real world in which the bomb is not going to go away."

But instead of completing that sentence in a Strangelovian way by extolling the possibilities of nuclear war, Nixon added, "We must redouble our efforts to reduce our differences with the Soviet Union, if possible. Where that is not possible, we must find ways to live with them rather than to die over them."

Those who have been close to Nixon tend to stress the complexity of the man and his thoughts.

"Don't generalize with this guy," warned former Nixon aide John D. Ehrlichman in an interview. "You will run a risk of being dead wrong if you do, because he's a very complicated mass of cells."

Historian Bernstein traces Nixon's notion of limits to American power to the Dwight D. Eisenhower era and argues that it provided Nixon with an overall strategy permitting selective "and often brutal" intervention in world affairs within a context of keeping the global peace with the Soviets.

This sense of limits still forms the core of Nixon's thinking. "We recognized that our two countries were locked in competition, and each of us was determined to protect his own country's interests," Nixon wrote in the *New York Times* last year, in an article discussing his three summit meetings with the late Soviet Premier Leonid I. Brezhnev. "But we also recognized that our countries shared certain common interests, which made it mutually advantageous for us to compromise or otherwise resolve an increasing range of our competing interests."

The antecedents of the Nixon foreign policy add credence to the claim by many Nixon associates that it was the President himself—not Henry A. Kissinger—who crafted the broad outlines of foreign policy in his Administration. They note, as an example, that he first advocated the opening to China in a *Foreign Affairs* magazine article in 1967, before he had ever met Kissinger.

Citing that and other examples of Nixon's leadership, historian Hoff-Wilson refers to Kissinger as "a glorified messenger boy."

"He has grabbed all of the credit that he possibly could, and without merit," Hoff-Wilson said. "I believe on my reading of the record that the prolonged negotiations over Vietnam were really part of Kissinger's egomaniacal tendency to prolong negotiations. The shuttle diplomacy in the Middle East fell apart."

The attempt to apportion credit or blame between Nixon and Kissinger will likely be the major point of contention in future assessments of that Administration, according to historian Dallek.

But Dallek said it will not be possible to definitively answer that question or to revise current estimates of Nixon until the release of more documents from the Nixon White House.

Forty-two million documents from the Nixon era are currently in the custody of the General Services Administration, but the vast majority have not been made public. Last month, a federal judge in Washington acceded to the request of former Nixon aides and temporarily blocked the release of 1.5 million documents; the aides had complained that the documents were private communications and ought to be shielded under the Privacy Act.

At this point, only Nixon and those persons he designates have access to those files. Ehrlichman is one who was granted access by Nixon.

Ehrlichman said that Nixon's image as the prime architect of his Administration's foreign policy will be enhanced at Kissinger's expense once the remaining White House tapes and other documents are released.

To illustrate his point, Ehrlichman supplied the *Los Angeles Times* with 1,000 pages that had been released to him from the U.S. Archives, which contain notes of daily White House meetings of the President and his top staff. In those entries, it is clearly a matter of Nixon calling the shots on foreign policy, down to detailed instructions to Kissinger even when the latter was off on one of his stints at shuttle diplomacy.

Those papers, as was the case with earlier releases of Nixon tapes and documents, suggest two extremely different views of the man. On the one hand, there is Nixon the consummate statesman, knowledgeable about the world, well prepared for his meetings with other heads of state, and capable of a cool, dispassionate approach to bargaining.

But the notes also reveal another, less stable Nixon, on one occasion apparently so drunk that Air Force One had to circle Andrews Air Force base until the President sobered up enough to approve a controversial press release.

Future historians will have to sort out the two Nixons in any reappraisals of the man and his Administration. And clearly there were two Nixons.

As Nixon's former speechwriter, Raymond K. Price Jr., put it, "Between the anguished, cornered Richard Nixon of the Watergate transcripts and the confident, self-assured Richard Nixon speaking the language of power, the contrast is as stark as it was between his return in triumph from Peking and his departure in disgrace to San Clemente. Both are part of the man. Both are part of the record."

❧

My profile of Richard Nixon after interviewing him in June 1984 ran in the Los Angeles Times *on July 1, 1984 under the headline, "U.S.-Soviet 'Star War' Studies Urged by Nixon."*

FORMER PRESIDENT RICHARD M. NIXON HAS URGED THE United States and the Soviet Union to share research on "Star Wars" missile systems because, otherwise, such defensive weapons could fuel fears that they might be used as a "shield" for a nuclear first strike.

In a wide-ranging interview with the *Los Angeles Times* last week, Nixon not only called for pooling resources in this top-secret weapons research but predicted that the "Star Wars" system initiated by President Reagan would offer the United States little protection against a nuclear attack by the Soviet Union. "When you have 10,000 of these damn things [nuclear warheads], there is no defense," Nixon said.

The former President seemed fit and relaxed during a two-and-a-half-hour interview in his office in the Federal Building in lower Manhattan. Despite a reputation for avoiding small talk, Nixon began the interview by discussing surfing on California beaches and ended by commenting on the recent birth of his granddaughter.

It was understood in advance that the interview would concentrate on foreign policy issues and would not deal with the Watergate scandal that forced Nixon's resignation from office nearly ten years ago, on August 9, 1974. In his office, where he is surrounded by mementos of his foreign policy triumphs—including photographs of himself with dozens of heads of state—there are few reminders of harder times.

During the interview, the former President:

- Denied that the 1970 U.S. invasion and bombing of Cambodia were politically motivated, as implied in a document provided to the *Times* by his former White House domestic adviser, John D. Ehrlichman.
- Acknowledged some policy differences with Reagan, but said the President is not part of "the kook right" and will probably be reelected in November, although the election could be close if there is an economic downturn.
- Said that he opposes the use of U.S. troops in El Salvador or Nicaragua.
- Assessed the role played by former Secretary of State

President Nixon and Scheer during their interview in his office

Henry A. Kissinger in his Administration and said it was he, not Kissinger, who initiated the groundbreaking February 1972 trip to China.
•Said that President Dwight D. Eisenhower considered using nuclear weapons in Korea and Vietnam.

Nixon would not join former President Jimmy Carter and his own former arms control adviser, Gerard C. Smith, in condemning Reagan's "Star Wars" weapons. Likening Reagan's support of "Star Wars" to President Harry S. Truman's decision to build the hydrogen bomb, Nixon said the United States would have to develop such weapons in the absence of a cooperative agreement with the Soviet Union, out of fear that the Soviets would do it on their own. Reagan has requested $1.87 billion for research and development of "Star Wars" weapons in fiscal 1985; final congressional action is pending.

But Nixon expressed skepticism about the effectiveness of defensive missile systems. The controversial "Star Wars"–type weapons, which would employ laser or other high-energy beams to attack incoming missiles, would be overwhelmed by the vastly greater numbers of offensive missiles that can be deployed by either the United States or the Soviet Union, he contended.

Such weapons will be effective, at best, against third powers that possess more limited nuclear arsenals than the superpowers, Nixon suggested. And for that reason, he said, the superpowers have a common stake in the development of some version of the weapons but an even greater interest in pooling their resources to avoid suspicion that these weapons are part of an offensive strategy.

Calling attention to what he considered the inherent

dangers of defensive weapons, the former President said such systems "would be destabilizing if they provided a shield so that you could use the sword"—that is, if either superpower thought its opponent, because of the existence of a defensive system, felt free to launch a first strike.

Predicting a summit conference after the November election, "no matter who is elected," Nixon said, "I strongly feel we should put all offers on the table to share research on defensive weapons—so they're not a shield."

Nixon denied that his controversial 1970 attack on Cambodia, which touched off student demonstrations nationwide, had been politically motivated. He was shown a copy of a page from the calendar of Ehrlichman, then his domestic adviser, recounting an April 25, 1970 conversation between Kissinger and Ehrlichman which indicated the U.S. invasion and bombing of Cambodia were undertaken to improve his standing in the polls.

The calendar item, which Ehrlichman provided the *Times*, said:

> *HAK [Kissinger] phones—I go down and he shows me Cambodian attack plans—I urge both on. [President's] leadership quotient very low and he's not gaining on domestic side— needs a bold stroke—HAK says he'll tell [President] my opinion.* [Ehrlichman used the mathematical symbol "pi" to refer to Nixon.]

Five days later, on April 30, Nixon sent U.S. troops into Cambodia and authorized the U.S. bombing of that country to support South Vietnamese ground operations against North Vietnamese and Viet Cong sanctuaries there.

After reading the note from Ehrlichman's calendar,

Nixon said that Ehrlichman was a political adviser who might have focused on the electoral advantages of the invasion. But Nixon insisted, "We did Cambodia for military reasons," and would not elaborate.

The former President, who said he has frequent contact with high officials in the Reagan Administration and talks on the telephone with Reagan himself, said, "Reagan would like to be remembered as a man of peace." Nixon predicted progress on arms control if Reagan is reelected.

Nixon expects "a close election," particularly if there is an economic downturn during the closing weeks of the campaign, but he expressed confidence that Reagan would eventually triumph.

"I marvel at Reagan's stamina, the irrepressible goodwill that he exudes," the former President said. "He's in touch with the masses of the country. The sleaze factor [a reference to alleged financial wrongdoing involving Reagan Administration officials] is not an issue. When you don't have a war, there's no foreign policy issue. The economy is the only issue; if it slows down, then it [the election] will be close."

Claiming that the Iranian hostage crisis and the problems it created for then-President Jimmy Carter were an exception to the rule, Nixon said: "You can make foreign policy an issue against a President because he controls that. But domestic [issues] nobody can control."

He conceded that "my views are more centrist" than Reagan's, but sought to downplay their differences. "I would not put him [Reagan] over on the kook right—they are an embarrassment to him," Nixon said. "He's on the responsible right." Nixon defined his own stance as that of "a pragmatic centrist."

The former President expressed approval of a recent softening in Reagan's previously harsh criticism of the policy of *détente* he and Kissinger pursued. Restating his own position that the United States should not seek nuclear superiority over the Soviets, Nixon noted that Reagan recently expressed the same view. As a result, Nixon said with a slight smile, the plank in the 1980 Republican platform calling for superiority "will have to be adjusted [at the Republican National Convention in August] to reflect the President's view."

While studiously avoiding direct criticism of the Reagan Administration, he challenged the confrontational stance toward the Soviet Union frequently espoused by the President and his key advisers.

"Periods of confrontation strengthen dictatorships, and periods of peace weaken them," he said, adding: "There would not have been a Solidarity movement in Poland were it not for *détente*. If you have a world of constant confrontation, then change will not be possible."

Recalling his own trips to Hungary in 1963 and in 1982, Nixon said the changes in that Communist country are like "night and day because of contact with the West."

He called for a "live-and-let-live middle ground" between those who want to destroy the Soviet system and those he termed naïve about its aggressive intentions.

"We have to recognize that we are never going to be friends, but we cannot afford to be enemies," Nixon said of the Soviets. Despite what he called his "hard-line background," he said, "I've always had a somewhat more subtle approach to the Soviet bloc—never have seen it as monolithic."

He cited his early support of Yugoslavia's efforts to follow an independent Communist course. But Nixon conceded that he had viewed China as simply part of the Soviet bloc until 1966, and that he was "five years late" in acknowledging the Sino-Soviet split of the early 1960s. He noted, however, that Reagan thought the Sino-Soviet split might be a Communist ploy to confuse the West as late as the 1980 campaign.

Nixon criticized those opponents of *détente* who believe the Soviet system will collapse if put under the economic strain of an arms race. "It will not happen," he said, because the Soviet leaders "are good at getting power and keeping it."

The Soviets are very interested in arms control because of their internal economic problems and their estrangement from the successful Western economic powers, Nixon said.

While supporting Reagan on aid to the rebels fighting the Sandinista government in Nicaragua, who are called *contras*, Nixon warned that such assistance "should not be a prelude to an American Involvement" of U.S. troops. He said he was also strongly opposed to the use of U.S. troops to fight in El Salvador, for, although "they could win, the moment they left, it [the government] would collapse."

More important than military aid to Central America, he said, "is what we do economically. It's a question of trade, interest rates, and aid."

He called on Reagan to develop an economic aid program in conjunction with Western Europe and Japan for the Third World, which he defined as "the real battleground" between the United States and the Soviet Union. He predicted that "if people continue to be mired down in poverty, they will have revolution" because "if the choice is revolution or staying where they are, they will take revolution."

Nixon said that "the Soviets have lost the ideological battle [in the Third World]—Marxism does not work—but the West has not won it . . . Nuclear weapons are irrelevant to the solution of Third World problems."

Recalling his years as Vice President under Eisenhower, Nixon acknowledged that during the Korean War, "there is no question that Eisenhower considered [using] nuclear weapons" to stop the Chinese advance down the Korean peninsula. "[Secretary of State John Foster] Dulles carried the message to China through India," he said.

"It was a credible threat then, but not today," Nixon added. "What American President, in order to protect the Third World, is going to threaten the Soviet Union with nuclear weapons?"

Nixon also noted that the Eisenhower Administration had considered the use of nuclear weapons "as shock treatment" in Vietnam, to aid the French forces embattled at Dien Bien Phu in 1954. He said that he personally opposed their use and favored massive conventional bombing by the United States instead. Eisenhower rejected both alternatives.

Nixon now stresses peaceful alternatives to military intervention by the United States in the Third World. He noted approvingly that President Reagan, in his trip to China in April, emphasized the economic rather than military connection with that country.

Observing that China is only a "mini-nuclear and conventional military power" that would require "astronomical funds" to become a major military power, Nixon said, "We should avoid any appearance of attempting to build China into a superpower to balance Russia." In mid-June, the Reagan Administration tentatively agreed to sell sophisticated anti-tank and anti-aircraft missiles to Peking.

Without mentioning these sales, Nixon said, "A U.S.-China military alliance will only have the effect of being unnecessarily provocative to the Soviet Union."

Nixon, whose first trip to Peking in 1972 ended a quarter-century of hostility between the United States and China, warned that "it is stupid and destructive" to suggest that a war between China and the Soviet Union might benefit U.S. interests. Any war between the two Communist powers "will inevitably be a world nuclear war," he said.

He cautioned against any attempt to play China off against the Soviet Union, contending that "we should never use the China card," because it is a "put-down" of the Chinese people. "Nobody wants to be a card. Let them understand that we would want a relationship even if there were no Russia."

Nixon called for a balanced approach to relations with China and the Soviet Union. "China is just as totalitarian as the Soviet Union—more so, because it's in an earlier stage of communism," he said. "But the idea that we cannot have a constructive relation with China or Russia until they change internal policy is madness."

While the Helsinki Accords of 1975, establishing international human rights standards, did provide a basis for pressuring signatory nations, including the Soviet Union, to abandon repressive measures at home, Nixon contended that it is counterproductive to make trade or other policies contingent on internal Soviet changes.

Singling out the 1974 Jackson-Vanik Amendment, which denied most-favored-nation trade status to Communist nations unless they allowed free emigration, Nixon called it "a major mistake." He claimed that the amendment, sponsored by the late Senator Henry M. Jackson (D-Washington) and former Representative Charles A. Vanik (D-Ohio), ended rather than encouraged substantial immigration of

Soviet Jews to Israel. "We went from 36,000 Jewish emigrants a year to nothing," Nixon said.

"In private conversations with [Soviet President Leonid I.] Brezhnev, I made it clear that we were concerned about this problem," he added. "I felt very strongly about Jewish emigration. Henry [Kissinger] did, too—after all, he has that background. We were not selling out Jewish people with our *détente* policy, because we felt that with the new relationship we would be in a better position to bring about change."

Noting that American Jewish organizations had lobbied hard for the Jackson-Vanik Amendment, Nixon said Congress should have resisted such pressure. "It's the responsibility of statesmen to make pressure groups understand," he said.

As a more recent example of politicians' caving in to pressure groups, he cited the proposal of Democratic presidential candidates Walter F. Mondale and Gary Hart to move the U.S. Embassy in Israel to Jerusalem from Tel Aviv. Nixon criticized their proposal, saying "that would make it impossible for the United States to play the role of peace broker" between Israel and the Arab nations that claim Jerusalem as their spiritual capital.

On Kissinger, Nixon emphatically declared that the decision to reopen relations with China had been his alone and was not initiated by Kissinger, then his National Security Adviser and later his Secretary of State.

Kissinger, who has received much of the credit for the China overture, "played an indispensable role" by setting up the trip, the former President said. "But as far as the decision was concerned, I had made up my mind before coming to office" to reopen relations with China, he added.

Nixon cited an article he wrote for *Foreign Affairs* magazine advocating the establishment of relations with China in 1968, before he had discussed the issue with Kissinger.

"I never had a conversation [about China] with Kissinger until after I came into office," Nixon said. "One of my first memos was to Henry Kissinger on China—I wanted it studied, so he did . . . Bill Safire [a former Nixon speech writer] used to climb the wall about Henry's getting the credit. I said it doesn't matter."

Nixon made light of Kissinger's tendency to claim credit for the major foreign policy achievements of the Nixon Administration in his voluminous writings, which the former President said "are a little long for me."

But he noted: "Everybody writes his own self-serving book. We all see it from our own vantage point. I have never plowed through the Kissinger ones or [former White House Chief of Staff Alexander M.] Haig's."

Nixon laughed and quoted British Prime Minister Winston Churchill as having said, "History will be kind to me because I intend to write it." Nixon, who has produced four books since leaving office, will soon begin work on his version of the Vietnam War. "I write my own and read few others," he said with a smile.

Citing the "Nixon Doctrine" as the seminal foreign policy contribution of his Administration—it acknowledged the limitations on U.S. military power in a multipolar world—Nixon noted that he first enunciated this doctrine in an extemporaneous press briefing on a trip to Guam in the first year of his first term in the White House. "Kissinger was startled when I said it," he recalled. "I articulated it on my own. I had not discussed it with him. It had not been discussed in the NSC [National Security Council]."

He acknowledged that Kissinger had "parallel" ideas about the new balance of power. But he said that he personally developed those ideas through his travels and conversations with world leaders, particularly French President Charles de Gaulle and West German Chancellor Konrad Adenauer, before ascending to the presidency.

"I thought it was very important to recognize that the world is multipolar, not bipolar, and the more multipolar, the better it is for the United States," Nixon said.

Nixon likened the world to "a great forest" in which there are the "great trees—the U.S., Western Europe, Japan, the Soviet Union, and China." Then there are the "saplings," such as Brazil and Argentina, that might grow up to be great trees. Finally, there are the smaller nations, "the creepers," Nixon called them, that "don't have the resources or background to become anything but creepers."

While Nixon seemed supremely self-assured and content with his perception of his place in history, he made a wry face at the mention of books by former *New York Times* reporter Seymour Hersh and others who have been less than flattering in their treatment of his Administration.

"We develop images," Nixon said of the books about him. "Once they paint a picture, it is difficult to move away from it."

JIMMY CARTER'S
LUSTFUL HEART

Y ES, AS YOU PROBABLY KNOW ALREADY FROM GORE Vidal's foreword, I am the guy who Jimmy Carter talked to about lust in his heart. I bring it up now because that entire episode into which I blundered during his 1976 presidential campaign provides an important clue to the makeup of this most interesting, well-intentioned, but perplexing man.

Well-intentioned is actually the last label that I would have chosen to describe the future President back then in Carter's living room in Plains, Georgia, as I concluded an interview that had extended over months of grueling campaigning in the Democratic Party primaries. The sensation following *Playboy* magazine's publication of the interview (reprinted on page 56), which hit newsstands in October 1976, was largely centered around Carter's reference to sexual lust, and on the fact that the Democratic Party nominee for President would even consent to a *Playboy* interview in the first place. In retrospect, the interview's significance is far greater as a harbinger of the fundamentalist Christian rhetoric that was beginning to inflame the political climate.

The interview began months earlier, well before Carter received his nomination at the Democratic National Convention on July 15, 1976 at Madison Square Garden in New York City. A relatively unknown ex-Governor of

Georgia, Carter had followed the advice of campaign operatives and agreed to my suggestion to use the *Playboy* interview as a vehicle to convince the party's liberal base that his
Southern religious roots would not stand in the way of his
claim to a progressive political outlook. I was the former editor of *Ramparts* magazine, which was known for its strong
opposition to the Vietnam War, and I therefore represented a
link to the 1960s protest veterans who were suspicious of the
candidate.

By the time we completed the interview, however,
Carter had already won his party's nomination, and the very
idea of appearing in *Playboy*—let alone the substance of
what he had said to me—would prove to be a huge political
embarrassment.

At the time of our last session, although neither he nor
his campaign handlers, including his press secretary Jody
Powell, realized it, Carter no longer needed *Playboy*. In the
general election, it was now crucial for Carter to appeal to
more conservative voters, for whom *Playboy* was anathema.
He would lose with those voters merely by appearing in the
pages of a publication that, even though it could make a good
claim to running many serious articles and important works
of fiction, was viewed largely as a skin magazine.

Difficult as it may be to imagine now, in those days it was
the Democratic candidate Carter who was wearing religion
on his sleeve and prattling on about family values and being
a born-again Christian. Because of his post-presidential
actions and advocacy, particularly his celebrated concern for
human rights and the poor throughout the world, it is also
difficult to recall that Carter came to office as a representative of his party's still-powerful conservative Southern wing.

Carter was the last of the Cold War Democrats, although

he didn't want to be regarded that way by his party's core constituency, still recoiling from decades of raw images of the Vietnam debacle. As it turned out, the party's liberal base was right to be suspicious, for as President, Carter aggressively pursued the outdated military interventionist policies that had marked Democrats during the 1960s as the war party of Lyndon Johnson.

Toward that end, Carter relied primarily on the views of one of the nation's most pronounced Cold War hawks, Zbigniew Brzezinski. It was Brzezinski, the embittered son of an exiled former Polish diplomat, who was largely responsible for enlisting Carter in the revival of a Cold War that had been sputtering into extinction.

Presidents Richard Nixon and Gerald Ford had vigorously pursued arms control and other elements of *détente* with the Soviet Union, as well as the opening to Red China. The devil image of the worldwide Communist menace had been brought down to earth and was increasingly viewed by mainstream America as a fragmented collection of nationalist leaders with whom we could do business. For all of the warm, fuzzy feelings that I and many others now have for Carter, as President he began chipping away at the progress of his Republican predecessors in bringing rational, as opposed to jingoistic, discourse into consideration of foreign policy.

The consequences of some of Carter's policies as President—particularly his manipulation of the Soviet incursion into Afghanistan to distract from the impasse with Iran over the seizure of American hostages—were disastrous. The Islamic revolution, so disturbingly manifested in Iran, was spread throughout the world far less by the preaching of the Shiite Ayatollahs than by the drive of Sunni fundamentalists to wage holy war against the Soviets in Afghanistan.

Although few have noted the direct line between the Carter Administration and the horror of the 9/11 attacks, there is little doubt that Carter's anti-Soviet policies had a massive and destabilizing impact that will most likely continue to haunt us well into the future. In an attempt to inflict on the Soviets their own Vietnam—as Brzezinski admitted a decade later to the French publication *Le Nouvel Observateur*—Carter played midwife to what George W. Bush's apologists have come to call *Islamo-Fascism*.

The venue for this Cold War revival was Afghanistan, and it was quite a stretch to take the Soviets' clumsy meddling in their neighbor's politics as an invitation to launch such a dangerous policy. Extremely dangerous in that moment because it derailed arms control and in its place brought on a massive spiraling of the nuclear threat. But even more significant to the post-9/11 trauma that now grips this nation's political agenda, the Carter Administration sparked a chain of events that ushered the Muslim fanaticism of Al Qaeda into existence.

I interviewed Senator Bob Dole for the *Los Angeles Times* in January 1980, when he was fashioning himself as an early challenger to Carter's reelection bid. The Iranian revolution had occurred on Carter's watch, and the fact that U.S. personnel were being held hostage in Tehran threatened to dominate the campaign and bring about Carter's defeat. Dole began our interview with a clear denunciation of Carter for using the Soviets' moves in Afghanistan to draw attention away from the Iran debacle, which had made the President appear impotent. Dole explained: "I see it as a diversion from the Iran thing—the hype is running out, there's not much more mileage in Iran unless the hostages are freed, so while they're trying to figure out some way to pull that off, you'd better focus on some other explosive thing like Afghanistan."

Dole was brilliant in his analysis, employing language that poignantly outlined a wicked failure of every modern President: playing political games without concern for the real cost in innocent lives lost and scarce resources wasted. No President in recent memory has resisted the exploitation of patriotism for partisan political purpose.

Dole summarized the Carter Administration's escalating response to the Soviets: "Suddenly it's got the people thinking about patriotism and sacrifice. I asked Zbigniew Brzezinski, 'Isn't there a lot of focus on Afghanistan, maybe to take a little of the focus off Iran?' Well, he didn't say yes or no, but I think I got the message. I think there is a little diversion going on . . ."

The diversion, including a dramatic U.S. boycott of the 1980 Moscow Olympics, was part of a campaign to cast the Soviet presence in Afghanistan as some brazen new power grab, when in fact it was all too typical of a pattern of vast Russian floundering. The Soviet intervention that Carter jumped on was, according to Dole, not that big a deal: "[S]ince '78, they, the Russians, have controlled Afghanistan. And I wonder about the word 'invasion'—I guess it's an invasion, but they've had the country for twenty months. Suddenly it's like it's just happened overnight—and this great friend of the West has been taken over by the Soviets."

Dole was correct in his claim that Carter used the Soviet intervention to draw attention from the Iranian hostage crisis. As we now know all too well, it was the very real fundamentalist Muslim threat—rather than the exaggerated Soviet one—that needed to be dealt with. The current torment of Islamic zealotry begins with that fateful U.S. decision to side with the fundamentalists in Afghanistan, recruiting fanatics from throughout the Arab world and funding a bloody religious war. It was a reckless policy, rousing fundamentalists against the Soviet-backed secularists, inflaming religious passions, and years later resulting in the obliteration of the World Trade Center. As the bipartisan 9/11 Commission Report released publicly on July 22, 2004 amply documents, Osama bin Laden was one of *our* freedom fighters in Afghanistan. The Al Qaeda movement was a direct outgrowth of a madly irrational sideshow to Carter's reelection bid.

Ironically, when I had asked Carter during our 1976 *Playboy* interview what would prevent his leading the U.S. into a Vietnam-type quagmire, he stated that he wouldn't "lie," as Lyndon Johnson had. At the time, I thought this was the most truly controversial statement in the interview—not the "lust" quote that was so widely publicized. Johnson's widow, Lady Bird, felt the same way, and she initially refused to meet with Carter when he landed in Dallas soon after the interview was published. Sadly, Carter went on to commit the same lie of inventing a national security threat—with dire consequences.

In short, Carter refused to learn the lesson of Vietnam at the same moment when many in his own party were demanding a break from its hawkish stance. Instead, he compounded the woeful course set by Lyndon Johnson of attempting to have both guns and butter, sacrificing the idealism of the war on poverty to the demands of a divisive and erroneous foreign policy.

But we can't say we weren't warned, for the Carter campaign stressed the man's military background and hawkish views. The campaign also represented an attempt to co-opt the conservative-values rhetoric of the religious right.

Though still of relatively minimal political impact—since most of the Southern evangelical movement remained deliberately suspicious of both political parties—the emerging "Christian right" was very much on the radar of the Georgian candidate. It had long existed as an essential ingredient of Southern racism; the Carter people, of course, steadfastly rejected this divisiveness, but they did attempt to seize upon its "moral values" allure.

To understand just why biblical references to morality and "lust" cropped up in our interview, it is necessary to capture the mood of the South during the 1970s. In the early years of the decade, President Nixon had boldly launched his "Southern strategy," using Lyndon Johnson's civil-rights legislation to split white voters away from the Democratic Party.

The challenge that Nixon faced in employing this tactic was to avoid invoking blatant racism, which would turn off many moderate Republican voters throughout the country. Thus was born the code language of so-called "family values," the appeal to "normal Americans" that cloaked a racist division of the Southern vote in biblical language. Although he stressed that he represented a post-racist South, Carter was as blatant in exploiting fundamentalist imagery as any politician since.

That was another reason I was initially skeptical of a man whom I, along with much of the world, regard today with admiration and deep respect. I pay this tribute despite a decades-long skirmish with the man, not over the accuracy of my interview transcript, but whether or not he knew the tape recorder was on.

The recorder was on and quite visibly so, but it is a measure of the man's complexity that while he does not disown his words (which hold up splendidly today as a relatively sane expression of the Baptist religion), he nonetheless dissembles as to why and how he came to say them. After all, the appearance of those words in *Playboy* made him look amateurish and almost cost him the 1976 election. It is not all that useful to revisit the specifics of what transpired in the closing moments of an interview conducted haphazardly over several months, and I will accept what Carter said in our last exchange of letters on the subject: "I can see the reason for your concern about my use of the word 'surreptitious' in describing your continuing to record our conversation for *Playboy*. This was an unfortunate choice of a word, implying that you deliberately misled me about whether the interview was over. The fact is that you and I have an honest difference of memory about these few minutes together . . . I've never meant to impugn either your integrity or the accuracy of your reporting."

Let's chalk the episode up to the overreaching of Carter's handlers in manipulating the news media. They had been successful far beyond their expectations in dressing up the former Governor of a small state to appear as a larger-than-life player on the world stage. Regrettably, Carter was not really ready for that role until *after* he had served as President.

⚬

The following is my most widely publicized presidential interview, published in Playboy *in November 1976 (Copyright ©1976* Playboy. *Reprinted with permission. All rights reserved.)*

THE BIOGRAPHICAL DETAILS ARE ALL TOO FAMILIAR BY NOW and, indeed, may seem a little pointless this month. If

JIMMY CARTER

12/13/96

To Robert Scheer

I can see the reason for your concern about my use of the word "surreptitious" in describing your continuing to record our conversation for <u>Playboy</u>. This was an unfortunate choice of a word, implying that you deliberately misled me about whether the interview was over.

The fact is that you and I have an honest difference of memory about these few minutes together. I thought that the interview had been concluded and did not realize that the tape recorder was still going. You have explained that you thought I was aware of the conversation being on the record.

I've never meant to impugn either your integrity or the accuracy of your reporting. In including this explanation in my most recent book, <u>Living Faith</u>, I intended to explain in a somewhat humorous way the difficulty of interpreting theological or religious beliefs in an abbreviated way to a general audience - especially to readers of that particular article.

If convenient for you, I look forward to seeing you on my upcoming visit to Los Angeles.

Best wishes,

Jimmy Carter

Jimmy Carter is elected President of the United States a few weeks from now, the facts about where he spent his youth, how he was educated, and the way he came out of nowhere to capture the Democratic nomination will soon enough be available in history books and on cereal boxes.

What will be less available and less familiar is what kind of person Carter is. To many Americans, the old charge that he was "fuzzy" on the issues may be less accurate than the persistent feeling that he is fuzzy as a personality. Even this late in the campaign, Carter remains for many an unknown quantity.

When Carter agreed to do a "*Playboy* interview," we decided we'd try our best not to add to all the hype that always gushes forth during a presidential campaign. We wanted to pit him against an interviewer who would prod him and challenge him and not be afraid to ask irreverent questions. Our choice of interviewer was natural: Robert Scheer, the Bronx-born, Berkeley-based journalist who in the past years has done interviews with California Governor Jerry Brown for *Playboy* (which was widely regarded as the earliest and most thorough exposure of Brown's curious politics and beliefs) and both William and Emily Harris for *New Times* (which provided crucial evidence in the trial of Patty Hearst).

For three months, Scheer dogged the footsteps of the peanut farmer who would be President, scrambling aboard press planes, sleeping in motels, hanging out with the pack of journalists that grew in size as the campaign gathered momentum. With the support of Carter's young aides—notably, press secretary Jody Powell and campaign manager Hamilton Jordan—Scheer and *Playboy* managed to log more hours of recorded conversations with the candidate than any other publication or news medium—a fact Carter joked about at the final session. After writing the accompanying article about his experiences and about Carter, a very exhausted Scheer filed this report:

It was the day after the Democratic Convention in New York City. Jody Powell was harried.

"Listen, Scheer, I'm not going to kid you. Now that he's the nominee, I've got over 700 requests from all over the world for interviews. He's told me to cut back, but I've got a prior commitment to you guys and I'm going to honor it. So hop a plane down to his place in Plains. We'll just cut out an appointment with some future Secretary of State."

Jody keeps his sense of humor even when he's harried. I had already logged hours of tape with Carter under conditions that were never less than chaotic. Our conversations had started when his chances were shakier and his time slightly more available. But, as Jody had said, once he became the nominee, it was going to be even tougher.

Some of our sessions were as short as half an hour on board the campaign plane, with the roar of engines and the pilot's announcements adding to the frenzy. Playboy and I both hung in there through the months, taking (and paying for) flights halfway across the country on the tentative promise of yet one more hurried chat. After all the baggage searches by the Secret Service and the many times I'd had to lurch up an airplane aisle, fumbling with my tape recorder, I was looking forward to a leisurely conversation with Carter at his home after the nomination.

Earlier this year, when I was working on the interview with Governor Jerry Brown, my Playboy editor, Barry Golson, had joined me for the final sessions at the Governor's office in Sacramento. It had produced interesting results—I, the aggressive Berkeley radical, Golson, the Eastern diplomatic Yalie. We felt the Mutt and Jeff technique would be valuable with Carter as well, so Golson and I traveled to Plains for the final session.

Down in Plains, everything was normal. Brother Billy Carter was in his blue overalls, leaning against a storefront, drawling about this and that to one of the locals who hadn't been up to New York City for the big show. We drove past the Secret Service barricades, past daughter Amy's lemonade stand, and parked in front of the Carter home. As we entered the front door, the candidate, dressed in rumpled work clothes and dusty clodhoppers, was ushering out an impeccably dressed six-man contingent from Reader's Digest.

As we said hello and sat down in his living room to adjust our tape recorders, I remarked to Carter that he must be in a puckish mood, talking to both the Digest and Playboy on the same afternoon. Carter flashed us every one of his teeth: "Yeah, but you guys must have some kind of blackmail leverage on Jody. I've spent more time with you than with Time, Newsweek, and all the others combined."

It was a flattering opening shot, but probably more canny and less casual than it sounded. A week earlier, during the Democratic Convention, Golson had bumped into Jordan at a party in New York. Neither of them was entirely sober, and they discussed the interview. Golson said something about all the time Carter had spent with me. Jordan replied, "We wouldn't do it if it weren't in our interest. It's your readers who are probably predisposed toward Jimmy—but they may not vote at all if they feel uneasy about him."

For me, the purpose of the questioning was not to get people to vote for or against the man, but to push Carter on some of the vagueness he's wrapped himself in. We tried to get beyond the campaigner to some of the personal doubts and confusions—as well as the strengths—of the man himself. Throughout my months on the campaign trail, I found Carter impatient with social chitchat and eager for challenging questions. He is thin-skinned, as others have reported, and he'll glare at you if he doesn't like something you've asked. But he can take it as well as dish it out and, unlike many other politicians I've interviewed, he'll eventually respond directly to a question if you press him hard enough. The

best evidence of this is contained in the final portion of the inter-
view, an open and revealing monologue that occurred because we
happened to ask him one last question on a topic about which he's
become impatient and frustrated.

Oh, just incidentally, there's one bit of folklore about Jimmy
Carter whose authenticity I can vouch for. When I've had a rough
day, I've been known to toss down a drink or four, and I wondered
what Carter did when he needed replenishment. I got my answer
during one short session as I slipped into the plane seat next to him
after he'd had a miserable day on the hustings. Between answers,
he would gobble down handfuls of peanuts at about the same rate
at which I drink. Different strokes, I thought.

PLAYBOY After nearly two years on the campaign trail, don't
you feel a little numbed by the routine—for instance, having to give the same speech over and over?

CARTER Sometimes. Once, when I was campaigning in the
Florida primary, I made twelve speeches in one day. It was
the worst day I ever had. But I generally have tried to
change the order of the speech and emphasize different
things. Sometimes I abbreviate and sometimes I elaborate.
Of twenty different parts in a speech, I might take seven or
eight and change them around. It depends on the audience—black people, Jewish people, *chicanos*—and that gives
me the ability to make speeches that aren't boring to myself.

PLAYBOY Every politician probably emphasizes different
things to different audiences, but in your case, there's been
a common criticism that you seem to have several faces,
that you try to be all things to all people. How do you
respond to that?

CARTER I can't make myself believe these are contrivances
and subterfuges I've adopted to get votes. It may be, and I

can't get myself to admit it, but what I want to do is to let people know how I stand on the issues as honestly as I can.

PLAYBOY If you feel you've been fully honest, why has the charge persisted that you're "fuzzy" on the issues?

CARTER It started during the primaries, when most of my opponents were members of Congress. When any question on an issue came up, they would say, "I'm for the Kennedy-Corman bill on health care, period, no matter what's in it." If the question was employment, they would say, "I'm for the Humphrey-Hawkins bill, no matter what's in it." But those bills were constantly being amended!

I'm just not able to do that. I have to understand what I'm talking about, and simplistic answers identifying my position with such-and-such a House bill are something I can't put forward. That's one reason I've been seen as fuzzy.

Another is that I'm not an ideologue and my positions are not predictable. Without any criticism of McGovern, if the questions had ever come up on abortion, you could pretty well anticipate what he was going to say. If it were amnesty, you could predict what McGovern was going to say about that. But I've tried to analyze each question individually; I've taken positions that to me are fair and rational, and sometimes my answers are complicated.

The third reason is that I wasn't a very vulnerable opponent for those who ran against me. Fuzziness was the only issue Congressman Udall, Senator Church—and others that are hard to remember now—could adopt in their campaigns against me. I think the drumming of that factor into the consciousness of the American voter obviously had some impact.

PLAYBOY Still, not everybody's sure whether you're a conservative in liberal clothing or vice versa. FDR, for instance, turned out to be something of a surprise to people who'd voted for him, because he hadn't seemed as progressive before he was elected as he turned out to be. Could you be a surprise that way?

CARTER I don't believe that's going to be the case. If you analyze the Democratic Party platform, you'll see that it's a very progressive, very liberal, very socially motivated platform. What sometimes surprises people is that I carry out my promises. People ask how a peanut farmer from the South who believes in balanced budgets and tough management of government can possibly give the country tax and welfare reform, or a national health program, or insist on equal rights for blacks and women. Well, I'm going to *do* those things. I've promised them during the campaign, so I don't think there will be many people disappointed—or surprised—when I carry out those commitments as President.

PLAYBOY But isn't it true that you turned out to be more liberal as Governor of Georgia than people who voted for you had any reason to suspect?

CARTER I don't really think so. No. The *Atlanta Constitution*, which was the source of all information about me, categorized me during the gubernatorial campaign as an ignorant, racist, backward, ultraconservative, rednecked South Georgia peanut farmer. Its candidate, Carl Sanders, the former Governor, was characterized as an enlightened, progressive, well-educated, urbane, forceful, competent public offical. I never agreed with the categorization that was made of me during the campaign. I was the same person before and after I became Governor. I remember keeping a check list, and every time I made a promise during the campaign, I wrote it down in a notebook. I believe I carried out every promise I made. I told several people during the campaign that one of the phrases I was going to use in my inaugural speech was that the time for racial discrimination was over. I wrote and made that speech.

The ultraconservatives in Georgia—who aren't supporting me now, by the way—voted for me because of their animosity toward Carl Sanders. I was the alternative to him. They never asked me, "Are you a racist or have you been a member of the Ku Klux Klan?" because they knew I wasn't and hadn't been. And yet, despite predictions early this year by the *Atlanta Constitution* that I couldn't get a majority of the primary vote in Georgia against Wallace, I received about eighty-five percent of the votes. So I don't think the Georgia people have the feeling I betrayed them.

PLAYBOY Considering what you've just said about the *Atlanta Constitution*, how do you feel about the media in general and about the job they do in covering election issues?

CARTER There's still a tendency on the part of some members of the press to treat the South, you know, as a suspect nation. There are a few who think that since I am a Southern Governor, I must be a secret racist or there's something in a closet somewhere that's going to be revealed to show my true colors. There's been a constant probing back ten, twelve years in my background, even as early as the first primaries. Nobody probed like that into the background of Udall or Bayh or other people. But I don't object to it particularly, I just recognize it.

(The answer was broken off and, at a later session, Carter returned to the question of the press and its coverage of issues. This time he was tired, his head sunk far back into his airplane seat. The exchange occurred during one of the late primaries.)

CARTER Issues? The local media are interested, all right, but the nation's news media have absolutely no interest in issues *at all*. Sometimes we freeze out the national media so we can open up press conferences to local people. At least we get questions from them—on timber management, on health care, on education. But the traveling press have zero interest in any issue unless it's a matter of making a mistake. What they're looking for is a forty-seven-second argument between me and another candidate or something like that. There's nobody in the back of this plane who would ask an issue question unless he thought he could trick me into some crazy statement.

PLAYBOY One crazy statement you were supposed to have made was reported by Robert Shrum after he quit as your speechwriter earlier this year. He said he'd been in conversations with you when you made some slighting references to Jewish voters. What's your version of what happened?

CARTER Shrum dreamed up eight or ten conversations that never took place, and nobody in the press ever asked me if they had occurred. The press just assumed that they had. I never talked to Shrum in private except for maybe a couple of minutes. If he had told the truth, if I had said all the things he claimed I had said, I wouldn't vote for *myself*.

When a poll came out early in the primaries that said I had a small proportion of the Jewish vote, I said, "Well, this is really a disappointment to me—we've worked so hard with the Jewish voters. But my pro-Israel stand won't change, even if I don't get a single Jewish vote; I guess we'll have to depend on non-Jews to put me in office." But Shrum treated it as if it were some kind of racist disavowal of Jews. Well, that's a kind of sleazy twisting of a conversation.

PLAYBOY While we're on the subject of the press, how do you feel about an issue that concerns the press itself—the right of journalists to keep their sources secret?

CARTER I would do everything I could to protect the secrecy of sources for the news media.

PLAYBOY Both the press *and* the public seem to have made an issue out of your Baptist beliefs. Why do you think this has happened?

CARTER I'm not unique. There are a lot of people in this country who have the same religious faith. It's not a mysterious or mystical or magical thing. But for those who don't know the feeling of someone who believes in Christ, who is aware of the presence of God, there is, I presume, a quizzical attitude toward it. But it's always been something I've discussed very frankly throughout my adult life.

PLAYBOY We've heard that you pray twenty-five times a day. Is that true?

CARTER I've never counted. I've forgotten who asked me that, but I'd say that on an eventful day, you know, it's something like that.

PLAYBOY When you say an eventful day, do you mean you pray as a kind of pause, to control your blood pressure and relax?

CARTER Well, yes. If something happens to me that is a little disconcerting, if I feel a trepidation, if a thought comes into my head of animosity or hatred toward someone, then I just kind of say a brief silent prayer. I don't ask for myself but just to let me understand what another's feelings might be. Going through a crowd, quite often people bring me a problem, and I pray that their needs might be met. A lot of times, I'll be in the backseat of a car and not know what kind of audience I'm going to face. I don't mean I'm terror-stricken, just that I don't know what to expect next. I'll pray then, but it's not something that's conscious or formal. It's just a part of my life.

PLAYBOY One reason some people might be quizzical is that you have a sister, Ruth, who is a faith healer. The association of politics with faith healing is an idea many find disconcerting.

CARTER I don't even know what political ideas Ruth has had, and for people to suggest I'm under the hold of a sister— or any other person—is a complete distortion of fact. I don't have any idea whether Ruth has supported Democrats or not, whereas the political views of my other sister, Gloria, are remarkably harmonious with mine.

PLAYBOY So you're closer to Gloria, who has described herself as a McGovern Democrat and rides motorcycles as a hobby?

CARTER I like them both. But in the past twenty or twenty-five years, I've been much closer to Gloria, because she lives next door to me and Ruth lives in North Carolina. We hardly saw Ruth more than once a year at family get-togethers. What political attitudes Ruth has had, I have not the slightest idea. But my mother and Gloria and I have been very compatible. We supported Lyndon Johnson openly during the 1964 campaign, and my mother worked at the Johnson county headquarters, which was courageous, not an easy thing to do politically. She would come out of the Johnson headquarters and find her car smeared with soap and the antenna tied in a knot and ugly messages left on the front seat. When my young boys went to school, they were beaten. So Mother and Gloria and I, along with my Rosalynn, have had the same attitudes even when we were in a minority in Plains. But Ruth lives in a different world in North Carolina.

PLAYBOY Granting that you're not as close to your religious sister as is assumed, we still wonder how *your* religious beliefs would translate into political action. For instance, would you appoint judges who would be harsh or lenient toward victimless crimes—offenses such as drug use, adultery, sodomy, and homosexuality?

CARTER Committing adultery, according to the Bible—which I believe in—is a sin. For us to hate one another, for us to have sexual intercourse outside marriage, for us to engage in homosexual activities, for us to steal, for us to lie—all these are sins. But Jesus teaches us not to judge other people. We don't say to another human being, "You're condemned because you commit sins." All Christians, all of us, acknowledge that we are sinful and the judgment comes from God, not from another human being.

As Governor of Georgia, I tried to shift the emphasis of law enforcement away from victimless crimes. We lessened the penalties on the use of marijuana. We removed alcoholism as a crime, and so forth. Victimless crimes, in my opinion, should have a very low priority in terms of enforcing the laws on the books. But as to appointing judges, that would not be the basis on which I'd appoint them. I would choose people who were competent, whose judgment and integrity were sound. I think it would be inappropriate to ask them how they were going to rule on a particular question before I appointed them.

PLAYBOY What *about* those laws on the books that govern personal behavior? Should they be enforced?

CARTER Almost every state in the Union has laws against adultery and many of them have laws against homosexuality and sodomy. But they're often considered by police officers as not worthy of enforcing to the extent of disturbing consenting adults or breaking into a person's private home.

PLAYBOY But, of course, that gives the police a lot of leeway to enforce them selectively. Do you think such laws should be on the books at all?

CARTER That's a judgment for the individual state to make. I think the laws are on the books quite often because of their relationship to the Bible. Early in the nation's development, the Judeo-Christian moral standards were accepted as a basis for civil law. But I don't think it hurts to have this kind of standard maintained as a goal. I also think it's an area that's been interpreted by the Supreme Court as one that can rightfully be retained by the individual states.

PLAYBOY Do you think liberalization of the laws over the past decade by factors as diverse as the pill and *Playboy*—an effect some people would term permissiveness—has been a harmful development?

CARTER Liberalization of some of the laws has been good. You can't legislate morality. We tried to outlaw consumption of alcoholic beverages. We found that violation of the law led to bigger crimes and bred disrespect for the law.

PLAYBOY We're confused. You say morality can't be legislated, yet you support certain laws because they preserve old moral standards. How do you reconcile the two positions?

CARTER I believe people should honor civil laws. If there is a conflict between God's law and civil law, we should honor God's law. But we should be willing to accept civil punishment. Most of Christ's original followers were killed because of their belief in Christ: They violated the civil law in following God's law. Reinhold Niebuhr, a theologian who has dealt with this problem at length, says that the framework of law is a balancing of forces in a society: The law itself tends to alleviate tensions brought about by these forces. But the laws on the books are not a measure of this balance nearly as much as the degree to which the laws are enforced. So when a law is anachronistic and is carried over from a previous age, it's just not observed.

PLAYBOY What we're getting at is how much you'd tolerate behavior that your religion considers wrong. For instance, in San Francisco you said you considered homosexuality a sin. What does that mean in political terms?

CARTER The issue of homosexuality always makes me nervous. It's obviously one of the major issues in San Francisco. I don't have any, you know, personal knowledge about homosexuality, and I guess being a Baptist, that would contribute to a sense of being uneasy.

PLAYBOY Does it make you uneasy to discuss it simply as a political question?

CARTER No, it's more complicated than that. It's political, it's moral, and it's strange territory for me. At home in Plains, we've had homosexuals in our community, our church. There's never been any sort of discrimination—some embarrassment but no animosity, no harassment. But to inject it into a public discussion on politics and how it conflicts with morality is a new experience for me. I've thought about it a lot, but I don't see how to handle it differently from the way I look on other sexual acts outside marriage.

PLAYBOY We'd like to ask you a blunt question: Isn't it just these views about what's "sinful" and what's "immoral" that contribute to the feeling that you might get a call from God, or get inspired and push the wrong button? More realistically, wouldn't we expect a puritanical tone to be set in the White House if you were elected?

CARTER Harry Truman was a Baptist. Some people get very abusive about the Baptist faith. If people want to know about it, they can read the New Testament. The main thing is that we don't think we're better than anyone else. We are taught not to judge other people. But as to some of the behavior you've mentioned, I can't change the teachings of Christ. I can't change the teachings of Christ! I believe in them, and a lot of people in this country do as well. Jews believe in the Bible. They have the same commandments.

PLAYBOY Then you as President, in appointing Supreme Court Justices—

CARTER I think we've pursued this conversation long enough—if you have another question . . . Look, I'll try to express my views. It's not a matter of condemnation, it's not a matter of persecution. I've been a Governor for four years. Anybody can come and look at my record. I didn't run around breaking down people's doors to see if they were fornicating. This is something that's ridiculous.

PLAYBOY We know you didn't, but we're being so persistent because of this matter of self-righteousness, because of the moral certainty of so many of your statements. People wonder if Jimmy Carter ever is unsure. Has he ever been wrong, has he ever had a failure of moral nerve?

CARTER Well, there are a lot of things I could have done differently had I known during my early life what I now know. I would certainly have spoken out more clearly and loudly on the civil-rights issue. I would have demanded that our nation never get involved initially in the Vietnam War. I would have told the country in 1972 that Watergate was a much more horrible crime than we thought at the time. It's easy to say in hindsight what you would have done if you had had information that you have now.

PLAYBOY We were asking not so much about hindsight as

about being fallible. Aren't there any examples of things you did that weren't absolutely right?

CARTER I don't mind repeating myself. There are a lot of those in my life. Not speaking out for the cessation of the war in Vietnam. The fact that I didn't crusade at a very early stage for civil rights in the South, for the one-man, one-vote ruling. It might be that now I should drop my campaign for President and start a crusade for black-majority rule in South Africa or Rhodesia. It might be that later on, we'll discover there were opportunities in our lives to do wonderful things and we didn't take advantage of them.

The fact that in 1954 I sat back and required the Warren Court to make this ruling without having crusaded myself—that was obviously a mistake on my part. But these are things you have to judge under the circumstances that prevailed when the decisions were being made. Back then, the Congress, the President, the newspaper editors, the civil libertarians all said that separate-but-equal facilities were adequate. These are opportunities overlooked, or maybe they could be characterized as absence of courage.

PLAYBOY Since you still seem to be saying you'd have done the right thing if you'd known what you know now, is it realistic to conclude that a person running for the highest office in the land *can't* admit many mistakes or moments of self-doubt?

CARTER I think that's a human circumstance. But if there are issues I'm avoiding because of a lack of courage, either I don't recognize them or I can't make myself recognize them.

PLAYBOY You mentioned Vietnam. Do you feel you spoke out at an early enough stage against the war?

CARTER No, I did not. I never spoke out publicly about withdrawing completely from Vietnam until March of 1971.

PLAYBOY Why?

CARTER It was the first time anybody had asked me about it. I was a farmer before then and wasn't asked about the war until I took office. There was a general feeling in this country that we ought not to be in Vietnam to start with. The American people were tremendously misled about the immediate prospects for victory, about the level of our involvement, about the relative cost in American lives. If I had known in the '60s what I knew in the early '70s, I think I would have spoken out more strongly. I was not in public office. When I took office as Governor in 1970, I began to speak out about complete withdrawal. It was late compared with what many others had done, but I think it's accurate to say that the Congress and the people—with the exception of very small numbers of people—shared the belief that we were protecting our democratic allies.

PLAYBOY Even without holding office, you must have had some feelings about the war. When do you recall first feeling it was wrong?

CARTER There was an accepted feeling by me and everybody else that we ought not to be there, that we should never have gotten involved, we ought to get out.

PLAYBOY You felt that way all through the '60s?

CARTER Yeah, that's right, and I might hasten to say that it was the same feeling expressed by Senators Russell and Talmadge—very conservative Southern political figures. They thought it was a serious mistake to be in Vietnam.

PLAYBOY Your son Jack fought in that war. Did you have any qualms about it at the time?

CARTER Well, yes, I had problems about my son fighting in the war, period. But I never make my sons' decisions for them. Jack went to war feeling it was foolish, a waste of time, much more deeply that I did. He also felt it would have been grossly unfair for him not to go when other, poorer kids had to.

PLAYBOY You were in favor of allocating funds for the South Vietnamese in 1975 as the war was coming to a close, weren't you?

CARTER That was when we were getting ready to evacuate our troops. The purpose of the money was to get our people out and maintain harmony between us and our Vietnamese allies, who had fought with us for twenty-five years. And I said yes, I would do that. But it was not a permanent thing, not to continue the war but to let us get our troops out in an orderly fashion.

PLAYBOY How do you respond to the argument that it was the Democrats, not the Republicans, who got us into the Vietnam War?

CARTER I think it started originally, maybe, with Eisenhower, then Kennedy, Johnson, and then Nixon. It's not a partisan matter. I think Eisenhower probably first got us in there thinking that since France had failed, our country might slip in there and succeed. Kennedy thought he could escalate involvement by going beyond the mere advisory role. I guess if there was one President who made the most determined effort, conceivably, to end the war by massive force, it was certainly Johnson. And Nixon went into Cambodia and bombed it, and so forth.

It's not partisan—it's just a matter that evolved as a habit over several administrations. There was a governmental consciousness to deal in secrecy, to exclude the American people, to mislead them with false statements and sometimes outright lies. Had the American people been told the facts from the beginning by Eisenhower, Kennedy, McNamara, Johnson, Kissinger, and Nixon, I think there would have been different decisions made in our government.

PLAYBOY At the Democratic Convention, you praised Johnson as a President who had vastly extended human rights. Were you simply omitting any mention of Vietnam?

CARTER It was obviously the factor that destroyed his political career and damaged his whole life. But as far as what I said at the convention, there hasn't been another President in our history—with the possible exception of Abraham Lincoln—who did so much to advance the cause of human rights.

PLAYBOY Except for the human rights of the Vietnamese and the Americans who fought there.

CARTER Well, I really believe that Johnson's motives were good. I think he tried to end the war even while the fighting was going on, and he was speaking about massive rehabilitation efforts, financed by our government, to help people. I don't think he ever had any desire for permanent entrenchment of our forces in Vietnam. I think he had a mistaken notion that he was defending democracy and that what he was doing was compatible with the desires of the South Vietnamese.

PLAYBOY Then what about the Administration that *ended* the war? Don't you have to give credit to Kissinger, the Secretary of State of a Republican President, for ending a war that a Democratic President escalated?

CARTER I think the statistics show that more bombs were dropped in Vietnam and Cambodia under Nixon and Kissinger than under Johnson. Both administrations were at fault; but I don't think the end came about as a result of

Kissinger's superior diplomacy. It was the result of several factors that built up in an inexorable way: the demonstrated strength of the Viet Cong, the tremendous pressure to withdraw that came from the American people, and an aroused Congress. I think Nixon and Kissinger did the proper thing in starting a phased withdrawal, but I don't consider that to be a notable diplomatic achievement by Kissinger. As we've now learned, he promised the Vietnamese things that cannot be delivered—reparations, payments, economic advantages, and so forth. Getting out of Vietnam was very good, but whether Kissinger deserved substantial diplomatic credit for it is something I doubt.

PLAYBOY You've said you'll pardon men who refused military service because of the Vietnam War but not necessarily those who deserted while they were in the Armed Forces. Is that right?

CARTER That's right. I would not include them. Deserters ought to be handled on a separate-case basis. There's a difference to me. I was in the Navy for a long time. Somebody who goes into the military joins a kind of mutual-partnership arrangement, you know what I mean? Your life depends on other people, their lives depend on you. So I don't intend to pardon the deserters. As far as the other categories of war resisters go, to me the ones who stayed in this country and let their opposition to the war be known publicly are more heroic than those who went and hid in Sweden. But I'm not capable of judging motives, so I'm just going to declare a blanket pardon.

PLAYBOY When?

CARTER The first week I'm in office.

PLAYBOY You've avoided the word *amnesty* and chosen to use the word *pardon*, but there doesn't seem to be much difference between the two in the dictionary. Could it be because amnesty is more emotionally charged and pardon is a word more people will accept?

CARTER You know, I can't deny that. But my reason for distinguishing between the two is that I think that all of those poor, and often black, young men who went to Vietnam are more worthy of recognition than those who defected, and the word *pardon* includes those who simply avoided the war completely. But I just want to bring the defectors back to this country without punishment and, in doing so, I would like to have the support of the American people. I haven't been able to devise for private presentation a better way to do it.

PLAYBOY Earlier this year, there was a report that as Governor of Georgia, you had issued a resolution that seemed to support William Calley after his trial for the My Lai massacre and that you'd referred to him as a scapegoat. Was that a misreading of your position?

CARTER Yes. There was no reason for me to mislead anybody on the Calley thing. I thought when I first read about him that Calley was a murderer. He was tried in Georgia and found to be a murderer. I said two things: one, that Calley was not typical of our American Servicemen, and two, that he was a scapegoat because his superiors should have been tried too. The resolution I made as Governor didn't have anything to do with Calley. The purpose of it, calling for solidarity with our boys in Vietnam, was to distinguish American Servicemen fighting an unpopular war. They weren't murderers, but they were equated, unfortunately, with a murderer in people's minds.

PLAYBOY In preparing for this interview, we spoke with your mother, your son Chip, and your sister Gloria. We asked them what single action would most disappoint them in a Carter presidency. They all replied that it would be if you ever sent troops to intervene in a foreign war. In fact, Miss Lillian said she would picket the White House.

CARTER They share my views completely.

PLAYBOY What about more limited military action? Would you have handled the Mayaguez incident the same way President Ford did?

CARTER Let me assess that in retrospect. It's obvious we didn't have adequate intelligence; we attacked an island when the Mayaguez crew was no longer there. There was a desire, I think, on the part of President Ford to extract maximum publicity from our effort, so that about twenty-three minutes after our crew was released, we went ahead and bombed the island airport. I hope I would have been capable of getting adequate intelligence, surrounded the island more quickly, and isolated the crew, so we wouldn't have had to attack the airport after the crew was released. These are some of the differences in the way I would have done it.

PLAYBOY So it's a matter of degree; you would have intervened militarily, too.

CARTER I would have done everything necessary to keep the crew from being taken to the mainland, yes.

PLAYBOY Then would you summarize your position on foreign intervention?

CARTER I would never intervene for the purpose of overthrowing a government. If enough were at stake for our national interest, I would use prestige, legitimate diplomatic leverage, trade mechanisms. But it would be the sort of effort that would not be embarrassing to this nation if revealed completely. I don't ever want to do anything as

President that would be a contravention of the moral and ethical standards that I would exemplify in my own life as an individual or that would violate the principles or character of the American people.

PLAYBOY Do you feel it's fair criticism that you seem to be going back to some familiar faces—such as Paul Warnke and Cyrus Vance—for foreign-policy advice? Isn't there a danger of history repeating itself when you seek out those who were involved in our Vietnam decisions?

CARTER I haven't heard that criticism. If you're raising it, then I respond to the new critic. These people contribute to foreign-affairs journals, they individually explore different concepts of foreign policy. I have fifteen or twenty people who work with me very closely on foreign affairs. Their views are quite divergent. The fact that they may or may not have been involved in foreign-policy decisions in the past is certainly no detriment to their ability to help me now.

PLAYBOY In some respects, your foreign policy seems similar to that established by Kissinger, Nixon, and Ford. In fact, Kissinger stated that he didn't think your differences were substantial. How, precisely, does your view differ from theirs?

CARTER As I've said in my speeches, I feel the policy of *détente* has given up too much to the Russians and gotten too little in return. I also feel Kissinger has equated his own popularity with the so-called advantages of *détente*. As I've traveled and spoken with world leaders—Helmut Schmidt of West Germany, Yitzhak Rabin of Israel, various leaders in Japan—I've discerned a deep concern on their part that the United States has abandoned a long-standing principle: to consult mutually, to share responsibility for problems. This has been a damaging thing. In addition, I believe we should have stronger bilateral relations with developing nations.

PLAYBOY What do you mean when you say we've given up too much to the Russians?

CARTER One example I've mentioned often is the Helsinki agreement. I never saw any reason we should be involved in the Helsinki meetings at all. We added the stature of our presence and signature to an agreement that, in effect, ratified the takeover of Eastern Europe by the Soviet Union. We got very little, if anything, in return. The Russians promised they would honor democratic principles and permit the free movement of their citizens, including those who want to emigrate. The Soviet Union has not lived up to those promises and Mr. Brezhnev was able to celebrate the major achievement of his diplomatic life.

PLAYBOY Are you charging that Kissinger was too soft on the Russians?

CARTER Kissinger has been in the position of being almost uniquely a spokesman for our nation. I think that is a legitimate role and a proper responsibility of the President himself. Kissinger has had a kind of Lone Ranger, secret foreign-policy attitude, which almost ensures that there cannot be adequate consultation with our allies; there cannot be a long-range commitment to unchanging principles; there cannot be a coherent evolution on foreign policy; there cannot be a bipartisan approach with support and advice from Congress. This is what I would avoid as President and is one of the major defects in the Nixon-Ford foreign policy as expressed by Kissinger.

PLAYBOY Say, do you always do your own sewing?

(This portion of the interview also took place aboard a plane. As he answered the interviewer's questions, Carter had been sewing a rip in his jacket with a needle and thread he carried with him.)

CARTER Uh-huh. *(He bit off the thread with his teeth.)*

PLAYBOY Anyway, you said earlier that your foreign policy would exemplify your moral and ethical standards. Isn't there as much danger in an overly moralistic policy as in the kind that is too pragmatic?

CARTER I've said I don't think we should intervene militarily, but I see no reason not to express our approval, at least verbally, with those nations that develop democratically. When Kissinger says, as he did recently in a speech, that Brazil is the sort of government that is most compatible with ours—well, that's the kind of thing we want to change. Brazil is not a democratic government: It's a military dictatorship. In many instances, it's highly repressive to political prisoners. Our government should justify the character and moral principles of the American people, and our foreign policy should not short-circuit that for temporary advantage. I think in every instance we've done that, it's been counterproductive. When the CIA undertakes covert activities that might be justified if they were peaceful, we always suffer when they're revealed—it always seems as if we're trying to tell other people how to act. When Kissinger and Ford warned Italy she would be excluded from NATO if the Communists assumed power, that was the best way to make sure Communists *were* elected. The Italian voters resent it. A proper posture for our country in this sort of situation is to show, through demonstration, that our own government works properly, that democracy is advantageous, and let the Italian people make their own decisions.

PLAYBOY And what if the Communists in Italy had been elected in greater numbers than they were? What if they had actually become a key part of the Italian government?

CARTER I think it would be a mechanism for subversion of the strength of NATO and the cohesiveness that ought to bind European countries together. The proper posture was the one taken by Helmut Schmidt, who said that German aid to Italy would be endangered.

PLAYBOY Don't you think that constitutes a form of intervention in the democratic processes of another nation?

CARTER No, I don't. I think that when the democratic nations of the world express themselves frankly and forcefully and openly, that's a proper exertion of influence. We did the same thing in Portugal. Instead of going in through surreptitious means and trying to overthrow the government when it looked like the minority Communist Party was going to assume power, the NATO countries as a group made it clear to Portugal what it would lose in the way of friendship, trade opportunities, and so forth. And the Portuguese people, recognizing that possibility, decided that the Communists should not lead their government. Well, that was legitimate exertion of influence, in my opinion. It was done openly and it was a mere statement of fact.

PLAYBOY You used the word *subversion* referring to communism. Hasn't the world changed since we used to throw words like that around? Aren't the West European Communist parties more independent of Moscow and more willing to respect democracy?

CARTER Yes, the world's changed. In my speeches, I've made it clear that as far as Communist leaders in such countries as Italy, France, and Portugal are concerned, I would not want to close the doors of communication, consultation, and friendship to them. That would be an almost automatic forcing of the Communist leaders into the Soviet sphere of influence. I also think we should keep open our opportunities for the East European nations—even those that are completely Communist—to trade with us, understand us, have tourist exchange, and give them an option from complete domination by the Soviet Union.

But again, I don't think you could expect West Germany to lend Poland two billion dollars—which was the figure in the case of Italy—when Poland is part of the Soviet government's satellite and supportive-nation group. So I think the best way to minimize totalitarian influence within the governments of Europe is to make sure the democratic forces perform properly. The major shift toward the Communists in Italy was in the local elections, when the Christian Democrats destroyed their reputation by graft and corruption. If we can make our own government work, if we can avoid future Watergates and avoid the activities of the CIA that have been revealed, if we can minimize joblessness and inflation, this will be a good way to lessen the inclination of people in other countries to turn away from our form of government.

PLAYBOY What about Chile? Would you agree that that was a case of the United States, through the CIA, intervening improperly?

CARTER Yes. There's no doubt about it. Sure.

PLAYBOY And you would stop that sort of thing?

CARTER Absolutely. Yes, sir.

PLAYBOY What about economic sanctions? Do you feel we should have punished the Allende government the way we did?

CARTER That's a complicated question, because we don't

know what caused the fall of the Allende government, the murder of perhaps thousands of people, the incarceration of many others. I don't have any facts as to how deeply involved we were, but my impression is that we were involved quite deeply. As I said, I wouldn't have done that if I were President. But as to whether or not we ought to have an option on the terms of our loans, repayment schedules, interest charges, the kinds of materials we sell to them—those are options I would retain, depending upon the compatibility of a foreign government with our own.

PLAYBOY To what do you attribute all those deceptions and secret maneuverings through the years? Why were they allowed to happen?

CARTER It was a matter of people just saying, Well, that's politics; we don't have a right to know what our government is doing; secrecy is OK; accepting gifts is OK; excluding the American people is OK. These are the kinds of things I want to change.

PLAYBOY It sounds as if you're saying Americans accepted indecency and lies in their government all too easily. Doesn't that make your constant campaign theme, invoking the decency and honesty of the American people, somewhat naïve and ingenuous?

CARTER I say that the American people are basically decent and honest and want a truthful government. Obviously, I know there are people in this country, out of 214,000,000, who are murderers. There are people, maybe, who don't want a decent government. Maybe there are people who prefer lies to truth. But I don't think it's simplistic to say that our government hasn't measured up to the ethical and moral standards of the people of this country. We've had better governments in the past and I think our people, as

I've said many times, are just as strong, courageous, and intelligent as they were two hundred years ago. I think we still have the same inner strength they had then.

PLAYBOY Even though a lot of people support that feeling, many others think it makes you sound like an evangelist. And that makes it all the more confusing when they read about your hanging out with people so different from you in lifestyle and beliefs. Your publicized friendship with journalist Hunter Thompson, who makes no secret of his affinity for drugs and other craziness, is a good example.

CARTER Well, in the first place, I'm a human being. I'm not a packaged article that you can put in a little box and say, "Here's a Southern Baptist, an ignorant Georgia peanut farmer who doesn't have the right to enjoy music, who has no flexibility in his mind, who can't understand the sensitivities of an interpersonal relationship. He's gotta be predictable. He's gotta be for Calley and for the war. He's gotta be a liar. He's gotta be a racist."

You know, that's the sort of stereotype people tend to assume, and I hope it doesn't apply to me. And I don't see any mystery about having a friendship with Hunter Thompson. I guess it's something that's part of my character, and it becomes a curiosity for those who see some mystery about someone of my background being elected President. I'm just a human being like everybody else. I have different interests, different understandings of the world around me, different relationships with different kinds of people. I have a broad range of friends: sometimes very serious, sometimes very formal, sometimes lighthearted, sometimes intense, sometimes casual.

PLAYBOY So when you find yourself at a rock concert or in some other situation that seems at odds with your rural, religious background, you never feel a sense of estrangement?

CARTER None. No. I feel at home with 'em.

PLAYBOY How did you get to feel this way without going through culture shock?

CARTER I have three sons, who now range from twenty-three to twenty-nine, and the oldest of them were very influenced by Bob Dylan in their attitudes toward civil rights, criminal justice, and the Vietnam War. This was about the period of time I was entering politics. I've been fairly close to my sons and their taste in music influenced my taste, and I was able to see the impact of Bob Dylan's attitudes on young people. And I was both gratified by and involved emotionally in those changes of attitudes.

Later, when I became Governor, I was acquainted with some of the people at Capricorn Records in Macon—Otis Redding and others. It was they who began to meld the white and black music industries, and that was quite a sociological change for our region. So as I began to travel around Georgia, I made contact a few days every month or two with Capricorn Records, just to stay in touch with people in the state, and got to know all the Allman Brothers, Dicky Betts, and others. Later on, I met Charlie Daniels and the Marshall Tucker Band.

Then I decided to run for President. I didn't have any money and didn't have any political base, so I had to depend substantially on the friends I already had. One of my potential sources for fundraising and for recruiting young volunteers was the group of recording stars I already knew. So we began to have concerts and I got to know them even better.

Of course, I've also been close to the country-music folks in Georgia, as well as the Atlanta Symphony

Orchestra. The first large contribution I got—$1,000—was from Robert Shaw, the music director of the orchestra. We've been over at the Grand Ole Opry a few times and gotten to know people like Chubby Jackson and Tom T. Hall.

PLAYBOY There's been a lot of publicity about your relationship with Dylan, whom you quoted in your acceptance speech at the Democratic Convention. How did that come about?

CARTER A number of years ago, my second son, Chip, who was working full-time in our farming business, took a week off during Christmas. He and a couple of his friends drove all the way to New York—just to see Bob Dylan. There had been a heavy snowstorm and the boys had to park several miles from Dylan's home. It was after Dylan was injured, when he was in seclusion. Apparently, Dylan came to the door with two of his kids and shook hands with Chip. By the time Chip got to the nearest phone, a couple of miles away, and called us at home, he was nearly incoherent. Rosalynn couldn't understand what Chip was talking about, so she screamed, "Jimmy, come here quick! Something's happened to Chip!"

We finally deciphered that he had shaken Dylan's hand and was just, you know, very carried away with it. So when I read that Dylan was going on tour again, I wrote him a little personal note and asked him to come visit me at the Governor's mansion. I think he checked with Phil Walden of Capricorn Records and Bill Graham to find out what kind of guy *is* this, and he was assured I didn't want to use him, I was just interested in his music.

The night he came, we had a chance to talk about his music and about changing times and pent-up emotions in young people. He said he didn't have any inclination to change the world, that he wasn't crusading, and that his personal feelings were apparently compatible with the yearnings of an entire generation. We also discussed Israel, which he had a strong interest in. But that's my only contact with Bob Dylan, that night.

PLAYBOY That brings us back to the reason so many people find it hard to get a handle on you: On the one hand, your association with youth culture, civil rights, and other liberal movements; and on the other, your apparent conservatism on many issues. Would you care to put it in a nutshell for us?

CARTER I'll try. On human rights, civil rights, environmental quality, I consider myself to be very liberal. On the management of government, on openness of government, on strengthening individual liberties and local levels of government, I consider myself a conservative. And I don't see that the two attitudes are incompatible.

PLAYBOY Then let's explore a few more issues. Not everyone is sure, for instance, what you mean by your call for tax reform. Does it mean that the burden will shift to corporations and upper-income groups and away from the middle- and lower-income groups, or are you talking merely about a simplified tax code?

CARTER It would involve both. One change I'm calling for is simplification, and the other involves shifting the income-tax burden away from the lower-income families. But what I'm really talking about is total, comprehensive tax reform for the first time since the income tax was approved back in 1913, I think it was.

It's not possible to give you a definitive statement on tax reform any time soon. It's going to take at least a year before we can come up with a new tax structure. But there are some general provisions that would be instituted that aren't there now. The income-tax code, which now comprises 40,000 pages, will be greatly simplified. Income should be taxed only once. We should have a true progressive income tax, so that the higher the income, the higher the percentage of taxation. I see no reason why capital gains should be taxed at half the rate of income from manual labor. I would be committed to a great reduction in tax incentives, loopholes, or whatever you want to call them, which are used as mechanisms to solve transient economic problems; they ought to be on a basis of annual appropriation or a time limit, rather than be built into the tax structure.

In any case, these are five or six things that would be dramatic departures from what we presently have, and they should tell you what side of the issue I stand on.

PLAYBOY Would one of those be increasing taxes for corporations, especially the overseas and domestic profits of multinational corporations?

CARTER No, I don't think so. Obviously, there have been provisions written into the law that favor certain corporations, including those that have overseas investments; I would remove those incentives. Tax laws also benefit those who have the best lobbying efforts, those who have the most influence in Washington, and the larger the corporations are, on the average, the smaller proportion they pay in taxes. Small businesses quite often pay the flat maximum rate, forty-eight percent, while some larger corporations pay as little as five or six percent. That ought to be changed.

But as far as increasing overall corporate taxes above the fifty-percent level, I wouldn't favor that. We also have the circumstance of multinational corporations depending on bribery as a mechanism for determining the outcome of a sale. I think bribery in international affairs ought to be considered a crime and punishable by imprisonment.

PLAYBOY Would you sympathize with the anticorporate attitude that many voters feel?

CARTER Well, I'm not particularly anticorporate, but I'd say I'm more oriented to consumer protection. One of the things I've established throughout the campaign is the need to break up the sweetheart arrangement between regulatory agencies and the industries they regulate. Another is the need for rigid and enthusiastic enforcement of the antitrust laws.

PLAYBOY To take another issue, you favor a comprehensive federal health care system. Why don't you just support the Kennedy-Corman bill, which provides for precisely that?

CARTER As a general philosophy, wherever the private sector can perform a function as effectively and efficiently as the government, I would prefer to keep it within the private sector. So I would like the insurance aspect of the health program to be carried out by employer/employee contribution. There would be contributions from the general fund for those who are indigent. I would also have a very heavy emphasis on preventive health care, since I believe most of the major afflictions that beset people can be prevented or minimized. And I favor the use to a greater degree of nonphysicians, such as nurses, physicians' assistants, and so forth. Some of these things are in conflict with the provisions of the Kennedy-Corman bill.

PLAYBOY Let us ask you about one last stand: abortion.

CARTER I think abortion is wrong and I will do everything I can as President to minimize the need for abortions—

within the framework of the decision of the Supreme Court, which I can't change. Georgia had a more conservative approach to abortion, which I personally favored, but the Supreme Court ruling suits me all right. I signed a Georgia law as Governor that was compatible with the Supreme Court decision.

PLAYBOY You think it's wrong, but the ruling suits you? What would we tell a woman who said her vote would depend on how you stood on abortion?

CARTER If a woman's major purpose in life is to have unrestricted abortions, then she ought *not* to vote for me. But she wouldn't have anyone to vote for.

PLAYBOY There seem to have been relatively few women in important staff positions in your campaign. Is that accurate?

CARTER Women have been in charge of our entire campaign effort in Georgia and in New York State outside New York City. Also in Nebraska, Kansas, a third of the state of Florida, and other areas.

PLAYBOY But whenever we hear about a meeting of top staff members, they almost always seem to be white males. Is that a failing in your organization?

CARTER I don't know about a failing. The three people with whom I consult regularly—in addition to my wife—are white males: Hamilton Jordan, Jody Powell, and Charles Kirbo. But we *do* have a lot of women involved in the campaign. We are now setting up a policy committee to run a nationwide effort to coordinate Democratic races, and fifty percent of the members of this committee will be women. But Jody has been my press secretary since 1970, and Hamilton and Kirbo were my major advisers in 1966. It's such an extremely stable staff that there's been no turnover at all in the past five or six years. But we've made a lot of progress, I think, in including women, and I think you'll see more.

PLAYBOY You mention very frequently how much you count on your wife's advice. Isn't there a strain during the campaign, with the two of you separated so much of the time?

CARTER Well, when I was in the Navy, I was at sea most of the time and I'd see her maybe one or two nights a week. Now, when I'm home in Plains, I see her almost every night. And if I'm elected President, I'll see her *every* night. So there is obviously a time to be together and a time to be separated. If you're apart three or four days and then meet again, it's almost—for me, it's a very exciting reunion. I'll have been away from Rosalynn for a few days and if I see her across an airport lobby, or across a street, I get just as excited as I did when I was, you know, thirty years younger.

We have a very close, very intimate sharing of our lives, and we've had a tremendous magnification of our life's purposes in politics. Before 1966, she and I were both very shy. It was almost a painful thing to approach a stranger or make a speech. It's been a mutual change we've gone through, because we both felt it was worthwhile; so no matter what the outcome of the election, the relationship between Rosalynn and me will be very precious.

PLAYBOY Did you both have the usual share of troubles adjusting to marriage?

CARTER We did at first. We've come to understand each other much better. I was by far the dominant person in the marriage at the beginning, but not anymore. She's just as strong, if not stronger than I am. She's fully equal to me in every way in our relationship, in making business decisions, and she makes most of the decisions about family affairs. And I think it was a struggle for her to achieve this degree of independence and equality in our personal relationship. So, to summarize, years ago we had a lot of quarrels—none serious, particularly—but now we don't.

PLAYBOY A lot of marriages are foundering these days. Why is yours so successful?

CARTER Well, I really love Rosalynn more now than I did when I married her. And I have loved no other women except her. I had gone out with all kinds of girls, sometimes fairly steadily, but I just never cared about them. Rosalynn had been a friend of my sister's and was three years younger than I, which is a tremendous chasm in the high school years. She was just one of those insignificant little girls around the house. Then, when I was twenty-one and home from the Navy on leave, I took her out to a movie. Nothing extraordinary happened, but the next morning I told my mother, "That's the girl I want to marry." It's the best thing that ever happened to me.

We also share a religious faith, and the two or three times in our married life when we've had a serious crisis, I think that's what sustained our marriage and helped us overcome our difficulty. Our children, too, have been a factor binding Rosalynn and me together. After the boys, Amy came along late and it's been especially delightful for me, maybe because she's a little girl.

PLAYBOY This is a tough question to ask, but because it's been such a factor in American political life, we wonder if you've ever discussed with Rosalynn the possibility of being assassinated. And, assuming you have, how do you deal with it in your own mind?

CARTER Well, in the first place, I'm not afraid of death. In the second place, it's the same commitment I made when I volunteered to go into the submarine force. I accepted a

certain degree of danger when I made the original decision, then I didn't worry about it anymore. It wasn't something that preyed on my mind; it wasn't something I had to
reassess every five minutes. There is a certain element of
danger in running for President, borne out by statistics on
the number of Presidents who have been attacked, but I
have to say frankly that it's something I never worry about.

PLAYBOY Your first answer was that you don't fear death. Why
not?

CARTER It's part of my religious belief. I just look at death as
not a threat. It's inevitable, and I have an assurance of
eternal life. There is no feeling on my part that I *have* to be
President, or that I *have* to live, or that I'm immune to danger. It's just that the termination of my physical life is relatively insignificant in my concept of overall existence. I
don't say that in a mysterious way; I recognize the possibility of assassination. But I guess everybody recognizes the
possibility of other forms of death—automobile accidents,
airplane accidents, cancer. I just don't worry.

PLAYBOY There's been some evidence that Johnson and
Nixon both seemed to have gone a bit crazy while they
were in the White House. Do you ever wonder if the pressures of the office might make *anyone* mentally unstable?

CARTER I really don't have the feeling that being in the
White House is what caused Nixon's or Johnson's prob-
lems. Other Presidents have served without developing
mental problems—Roosevelt, Truman, Eisenhower,
Kennedy, for instance. As far as I've been able to discern,
President Ford approaches—or avoids—the duties of the
White House with equanimity and self-assurance.

I think the ability to accept oneself and to feel secure
and confident, to avoid any degree of paranoia, to face

reality, these factors are fairly independent of whether or not one is President. The same factors would be important if someone were chief of police, or a schoolteacher, or a magazine editor. The pressure is greater on a President, obviously, than some of the jobs I've described, but I think the ability to accommodate pressure is a personal thing.

PLAYBOY We noticed your crack about President Ford's avoiding the duties of the White House. Do you agree with Senator Mondale's assessment, when he said shortly after the nomination that Ford isn't intelligent enough to be a good President?

CARTER Well, if you leave Mondale out of it, I personally think that President Ford is adequately intelligent to be President.

PLAYBOY And what about your presidency, if you're elected—will you have a dramatic first 1,000 days?

CARTER I would hope that my Administration wouldn't be terminated at the end of 1,000 days, as was the case with one Administration. I'm beginning to meet with key leaders of Congress to evolve specific legislation to implement the Democratic platform commitment. If I'm elected, there will be no delay in moving aggressively on a broad front to carry out the promises I've made to the American people. I intend to stick to everything I've promised.

PLAYBOY Thanks for all the time you've given us. Incidentally, do you have any problems with appearing in *Playboy?* Do you think you'll be criticized?

CARTER I don't object to that at all. I don't believe I'll be criticized.

(At the final session, which took place in the living room of Carter's home in Plains, the allotted time was up. A press aide

indicated that there were other appointments for which Carter was already late, and the aide opened the front door while amenities were exchanged. As the interviewer and the Playboy editor stood at the door, recording equipment in their arms, a final, seemingly casual question was tossed off. Carter then delivered a long, softly spoken monologue that grew in intensity as he made his final points. One of the journalists signaled to Carter that they were still taping, to which Carter nodded his assent.)

PLAYBOY Do you feel you've reassured people with this interview, people who are uneasy about your religious beliefs, who wonder if you're going to make a rigid, unbending President?

CARTER I don't know if you've been to Sunday school here yet; some of the press has attended. I teach there about every three or four weeks. It's getting to be a real problem because we don't have room to put everybody now when I teach. I don't know if we're going to have to issue passes or

Jimmy Carter and Scheer during one portion of the Playboy *interview; ©1976* Playboy

what. It almost destroys the worship aspect of it. But we had a good class last Sunday. It's a good way to learn what I believe and what the Baptists believe.

One thing the Baptists believe in is complete autonomy. I don't accept any domination of my life by the Baptist Church, none. Every Baptist church is individual and autonomous. We don't accept domination of our church from the Southern Baptist Convention. The reason the Baptist Church was formed in this country was because of our belief in absolute and total separation of church and state. These basic tenets make us almost unique. We don't believe in any hierarchy in church. We don't have bishops. Any officers chosen by the church are defined as servants, not bosses. They're supposed to do the dirty work, make sure the church is clean and painted and that sort of thing. So it's a very good, democratic structure.

When my sons were small, we went to church and they went, too. But when they got old enough to make their own decisions, they decided when to go and they varied in their devoutness. Amy really looks forward to going to church, because she gets to see all her cousins at Sunday school. I never knew anything except going to church. My wife and I were born and raised in innocent times. The normal thing to do was to go to church.

What Christ taught about most was pride, that one person should never think he was any better than anybody else. One of the most vivid stories Christ told in one of his parables was about two people who went into a church. One was an official of the church, a Pharisee, and he said, "Lord, I thank you that I'm not like all those other people. I keep all your commandments, I give a tenth of everything I own. I'm here to give thanks for making me more acceptable in your sight." The other guy was despised by the nation, and he went in, prostrated himself on the floor, and said, "Lord, have mercy on me, a sinner. I'm not worthy to lift my eyes to heaven." Christ asked the disciples which of the two had justified his life. The answer was obviously the one who was humble.

The thing that's drummed into us all the time is not to be proud, not to be better than anyone else, not to look down on people, but to make ourselves acceptable in God's eyes through our own actions and recognize the simple truth that we're saved by grace. It's just a free gift through faith in Christ. This gives us a mechanism by which we can relate permanently to God. I'm not speaking for other people, but it gives me a sense of peace and equanimity and assurance.

I try not to commit a deliberate sin. I recognize that I'm going to do it anyhow, because I'm human and I'm tempted. And Christ set some almost impossible standards for us. Christ said, "I tell you that anyone who looks on a woman with lust has in his heart already committed adultery."

I've looked on a lot of women with lust. I've committed adultery in my heart many times. This is something that God recognizes I will do—and I have done it—and God forgives me for it. But that doesn't mean that I condemn someone who not only looks on a woman with lust but who leaves his wife and shacks up with somebody out of wedlock.

Christ says, Don't consider yourself better than someone else because one guy screws a whole bunch of women while the other guy is loyal to his wife. The guy who's loyal to his wife ought not to be condescending or proud because of the relative degree of sinfulness. One thing that Paul Tillich said was that religion is a search for the truth about man's existence and his relationship with God and his fellow man; and that once you stop searching and think you've got it made—at that point, you lose your religion. Constant reassessment, searching in one's heart—it gives me a feeling of confidence.

I don't inject these beliefs in my answers to your secular questions.

(Carter clenched his fist and gestured sharply.)

But I don't think I would *ever* take on the same frame of mind that Nixon or Johnson did—lying, cheating, and distorting the truth. Not taking into consideration my hope for my strength of character, I think that my religious beliefs alone would prevent that from happening to me. I have that confidence. I hope it's justified.

❧

Simultaneous with the publication of my interview with Jimmy Carter in November 1976, Playboy *printed the following essay, originally titled, "Jimmy, We Hardly Know Y'all." (Copyright ©1976 Playboy. Reprinted with permission. All rights reserved.)*

T HE MAN HIMSELF IS SITTING, SMILE IN PLACE, IN HIS STUdiously plain living room in front of a life-size portrait of his daughter, Amy, as though he were waiting for Norman Rockwell to appear. He is dressed in rumpled, down-home Levi's shirt and pants and is telling me and my *Playboy* editor that it would be a good thing to have a Southern Baptist as President, because it would be good for the young, the poor, blacks, women, and even those citizens who might be inclined to fornicate without the blessings of marriage. And once again, one wonders if Jimmy Carter is not too good to be true.

On one level, the man is simply preposterous. On another, he seems reasonable, sincere, and eminently sensible. It is difficult for me to believe that after four months of following him around the country, listening to the same speech five or six times a day, and after many hours of one-on-one conversation, I still nod in smiling agreement, like some kind of spaced-out Moonie, as another human being tells me he would never lie, would never be egotistical, doesn't fear death, would make federal government simple, workable, responsive to the average citizen, and that, in addition to doing away with the fear of death, he would do away with the fear of taxes.

As we stumble out into the muggy heat of Plains, Georgia, a movie-set hamlet of about eight buildings and what seem like two hundred photographers, all taking pictures of Jimmy's Central Casting mother, Miss Lillian, my editor tells me, "Hey, I really *like* the guy." Then, not thirty seconds later, he wonders aloud if we've been had. Which is how it always is with a James Earl Carter performance.

The ambiguity that one feels about Carter can be maddening. Is he one of the most packaged and manipulative candidates in our time or a Lincolnesque barefoot boy who swooped out of nowhere at a time when we needed him? Is he a rigid proselytizer who wants to convert the country to his own vision of small-town, Sunday-school values or just a guy who believes in his personal God and will let the rest of us believe whatever the hell we want? Is he a true populist from something called the New South or yet another creature of the Eastern Establishment?

Hanging Out with Carter's Act

When Carter is a winner—and he seems to be as I write this in the fall of 1976—all these doubts emerge: his puritanism, his waffling on key questions, the sense that he and his campaign are an inexorable machine that have made us all cave in without really testing him. There is also at times an insufferable arrogance that seems almost patrician. But despite all that, when defeat threatened, back in the primary days, I was drawn to the man.

One night during the Oregon primary, the press people traveling with Carter were put up at a third-rate hotel and that fact seemed symbolic of what was then thought to be the coming disintegration of his campaign. The other candidates, Frank Church and Jerry Brown, were staying at better hotels. We were staying where we were because Carter had made a last-minute desperation switch in his schedule to spend an extra weekend in Oregon. He was running scared.

Brown had won handily in Maryland and Church seemed well ahead in Oregon. It looked as if Carter was facing a third-place finish in this Western primary. All of which seemed to portend the resuscitation of Hubert Humphrey's political corpse. Sam Donaldson, the ABC television correspondent, sat slumped in a sofa in the seedy hotel lobby and announced to anyone who would listen, "I smell blood in the water." We asked him to elaborate. "I smell a loser," he said. "I have a very sensitive nose and James Earl Carter is a *loser.*"

Donaldson is a good reporter and the judgment was so definitively stated that I mulled it over and was surprised to find myself suddenly depressed by the prospect of Carter's defeat. I say this with some objectivity, because, on the surface, the man was further from my own political beliefs than some of his more liberal opponents; but I didn't want him to leave the political stage. It was a sense that he did, in fact, represent some new, needed force that I couldn't yet define—but that somehow ought to have its day.

The feeling grew as I spent time with Carter, his family, and his aides in the months leading up to his nomination. To start with his aides, I found it increasingly difficult to think of them as possessing that cold-blooded uniformity of the Nixon gendarmes. Press secretary Jody Powell, campaign manager Hamilton Jordan, speechwriter Pat Anderson, and pollster Pat Caddell just don't fit the Haldeman, Ehrlichman, and Mitchell stereotypes. They are effective packagers, but worries about the palace guard throwing up the gates around the White House seem to fade as one stays up all night drinking with them in some redneck bar.

Maybe I'm just being suckered in by too much rural Southern exotica, but there is something raw, spontaneous, and physical about the people around Carter that puts a limit on their malleability and opportunism. It causes them to fuck up in ways I find reassuring. On one such occasion, I was riding with Jody and his wife, Nan, from Plains to nearby Americus. A car behind crowded us too closely and then passed, narrowly missing us. Jody shouted, "That fucking asshole!" and took off after the car. It would have made a fine wire-service story: Carter's press secretary, a former football player, wipes up the street with some local toughs. Nan managed to cool him down, but it was clear to me that in that moment, Jody had stopped being a politician's aide. On another occasion, Jody and Pat Anderson got into a hassle with some locals over a rented car. Again, shouts and anger while the next President of the United States cooled his heels, waiting for Pat to show up with a draft of his acceptance speech.

One of Jody's more useful functions on the campaign is to serve as proof that one can have been born in a small Southern town, be a Baptist, serve for six years as Carter's closest aide, and still not be tight-assed. Add to that, Anderson, who has written a novel called *The President's Mistress*; Caddell, hip and fresh out of Cambridge; Gerald Rafshoon, his media adviser and something of a carouser; Greg Schneiders, a one-time Washington restaurateur who is Carter's administrative assistant—and it becomes clear that Carter has not applied his concern with the Ten Commandments to the behavior of his staff. They are, at least some of them, as hard-drinking, fornicating, pot-smoking, freethinking a group as has been seen in higher politics.

Here's an exchange I taped with Hamilton Jordan:

SCHEER Given the purity this campaign has projected, I find it odd that few of you guys go to church, that you all drink and mess around, and some of you even smoke dope. Isn't there a contradiction?

JORDAN No. Jimmy's not self-righteous. He's very tolerant. If he weren't, he just wouldn't have people like me and Jody and Rafshoon around him.

SCHEER So when you're with him, you don't feel as if you're with your Sunday-school teacher?

JORDAN No, I don't feel that way. I'd never expect him to tell me how I should act. If people are concerned about his trying to foist his personal views on other people or that he somehow expects others to follow some rigid code he adheres to—well, that's just not him. He obviously hasn't made us change our way of living. He differentiates his personal and religious views from his actions as a political official. Look, all the same people who are so goddamned concerned about Jimmy's religion were early supporters of Martin Luther King, Jr. His forum was Southern Baptist, too, but it happened to be black. This thing of Jimmy talking about religion was a result of the press's always bringing it up, not him. If you're in Boston and you're a politician, you try to get your picture taken with Cardinal Cushing. If you're in the South, you're usually a Baptist and you go to church a lot. So?

Once, during the early stages of the campaign, a couple of his aides who were married had met two women in the hotel lobby and were taking them to their rooms. The elevator stopped at a floor below theirs, the door opened—and in walked Jimmy and Rosalynn. Not a word was exchanged. The aides stared nervously at the ceiling of the elevator as the two ladies giggled nervously and nudged each other. I was told later that Jimmy never mentioned the incident to either aide.

So much for reassuring anecdotes. At least these are anecdotes I've plucked out myself. But a modern campaign doles out anecdotes like a priest dispenses Communion wafers. The pack of reporters covering the candidate is always in a holding pattern of desperate anticipation, each waiting to be singled out for the blessing of an exclusive anecdote. This is because, during a campaign, a candidate is rarely going to say anything clear or provocative about anything important and, as a result, "color"—which is really just the plural for anecdote—becomes all-important. When we came out of our last interview session with Carter, a UPI reporter approached the assistant press secretary. The reporter was on the "body watch," which, as it was explained to me, means that the candidate might croak or fart and if the reporter's not there to record it, his ass is on the line. The newsman knew we'd been interviewing Carter and said, "Hey, what did those guys ask him? I need one crumb—anything for my lead this afternoon—because I've got nothing so far." The aide took an insignificant comment from our interview and doled it out.

So let's take the "oral sex" anecdote that Jody reserved especially for me. (Previously, I'd been given a Bob Dylan-meets-Jimmy Carter anecdote, but it slipped out and ended up being printed elsewhere.) It seems that on a trip to Washington, then-Governor Carter, Rafshoon, and a state trooper guarding the Governor all went to a screening of the movie *Lenny*. During the performance, the trooper kept snorting and poking Rafshoon about the language and some of the steamier scenes. Carter just sat quietly, taking it in. When they got out, Rafshoon couldn't resist asking, "Say, Governor, do they have oral sex in Plains?"

Carter, after a pause, said, "Yep, but they don't call it that."

Which is a nice thing to know about Plains. But it's safe to say that the anecdote was reserved for a writer from *Playboy* and that Jody didn't offer it to, say, the people from *Reader's Digest* who preceded us that day. It served a purpose: to telegraph to the "typical" *Playboy* reader that Jimmy Carter is a regular guy. He may not use hip language, but he has hip thoughts. The same purpose was served when he dropped that Dylan quote into his acceptance speech at the convention— to do for the Dylan generation what a reference to Polish people did for those five million voters: tip them off that he was secretly one of them.

Well, compared with Ford, Carter *is* hip. And there's no doubt the people around Carter are good guys, quite the opposite from the cold technicians' image that has frequently been attached to them. I'd buy a used car from Jody or Hamilton—or from Jimmy, for that matter. After all, what he wants is for me to have a car as good and decent and as full of love as I deserve. I'm tired of cars and State Departments and CIAs that are lemons. But the trouble is that every time I feel good about the man, I can feel bad twenty minutes later when I remember that Jody wanted Wallace above all others to join Carter at the podium of the Democratic Convention and that, sure enough, there was Hamilton clapping politely for various Democratic politicians as they were called up to the podium, then clapping enthusiastically when Wallace's name was called. (From my conversations with Jody and Hamilton, I'm sure they were responding to a Southern outsider's having his day at the convention and not to Wallace's racist reputation. But it still made me nervous.)

So who is hustling whom? The problem is that one's judgments about Carter are necessarily fragmented because we have no sense of the depth of the man, of his experience and roots. He just came to us a winner. Carter's people are good at their business, so good that they've managed to cover the hard and interesting edges of the man. What we see is the packaging. The young men surrounding Carter let an occasional nugget drop for a particular constituency, then wrap him up again quickly. The manipulation of staged media events along with color results in lopsided opinion polls that will probably carry him to the White House, but when you look closely, you end up confused. His more liberal aides, such as Peter Bourne and Mary King, will tell you that he is a closet progressive, as Roosevelt was when he first ran, and that he has withheld disclosure of his full program: Once he's in the White House—whammo! Others, such as Charles Kirbo, a more traditional politician, will confide to *his* friends that he's really a closet conservative. And so speculation about Carter the man and Carter the President really hangs on an appraisal of where his gut feelings are coming from.

Reporters covering Jerry Ford or Ronald Reagan or Scoop Jackson soon stop looking for the "real" person behind the campaigner, because they realize that if they should happen to find him, he would be boringly similar to the one they've seen all along. But I have yet to meet a reporter who feels that way about Carter. He is intriguing, baffling, and perpetually confounding. Even to his family.

One afternoon, I was visiting with Carter's sister Gloria and her husband, Walter Spann, in their farmhouse about five miles down the road from Jimmy's home. Carter had remarked during the *Playboy* interview that he felt closer to Gloria than to his evangelist sister, Ruth. The remark confused me, because Gloria is loose and outgoing—as opposed to Jimmy—and supported McGovern, drives motorcycles, and doesn't seem to give much of a damn about her image. I had first met Gloria when I was over at Miss Lillian's. Carter's mother had told me that Gloria wasn't giving interviews. When Gloria walked in, I asked her if she'd make an exception. She shot me a look and said, "I'm not talking to any reporters unless they have jeans, boots, and a beard." I had two of the prerequisites.

"Look," I said. "I'm only wearing this suit because I thought that's what you do when you go calling on Southern ladies."

She laughed and said, "Well, I ain't no Southern lady, but you finish here and come by and see me and Walter. I'll give you some bourbon, but no interview."

At the Spann home, as the three of us sat drinking, my reportorial instincts got the best of me and I started inquiring about Walter's political beliefs. He was even blunter than Gloria: It was none of my business, he said, whom he preferred for President or if he voted at all. He added, "I like it fine if you're over drinking with us, but I don't want to be interviewed. I'm a farmer, not a politician. Jimmy's the politician."

Later, they became more talkative and let me take notes. Gloria said that she had always known Jimmy as a vibrant, adventuresome person. She said that as a child, he was given the nickname Hot by his father and that his sisters and brother still called him that privately. Hot seemed to fit Jimmy, she said, because he felt deeply and was always in a fevered rush to do significant things with his life. (The other family nicknames she mentioned seem appropriate as well. Gloria, the family free spirit, was called Gogo. Billy, the self-conscious redneck, was Buck. And faith healer Ruth was Boopy Doop.)

Gloria said it was "bunk" that Hot, or Jimmy, should be considered cold, ruthless, or unemotional. It was true that he had always taken himself seriously, but that the political life had made him become more guarded. At this point, late in the boozy evening, Walter broke in and said, "You reporters aren't going to get to know Jimmy, because he's onstage. He's been onstage ever since 1966, when he ran for Governor."

To which Gloria added softly but with affection: "He's been onstage longer than that."

At one point during the interview with Carter, as I was fumbling with my tape recorder, I mentioned that my talk with Gloria had led me to believe he was a more relaxed and less mechanical person than he seemed on the campaign trail. Was there going to be any time in his life for the sort of openness that Gloria described?

"Sure," he said. "I've always lived that way. Listen, we're having a fish fry Saturday afternoon and you're welcome to come. We're not inviting many people. We're going to drain my little pond and get some of the bigger fish out of there and then have a fry afterward. I think it would be a good time for you to just see a typical incident in the life of the Plains community."

Two hours after I spoke with Carter, Jody invited the entire press corps to the fish fry. The typical scene in the life of the Plains community turned into yet another media event flashed around the world by television. It was a mob scene, with reporters outnumbering locals four to one. Carter looked about as relaxed as one of the flapping fish in the drained pond.

But Carter does come from a delightfully informal family. On one earlier occasion, Gloria and Miss Lillian had invited me to go along for supper at a local diner. Gloria had carefully prepared two jars of liquid refreshment—one filled with Early Times bourbon and the other with water—so I "wouldn't get thirsty" on the way to dinner. While we were there, they playfully felt under my coat to see if I was wired for sound and became totally relaxed as they sipped on the bourbon and talked irreverently about the foibles of people in Plains.

The shame is, they get uneasy when they see how friendly and natural they come off in print. I hope Miss Lillian doesn't react to my description of her the way she responded to some of what's been published about her—and, my God, she does get wonderful press. Here is Miss Lillian talking to me about the media:

"Frankly, I don't like women interviewers. They're pushy, though one I had was just as sweet as she could be. Some of them, they freelance, and if what you say isn't interesting, they touch it up a bit. That one girl wrote an article and she said I had a drink in my hand and I waved it around in the air. I never had a drink with anyone who was interviewing me. Never. If I offered you a drink, I don't know whether you'd write it down or not, because I don't trust anybody. I know it's going to get worse and I'm prepared. I'm just kind of suspicious of a woman writer until I know where I stand. Most women are freelancers, did you know that? I'm besieged by publishers and I just tell everyone that Gloria is going to write my story. She's got all my letters and everything, isn't that right, Gloria?"

But the afternoon of the fish fry, another member of the family delivered an opinion of the press that was a bit less charming. I was on the porch chatting with Gloria and Walter. Jimmy had escaped from the other reporters and walked over to kiss Gloria on the cheek. He shook Walter's hand, too, but ignored my presence. We had recorded a number of conversations by then and it was an awkward moment for me, given the fact that he'd invited me over to see him in a "relaxed" frame of mind. But what made it even more awkward was that he began to speak about the press in unflattering terms to Gloria and Walter, as if I were not present.

"Guess it's hard for you to get away from all those reporters," Walter said. "They're like gnats swarming around."

Carter paused in his munching of a catfish and replied, "The press people are afraid I'm going to eat a fishbone and choke on it. They're afraid they won't have a picture when it happens." The tone wasn't bantering; it was more on the bitter side.

Now, it's true that the body watch doesn't want to miss anything and that that can get depressing for a candidate. But the press people hadn't climbed over any fences to get in—Carter had invited them because he wanted a folksy image of his fish fry beamed around the world. A part of Carter undoubtedly loves down-home fish fries. But another part of him wants to exploit the hell out of them.

And that's the dilemma: He uses the process and gets consumed by it. He cares for his mother, but, as the seventy-eight-year-old Miss Lillian told me, "When I came back from India [she was with the Peace Corps], Jimmy asked me to accept every single speaking engagement I could to help him get exposure." That's why he plays up Gloria, the motorcycle rider, to a bike-race audience in Oregon, and sister Ruth to church folk in South Dakota. That's why his son Chip will be sent off to attend a gay function in San Francisco while Dad is addressing a meeting of black ministers (during which he pronounces homosexuality "a sin").

It is not that Carter is shallow or exploitative, but rather that he and his staff have consciously decided to use—and thus to submit to—a process of campaigning that is inherently shallow and exploitative. One realizes that Carter is capable of dealing with complicated thoughts. One also senses that he is a good man who cares for his family; that he has real roots; that he is serious about fairly representing the American people. But it is a fact that his life in these past two years—and perhaps longer, as his sister suggests—has been one staged media event after another.

Carter would probably admit to being onstage, to being

packaged, and at times—when he becomes testy and stiff-necked—he seems to be grappling with the implications of this to his personality. When I brought it up with one of his aides, I was told that that was the precise reason Carter insists on returning to Plains every weekend during the campaign, even if only for one night. But, as a result, Plains itself has become a stage prop that he has prettified for us.

Offstage

The town of Plains has by now become sticky with media hype. It's what one Manhattan friend calls *cracker chic*. Residents and reporters alike have entered into a conspiracy not to disillusion visitors. Among the locals, "We wouldn't do anything to hurt Jimmy's chances" is the most common refrain. What we have are caricatures. There is a talkative old Miss Lillian, rocking on her porch, a lovable interview junkie; brother Billy, the redneck cracker; Rosalynn, the dutiful if uptight wife; cousin Hugh, the genial worm farmer; Jimmy's father, James Earl Carter, Sr., who died in 1953 and is rarely mentioned, except to say that he had Old South (i.e., racist and reactionary) ideas.

But, of course, as is the case with Jimmy himself, the scene is more complicated than that. Fewer solid colors; more gray. Southern rural life is no simpler than urban life. And if you throw in the extreme pressure of the civil-rights years, probably tougher. The folksy, innocent façade that surrounds Plains may be convenient to the Carter campaign, but it simply rewrites history.

Coincidentally, I had been through Plains sixteen years ago and felt the tension beneath the surface of this placid town. In 1960, I was driving through southwest Georgia with a group of people who wanted to integrate public facilities. I have a particular memory of a gas station in Americus where I stopped so a white companion could deliberately use the "colored" rest room. An ugly confrontation ensued.

Recently, I was riding around town with Walter and Gloria and I spotted what appeared to be the same gas station. I mentioned the 1960 incident to them and Walter said, "Did you do that? Hell, they should have blown your fool head off." I like Walter and I knew he was kidding. In fact, he's one of the few people around Plains who don't feel a need to ennoble the past.

And that's the point. Carter does. Just as the campaign packaging prevents one from seeing his complexities, his tolerance, and his tensions, so the whitewashing of the past prevents one from studying his real roots. His family have become town characters with stereotyped pasts, and his own past, though somewhat more closely examined, becomes a part of folklore. But to get a glimpse of the complexity of real life, there is no better case study than the crucible the Old South went through to become the New South: the civil-rights struggle.

There are two roads at the edge of Plains that meet at nearly right angles: One goes toward an integrated farm called Koinonia and the other leads to Americus. Both places were sources of the main shock waves from civil rights that reached the Carter family.

Americus has been much discussed in the press. It was once one of the meanest towns in the South, the scene of some of the ugliest demonstrations and acts of violence during 1963 and 1964. It was in Americus that Martin Luther King, Jr., was jailed and told to sweep the floors. Until not long ago, its bulletin boards displayed a letter from King "thanking" the jailers for their hospitality. What Carter did and did not do as a moderate and a supporter of Lyndon Johnson has been raked over the coals. He did not speak out forcefully during the '60s (and, indeed, took no position at all during the worst disturbances) but paid his dues as his family and he were taunted as "nigger lovers" during L.B.J.'s campaign. Americus is nine miles from Plains.

But Koinonia is something else. It is a raw nerve to both Jimmy and Miss Lillian. It has not been raked over the coals, because it is hardly mentioned. Koinonia was founded in 1942 by a progressive white couple named Clarence and Florence Jordan. It was a courageous attempt to show that an integrated communal farm run on Christian principles was a possibility in the Old South. It is seven miles from Plains.

When I questioned Miss Lillian about the Carters' relationship to the farm, I caught a rare flash of anger. "Why do you want to bring that up?" she snapped. "It's over with. You'd just stir up some of the wilder people around here, and then nobody knows what will happen."

The people who might stir things up around Plains are the same ones who gave Miss Lillian and Gloria a hard time back in 1964, when they worked for Johnson's election at the Americus headquarters. "Children yelled at me," Miss Lillian recalled, "and threw things at my car because Johnson was what they called an N-I-G-G-E-R L-O-V-E-R." Were they some of the same people who have turned to private schools to avoid integration? "Some of them," she admitted, "but they're not the nicest people in town."

Why Not the Best? is the title of Carter's autobiography. And the concept of the nicest, or best, people is the key to understanding Jimmy Carter, for it comes out of a patrician rural tradition of responsibility to which he is heir. The white elite who survived the civil-rights strife without losing their power either by overtly siding with the blacks or by taking racist stands formed the core of the New South that Carter personifies. It is moderate and pragmatic and, above all, patrician.

The Carters, after all, were patricians. Part of Jimmy's packaging includes reminiscences about his childhood in a home without electricity. Well, in the days before rural electrification, nobody much had it. But Earl, as Jimmy's father was known, owned four thousand acres, employed servants, and died with money in the bank. And to be patrician toward a radical experiment such as Koinonia meant to keep it at a proper distance without really siding against it.

Another personal coincidence: The period I spent nosing around Plains wasn't the first time I'd heard about Koinonia. I remember that when I left the gas station in Americus, I stopped to ask directions for the farm. I had read about it and stopped at a corner to naïvely ask a group of white men how to get to Koinonia. One of them sneered at me, "Why you want to go there, boy?" I chose to discontinue the dialogue. For the next few hours, there were many false starts up red-clay roads with flashlights shining on our California license plates and enormous dogs barking. I was about as scared as I've ever been, and to this day, I can't fathom the courage of blacks in Americus who decided to take a stand. Or the whites and blacks who dared to live together at Koinonia. That was the night I met Florence and Clarence Jordan, the founders of the farm.

Sixteen years later, on the Carter campaign, I met Hamilton Jordan and asked him if he was related to the Clarence Jordan I'd met years ago. Hamilton told me

Clarence, who died in 1969, was his uncle and "one of the two people in my life I have respected most," the other being Carter. Hamilton and I discussed Koinonia and his uncle for quite some time.

Hamilton has his roots in this southwest Georgia clay and reached adulthood during the worst of the racial turmoil. He recalls that he was a segregationist until "after Kennedy," but he was always awed by the idealism of his Uncle Clarence. He visited Koinonia as a kid and remembers: "Clarence had a tragic life, but he was a great, great man—a straight shooter, at peace with himself."

Hamilton, like Jimmy, played the proper, white-sheep role in his family. A crusader like Clarence was therefore a "loser," but one who was a challenge to the rest of the family. As Miss Lillian admitted, "Clarence was twenty years ahead of his time."

Clarence Jordan was a Baptist minister with a Ph.D. who, quite literally, practiced what he preached. The Christianity and brotherly love about which he spoke so eloquently from the pulpit included blacks, and it didn't take the townspeople of Plains long to figure that out. In 1942, he formed a small community of farmers and workers, black and white, in what was essentially a commune. The Klan paid its first visit that year. By the '50s, the powerful White Citizens' Council had moved on to boycotts, bombings, and shootings. The farm became famous in the middle '50s, when an Atlanta newspaper printed a cartoon showing the Koinonia barn with a lightning rod on its roof.

How did Carter, back from the Navy after his father's death in 1953, respond to the farm? "I went there several times in the '50s and '60s," he told me. "They couldn't get anyone else to shell seed for them, and I did. I went down there a couple of times to talk to Clarence Jordan . . . I knew Clarence Jordan when we were going through the years of integration."

I checked his recollection with that of Clarence's widow, Florence, who still lives on the Koinonia farm. "It's not that I want to throw a monkey wrench into his campaign," she told me, "because most of us will probably vote for him. But it does seem kind of bad when a reporter calls here on the basis of Jimmy's having said he used to visit here and knew us. I have to say I'm sorry, but I don't even know the man. I've never met him, and we've been living down the road for thirty-four years. People came here from all over the world, but he hasn't come seven miles."

In that same conversation, she told me that there were people who had been friendly to the Koinonia folks, but that most of them had been forced to leave the area because of the social pressure. No one else in the county offered support. "They would lose their business or lose their friends," she said sadly, "and that was more important than their Christian beliefs. That was true of most people in the county and [Jimmy] was no different."

I went back to Carter and pinned him down on what stand he *had* taken when he heard about the shootings and bombings at Koinonia. "I didn't shoot at them or throw bombs," he replied, in what I believe was a sarcastic tone.

"I know," I said, "but did you speak out against it?"

"There was a general deploring of violence," he replied, "and the grand jury investigated it, and I think everybody was embarrassed by it. It was done—if it was done—by a fringe element. This was a time, I'd say, of very radical elements on both sides."

If Florence wasn't lying to me about Jimmy's visits to

Koinonia, then Jimmy was. Since the shootings are vastly documented, his hedge—"if it was done"—is chickenshit. And his answer to my question about whether he'd spoken out—"There was a general deploring"—indicates his embarrassment at any but the most heroic image of his past. And, to top it off, the grand-jury investigation Carter referred to as a presumably impartial force is known to have been a McCarthy-type witch-hunt directed *against* Koinonia.

When I considered Carter's promises never to lie, his sanitized version of events in his past, and his stubborn refusal to admit to imperfection, the implications of this exchange angered me—which comes easily and self-righteously to a Northerner. But it almost caused me to overlook what I was seeking out: complexity. I stumbled across another unknown incident involving an early member of Koinonia, and it softened the impact for me.

It was Gloria who told me to look up Jack Singletary. Singletary came from a patrician family like Carter's in another part of Georgia. He attended the Naval Academy at the same time Carter did (though they did not know each other there) and served in the Navy. But when the postwar draft came along, Singletary refused to register on religious grounds. He had already joined Koinonia when he was sent to federal prison; upon his release, he went back to the farm. After a couple of years, he moved to his own farm nearby, without giving up Koinonia's progressive ideas. He became, in Gloria's words, "the white nigger of Plains."

Chatting with this remarkable Georgian, who I thought would have little good to say about a man who did not support him through Koinonia's terrible years, I was surprised to find that his memories of Carter were positive:

"Jimmy came home from the Navy and I ran into him on

the street, and he and Rosalynn invited me to their apartment, which had never been done. That was in '53 or '54. He told me that night that he shared my views in regard to the race question. He told me about the incident when he was an officer on a ship and the crew was on shore leave and was invited to an official function. A black sailor wasn't invited, so the whole crew didn't go. He was proud. He wanted me to know this."

Singletary related the story of the boycott against his family. The White Citizens' Council in Sumter County decided that no merchant should sell goods to any member of Koinonia, and that included Singletary.

"There was a little store down here—Mrs. Howell's store—and they circulated stuff that me and Koinonia were buying our groceries from her. So the sheriff and the Georgia Bureau of Investigation agent went to see Mrs. Howell. They told her that if she didn't quit selling to us, something was going to happen to her. But the only contact I was having with Mrs. Howell was that my oldest child was dying with leukemia and we didn't have a telephone. Mrs. Howell's store had the nearest telephone. We had taken our son to Sloan-Kettering in New York for treatment and we were keeping in touch with them by telephone about his medicine. I'd go down and use Mrs. Howell's telephone and I'd pay her telephone bill. Well, she told me that they had come to threaten her and that she was going to have to stop letting me use the telephone."

Singletary took his case to the local merchants' group, of which Carter was a member. The group decided to bend the boycott in Singletary's case, though it remained in force against the residents of Koinonia. They were good people, the merchants, and they weren't going to do something so inhumane as to deny help to a leukemic boy. It wasn't a great moment for Jimmy Carter, but it told the powerful White Citizens' Council where he and some of the best people stood.

There is even more to the Koinonia story that reflects on the Carter family and that invalidates the simple stereotypes we've been allowed to see. For instance, Singletary told me about a follow-up that changed my mind about Rosalynn, who doesn't get much credit for having taken courageous stands.

"Our little boy finally died of leukemia. It was when the boycott was on and we had our friends from Koinonia come over for the funeral. Rosalynn came the next morning and brought a ham. We invited her to stay and she did: We had a very informal Quaker-type service and put the body into a little box that Koinonia had made. We took it down to a little playground there where he had played and buried him without any remarks. Rosalynn left here, I'm told, really just all upset and went to Plains to see the Baptist preacher and bawled him out. He said he reckoned he'd be run out of town if he did it, but she made him come, so we finally had a graveside service. Now, that's a little insight into the kind of person she is, and I'm sure that Jimmy was with her."

When I told Rosalynn that I had been talking to Singletary, she said quietly, "Yes, that's right—they were heroic people. It took people from the outside to shake us up into seeing what was right. I have a lot of respect for those people." I don't care what I read about Rosalynn in the *Ladies' Home Journal* from now on: I'm prepared to admire her without being cynical.

As I began collecting other bits of evidence, many of them favorable to the Carters, from sources that seemed impartial,

I realized how superficially the press—with the connivance of the Carter campaign—had characterized these human beings. Earl Carter, for instance, turns out not to have been the hidebound racist he is made out to be. It was he, in fact, who first befriended Singletary, inviting him (on one occasion with a black friend) into the back of the store for a soda pop when such an act took courage. "Mr. Earl," as Singletary called him, also went into partnership with him to combine clover when no other farmers would even share equipment with Singletary. When Earl was dying in 1953 of cancer, Singletary was one of the two non–family members Earl asked to his bedside.

Billy Carter, the incorrigible cracker who still uses the word "nigger" when he's drinking with his old buddies at the gas station, took an unpopular stand against the church people in speaking out against the antiquated liquor laws. That much may not be surprising, but it was also he who financed a 1966 lawsuit against segregated private schools.

On the other hand, there is cousin Hugh, whom news people love to quote for bits of quaint philosophy. Hugh was the one who fought against the very desegregation initiative his cousins supported: He was also head of the board of deacons in the Baptist Church and in 1962 voted to keep blacks out of the church that Jimmy tried to integrate. And it wasn't just blacks he was opposed to. His board of deacons unanimously voted against admitting the Singletarys as church members, merely for associating with blacks. Singletary told me that the board had warned his family they weren't even welcome to visit the church. Needless to say, Jimmy and Rosalynn opposed Hugh's position on this, and Jimmy stood up in church the following Sunday to plead unsuccessfully for the admission of the Singletarys.

Nor is Miss Lillian the Central Casting figure she likes to play. For instance, we've heard a lot about the fact that she entered the Peace Corps at the age of sixty-eight, but usually in the context of an old lady going off on a lark. In one of our conversations, she revealed some of that condescending but well-intentioned patrician spirit that now marks Jimmy (I have condensed a much longer monologue):

"I went to India, which is a dark country with a warm climate, because I felt the South had been so awful to blacks that I wanted to go where I could help people who had nothing . . . I did a lot of family-planning work and had to explain to those poor people why it was necessary for them . . . If a man had more than three children, he had to have a vasectomy, which was fair. It was the only way to handle it, because those people are ignorant and the only outlet they have is sex . . . I listened to one of the women at the clinic explain to one of the men why he needed a vasectomy. I had seen some of the men almost lose their minds. You know, they could not believe that if they had the operation they would still be men, so I would see a lot of scenes of broken men . . . I would see some of the attendants holding men down on the tables for their operation, and I said, I can do better than that, so I must tell you what I did: I would stand at the man's head: he hadn't had a shot or anything, he had to stand it without anesthesia. I stood at his head and I got a pan of cold water and I would talk in a low, soothing voice and put rags on his head, and I would say, That's all right—I had a few words of Hindi that I could say to keep him calm . . . It hurts, you have to cut the thing in two, and, oh, that hurts. So that's what I did with the vasectomies."

My focus on the Carters' patrician spirit and on Koinonia and on civil rights isn't to raise the specter of intolerance or closet racism. It's pretty clear that Carter and most of his family were never racists—and were, on the whole, as courageous as any of the "best" families. But I do raise it to say that Carter and his family can't be capsulized as easily as they want to make us think. Despite Carter's acts of courage, he didn't *always* act courageously. He was caught in a terrible time and he was only human—which means he often didn't do the right thing. *But Jimmy Carter won't admit it.* The real heroes of the era were less than ten miles up the road in either direction from his home all his life, taking the most terrible punishment, and he won't admit that he shunned them like nearly everyone else. Like all of us.

Carter is addicted to the theory that we progress by stressing our virtues rather than by dwelling on failures; this is the major theme of his campaign speeches. There's undoubtedly some merit to this approach, but it seems to me that it excludes serious learning from past error.

The mythologizing of the past leads naturally to the prettification of present-day Plains. Right here, in brother Billy's fire-prone gas station and cousin Hugh's antique store, when the talking and drinking get going, one still finds considerable contempt for "niggers." I was with Billy when he pointed out a hulking, mean-looking local and explained, "He's a John Bircher—used to be in the White Citizens' Council. John Birch is real big around here. They've taken over from the Council and the Klan."

Plains and Americus are no better or worse than many other places, but hanging out in these towns makes you wonder where Jimmy gets off extolling the virtues of small-town living, as he often does. It merely leaves the rest of us feeling guilty, hankering for some sort of idyllic golden age that never existed. "Why not the best?" is a reasonable question if it is made clear that the best doesn't exist, that it's something we can only aspire to. And it is this self-righteous, sanctimonious, smiley side of Jimmy Carter that gets to me, because it miseducates us about the real problems we face in trying to become the best. Carter frequently promises that he will never lie to us, but his power-of-positive-thinking stance is itself a lie. We are not all "full of love." We don't "all want the same things." His version of the good life, filled with churches and sermons, would bore a lot of people—including those in his hometown.

I remember one afternoon in a small town in Oregon during the primary campaign when there was a convention of barbershop quartets. I didn't mind it until several of the quartets approached Carter and serenaded him with a syrupy rendition of "Dixie." Carter began to speak about how the scene was exactly the same in Plains, where people sit around on the grass and listen to music, and said that that was what the good life was really like. It was such a cloying performance all around that I began muttering incoherently about the need for a little perversity in everybody's life. I asked one of the singers whether he believed in all this small-town goodness that he represented, fully expecting to be punched out. His answer restored my faith in America much more than anything Carter said that day. "Hey, man," he said in a pleasing tenor voice, "this is *camp!*"

Kids are being busted right now in Plains for hard drugs. Carter's nephew is a hard-drug user and homosexual who is serving time in a California jail for armed robbery. Rosalynn told me that her friend's sixteen-year-old son is serving time in prison on a marijuana charge. In August, a twenty-eight-year-old puritan named Randy Howard was elected Sumter County sheriff on the basis of his record as a one-man narc squad, hassling half the younger population. Howard claims that organized crime has moved into the area with drugs, pornography, and gambling. He says alcoholism remains the number-one problem in the area.

The hypocrisy about booze is extreme. One hot night, when Carter and Walter Mondale were scheduled to speak at the Plains railroad depot, I went over to brother Billy's gas station to get a six-pack and then went back to the rally, only to be told by Buford Reese, a local Carter man, "Friend, would you put that away on behalf of the community?" We in the press giggled. But later I felt sorry for Buford and for Howard (who had told me that he never touches alcohol and doesn't think people need anything more than Coca-Cola), because their sincerity cannot possibly withstand their daily experiences with the reality of life in Sumter County. Hell, the next President's brother sells beer late into the night and his mother has been known, as are many older Southern ladies, to pick up a half-pint of harder stuff. (It always had to be bought in half-pint bottles or the liquor-store people, and therefore anyone else, might get the wrong idea.) But who *needs* this guilt?

Evidently it serves a purpose. The way Jody Powell explains it, life in these towns is so intimate and passions so close to the surface that certain fictions must be maintained as social restraints. There are just certain things that the "best people" ought not to be seen doing or everything else will fall apart. Although everyone knows that the contradictions are there, it is important to conceal them. And it is this principle that Jimmy Carter has made the mainstay of his drive for the presidency. In the wake of Watergate and the

myriad other revelations about the seamy side of government, Carter has proceeded to conduct himself as one of the
best people who will not lie, cheat, screw around, gamble, or
in any other way reflect a disheveled and chaotic spirit.
Carter decided, as he states in his autobiography, to carry on
"in the tradition of the best people," and that's just what he's
been doing. His daddy had done the same and his momma
took over after his daddy's death. They consciously attempted
to publicly embody a high standard of morality as a playing
out of their historic role as one of the leading families. It is
therefore understandable that Jimmy has now extended that
principle to national politics. What has startled everyone is
that because of the particular disarray of American government, at this moment, that old style fulfills a national need.

The limit of this stance is that it is based on paternalism.
It assumes that the best people are the source of cultural and
moral wisdom. And although they have an obligation to help
educate the rest of us, we don't stand much of a chance of
getting educated. Hence, they will have to lead, cajole, and
manipulate us sinners into being better than we are. That is
why Jimmy appears fuzzy on the issues: He can't tell us too
much or we might prevent his gaining power to do the right
thing.

Will Carter Kick Ass?

> If, after the inauguration, you find a Cy Vance as Secretary of
> State and Zbigniew Brzezinski as head of National Security,
> then I would say we failed. And I'd quit. But that's not going
> to happen. You're going to see new faces, new ideas. The gov-
> ernment is going to be run by people you have never heard of.
> —Hamilton Jordan

By the time I'd finished my Southern odyssey, it seemed to me that despite all the contradictions I'd found, most of the fears of Carter's liberal critics appeared unwarranted. A Carter presidency will probably be strong on civil liberties and civil rights. Blacks and women will probably be amply sprinkled throughout the higher levels of his Administration (though it hasn't yet happened in his campaign staff), and freethinkers won't be thrown into jail. On the contrary: Just as Nixon, secure in his right flank, was able to open relations with China, Carter's Bible base will probably permit him to extend our basic freedoms. If his current staff becomes the palace guard, it might even be fun.

But now that we have looked at Carter as a Southern patrician, what about his constant campaign cries against "political and economic elites," against "big shots"? Aren't successful Southern politicians part of the political elite? And when they're backed by large Southern-based corporations, aren't they part of the economic elite? Carter has a particularly close relationship with Coca-Cola board chairman J. Paul Austin, who organized fundraising and businessmen's groups for him. There was even some trouble when the press reported that Carter had taken a couple of trips abroad that were paid for by Coke. And while it's true that Coke is based in Atlanta and Pepsi is in Purchase, New York, both are huge multinational corporations with similar positions on foreign policy.

What got me thinking about all this was a campaign stop in Fayetteville, Arkansas. Carter was delivering his speech and I was chatting with Pat Anderson, his speechwriter, at the windswept airport. There was also a contingent of beauty contestants brought up onto the podium. I'd just interviewed

Miss Poultry—honest to God—out of a fear that I'd go crazy if I had to listen to Carter's speech one more time.

SCHEER Miss Poultry, I wonder if you could tell us your position on foreign policy?

MISS POULTRY I'm sorry, we're not allowed to have positions. It's against the rules.

I turned to Anderson to ask him *his* position on foreign policy; I figured I'd have better luck with him, since he'd been jotting down notes for Carter's upcoming speech before the Foreign Policy Association in New York. Anderson waved me aside and said, "Later, I have to check this speech out with Brzezinski."

Check it out with Brzezinski? That was when I flashed back to the fact that the first time I'd ever really heard of Jimmy Carter wasn't over beers in some redneck bar with the likes of Jody Powell or Hamilton Jordan, but in Mount Desert, Maine, with none other than Zbigniew Brzezinski.

It was the summer of 1975 and I was researching an article on the Rockefellers, who vacation on the coast of Maine. I'd met Zbig and his wife and they'd asked me over to their twenty-seven-room house just down the road from David Rockefeller's place. I found that Zbig had been sponsored by David Rockefeller in much the same way that Henry Kissinger had been sponsored by Nelson Rockefeller. ("With one important distinction," Zbig cautioned. "Henry worked for Nelson as an employee and I work with David as an associate.")

It was back then that Brzezinski told me that he favored a former Governor of Georgia as the Democratic candidate. I was surprised. Why a Georgian peanut farmer who was supposed to be a grassroots populist should have earned the enthusiasm of an Establishment intellectual like Brzezinski was a mystery to me.

Well, it turned out that Brzezinski and Carter had a relationship going back to 1972, when David Rockefeller asked the then-Governor of Georgia to join the new international-elite organization that he was forming called the Trilateral Commission. Carter told me he was never to miss a meeting of the Trilateral Commission during the next three years and that he received his basic foreign-policy education under its auspices. It is also clear that during this period, Carter was able to impress David Rockefeller, who is part of the group that runs things in this country. Carter had already decided to run for the presidency, remember. Rafshoon, his media specialist, told me during the campaign that Carter's selection to the Trilateral Commission was "one of the most fortunate accidents of the early campaign and critical to his building support where it counted." It is also the source for the main foreign-policy ideas in the Carter program. Which should be enough of a buildup to justify the question: What is a Trilateral Commission?

Essentially, the Trilateral Commission is a group of political and financial bigwigs from Western Europe, Japan, Canada, and the U.S., formed to provide a common negotiating position for the industrialized capitalist nations. David Rockefeller was instrumental in its founding. It's as much of a political *and* an economic elite as you can find.

The Rockefeller family has long had a propensity for establishing foundations, commissions, think tanks, and study groups. These basically involve using tax-free dollars to buy up high-priced intellectual talent in order to develop social programs that ostensibly meet the public's needs while maintaining (a darker spirit might suggest "extending") the interests of the Rockefellers. The original Rockefeller Brothers Reports and, more recently, Nelson's Commission on Critical Choices for Americans, are examples of the process. David happens to have taken an interest in foreign affairs: The New York Council on Foreign Relations, of which he is the chairman, is one of his pet projects. The CFR was directed for twenty-five years by David's college roommate, one George Franklin, who left the CFR at David's behest to form the Trilateral Commission.

Franklin told me that he was the person who first hired an enterprising young Harvard professor to work for the council and, after eight years of heading up or participating in council studies, Henry Kissinger went on to do quite well in government service. Kissinger and Brzezinski were in the same class at Harvard Graduate School. Although both have been Rockefeller/Franklin protégés, they try to avoid speaking to each other, which is more of a reflection of their egos than of any serious policy differences between the two men. Franklin and David like them both and one suspects they don't really care which one is Secretary of State.

Carter has made an issue of his differences with Kissinger's foreign policy, but given his reliance on the Trilateral Commission and Brzezinski, he must have had to dig for differences. Since there aren't many, he decided to attack Kissinger's "Lone Ranger" methods. But it doesn't add up to much in the way of real dissimilarities.

Also, Jimmy Carter, the man who now says the war in Vietnam was terrible and racist, has chosen the Trilateral Commission's Samuel Huntington as one of his advisers. Huntington's main claim to fame is that he came up with the forced-urbanization program for Vietnam, which meant bombing the countryside to "dry up the sea of people" around the Viet Cong. Carter is also relying on Paul Nitze, who, as nearly as I can tell, has been shouting, "The Russians are coming!" since the days of the last czar.

It makes you wonder if we aren't safer with Kissinger. Henry's balance-of-power ideas may be old-fashioned and dangerous, but are we better off with Brzezinski's slightly different notions of a gathering of the powerful—which is what the Trilateral approach is all about? When the Democratic Party elite return from exile with Carter (and they probably will: I saw most of them pop up while I traveled on the press plane during the campaign, and we all know about the trek they took from Harvard to Plains after the nomination), they'll want to do something to outdistance Kissinger's mark. They'll want to be spectacular. So here we go again: the best and the brightest, part two.

Against that prognosis, all I had to go on as I pulled out of my odyssey was the assurance by sister Gloria and Carter's son Chip that they'd lead a demonstration if Carter got us into another Vietnam. That, and the assurance by Carter's young aides that our next President is a committed Georgia populist who will never cave in to the Eastern Establishment. And, to be fair, Carter himself has said that on principle he is against military intervention in foreign countries.

Still, if Brzezinski doesn't become Secretary of State, it's only because you can't have two accents in a row. As in Kissinger's case, he'll probably first do a stint as National Security Adviser. Zbig is better informed and more reasonable than most of the Establishment figures Carter has gone to, but when I talked with Zbig that summer in Maine, he made it clear that to him, Carter was no Georgia populist who would rock any boats. He seemed to judge him an urbane thinker who had passed muster with the Establishment.

So which is it going to be—some fresh new faces or the old gang from Harvard? Or, put another way, can a millionaire from southwest Georgia who was raised to care about the poor and wants government to be returned to the people do so without kicking ass?

Is Jimmy Carter too good to be true? I still don't know, because I hardly know him. But I do have one more anecdote to throw into the hopper.

A couple of nights before he was to give his acceptance speech in New York, Jimmy Carter was sitting in his expensive suite with Anderson, Caddell, Powell, and Rafshoon. He was reading his speech aloud and stopping every few sentences to get their reaction. When he got to the section blasting political and economic elites, one of his aides suggested it be cut: It was too controversial. (In fact, the *New York Times* attacked that portion of the speech a few days later as "demagogic" and "populist.") Up in his hotel room, Carter thought for a minute, looked around the room slowly, and said, "No. I have a very strong visceral feeling about that and I want to use it."

After all these months, after all the ambiguity and the packaging and the rewritten history, my visceral feeling is that Jimmy Carter has those visceral feelings.

It's also my favorite anecdote.

RONALD REAGAN'S
OBSCURE COMPLEXITY

THE FIRST TIME I INTERVIEWED RONALD REAGAN, IT WAS in a motel room in a Northern California farming community, where he had come to campaign in his first successful run for Governor. I had been sent to the motel room by Reagan's press aide and promptly fell asleep in an overstuffed chair, only to be inadvertently awakened minutes later by the man himself, who was busy changing his pants. When he discovered that I was there with him in his room, he was more curious than startled—which says quite a bit about a movie star who had every reason to be apprehensive at the sudden appearance of a stranger.

Even better, once Reagan realized that I was the editor he had been scheduled to meet from that dreaded radical magazine *Ramparts*, he simply laughed. I don't think he typed me, and I tried to return the favor. After a rather lengthy interview, I came away favorably impressed with the man, recognizing that the Bonzo movie mantle was wrongly dismissive, and I correctly predicted in *Ramparts* that he would defeat two-term Governor Pat Brown.

Not that Pat Brown deserved to be defeated; his tenure in California from 1959–1967 did more to make the Golden State golden than the efforts of any other political leader of that era—via massive infrastructure investment, including water, highway, and university expansion.

But Reagan knew well how to play on voters' fatigue with Brown, mixing an anti-tax orientation with the red-meat patriotism that would become a staple of the Reagan revolution.

I liked Ronald Reagan, despite the huge divide between us politically. He was a charming old pro who gave me hours of his time in a series of interviews continuing on into his run for the presidency. After *Ramparts*, I interviewed him for the *Los Angeles Times* and other mainstream outlets, but I believe he was so consistently generous with his time simply because he enjoyed the give-and-take. He never pulled rank by nodding to a press aide to end the interview, even when many other reporters were waiting for him on the same plane. Perhaps I was charmed beyond the wisdom of his words, for I often found myself defending the Gipper when confronted with an East Coast pundit determined to denigrate anyone (especially movie stars) from my adopted state. Now, looking back at his record, I am dismayed that I warmed to the man as much as I did.

The fact is, Reagan abandoned the Roosevelt New Deal—which he admitted had saved his own family during the Great Depression—in favor of massive corporate welfare. His paymasters at Warner Brothers, General Electric, and on the conservative lecture circuit inculcated in him an excessive faith in the morality of the corporate sector. Though Reagan the man was hardly mean-spirited, Reagan the politician utterly betrayed the social programs and trade unionism in which he once believed so fiercely.

Let's start with his leadership of California, where he launched attacks on the state's once-incomparable public universities and devastated its mental health system. Foreshadowing his trumped-up invasion of tiny Grenada, Governor Reagan ordered the National Guard to teargas Berkeley.

Over time, it also became increasingly clear that although the man wasn't unintelligent, his ability to mingle truth with fantasy was frightening. At different points, Reagan—who infamously said that "facts are stupid things"—falsely claimed to have ended poverty in Los Angeles; implied he was personally involved in the liberation of Europe's concentration camps; argued that trees cause pollution; insisted that the Hollywood blacklist, to which he had contributed names, never existed; described as "freedom fighters" both *contra* thugs in Nicaragua and the religious fanatics in Afghanistan who would later become Al Qaeda; and reasoned that fighting a "limited" nuclear war was a viable option.

But to see Ronald Reagan as merely a bumpkin—which many in the media did—was to very much underestimate him. Like Nixon, the Teflon President was a survivor who'd come up the hard way, and many journalists and politicians who didn't understand this were perpetually surprised by his resilience and political savvy. He was generally compliant with his handlers, yet any time campaign pros or rigid ideologues got in the way of his or Nancy's instincts, they were summarily discarded.

Even when his ideas were silly, his intentions often seemed good. Reagan touted one of his dumbest and costliest pet projects, the "Star Wars" missile-defense program (which he first alluded to when I interviewed him for the *Los Angeles Times* in 1980), as a peace offering to the Soviets.

And his legendary ability to effectively project an upbeat, confident worldview masked many of the negative consequences of his policies. For example, he made the terrible mistake of willfully ignoring the burgeoning AIDS epidemic at a time when action could have saved the lives of millions. Unlike many right-wingers, however, he was not driven by homophobia. Instead, Reagan allowed AIDS to spread for the same reason he pointedly savaged policies targeted at reducing poverty: He was genuinely convinced that government programs exacerbated problems—unless they catered to the needs of the businessmen he had come to revere.

In the White House, he ran up more debt than any previous President, primarily to serve the interests of what Republican President Eisenhower had, with alarm, termed the "military-industrial complex." (George W. Bush has broken the Gipper's debt record.)

Apologists for this waste argue that throwing money at the defense industry broke the back of the Soviet Union and ended the Cold War. But the Soviet Union was already broken, as Mikhail S. Gorbachev acknowledged quite freely when he came to power in the 1980s. What Reagan *does* deserve considerable credit for is ignoring the dire warnings of his own hawks and responding enthusiastically to Gorbachev during their historic Reykjavík summit in October 1986, where the two leaders called for a nuclear-free world.

Let it be remembered, then, that in the closing act of his presidency, Reagan embraced the peacemakers, rejecting the cheerleaders of Armageddon, and was loudly castigated by the very neoconservatives—most vociferously Richard Perle—who have claimed the Reagan mantle for the post–Cold War militarism of the George W. Bush Administration.

All in all, a far more complicated man than the one who foes and celebrants alike remember. Reagan had his share of dumb statements and obtuse positions, but they were balanced by worthy gut instincts. What is most often forgotten about Reagan, primarily because of his acting career, is that his was a life not merely acted but lived. Reagan's early years were quite troubled, and the scars incurred very much informed his performance as an actor on the political stage. Capturing his essence still eludes us today, even after all of the memoirs and other accounts by those who knew him (or pretended to know him).

The only person capable of fully capturing the man's essence is Nancy Reagan, and she isn't talking. But I did have one memorable encounter with her long after the presidency, when her husband was too ill to appear at yet another memorial outpost to his stunning career. The event took place at one of the former President's preferred quiet corners in the world of glitz—a floor of the Century Plaza Hotel in Los Angeles that had been the scene of a number of his political triumphs, and which was now adorned with plaques and other Reagan memorabilia and was being dedicated in his honor.

I had always liked Mrs. Reagan and had written favorably about her when she was maligned by former Treasury Secretary Don Regan and others, and she greeted me warmly that day in the Century Plaza. After the ceremony, I wrote a short piece attempting to capture something of the spirit of Ronald Reagan. I was pleased when I soon thereafter received a little note from her (reprinted on the following page) thanking me for my evaluation of her husband, a column she later distributed at a meeting in the Ronald Reagan Presidential Foundation & Library. I take it as an indication from Nancy that I managed to get right at least part of the story of her infuriatingly obscure husband.

Yes, *obscure* is the right word. Honed by the terrors of an alcoholic father and his Warner Brothers studio bosses, and later by his political handlers, Reagan kept much to himself that was not needed for the part he was playing at any given moment. He was always aware that he was onstage and was determined not to let his own sensibilities damage his role.

Even so, he still had those obsessively felt sensibilities, and to the end, for better or worse, they drove him. The failure to give Reagan his due as a complex human being is what has undermined the efforts of many of his biographers, both critical and fawning, for the man himself was always more interesting, albeit maddeningly elusive, than the one he presented.

❧

The following profile of Ronald Reagan, based around my multiple interviews with him, was titled "The Reagan Question" and published by Playboy *in August 1980.*

I T WAS FRIDAY, SO ACCORDING TO THE SCHEDULE, IT MUST have been Augusta, Georgia—steamy, sultry, and dull—where we met the two ladies in the hotel lobby, wearing the current thigh-revealing, split-skirt fashion they were showing in New York. They sported the Reagan straw hats and buttons but also the pushed-up-cleavage look that one often finds at Republican dinners, a throwback to the '40s tease who played opposite Ronald Reagan the actor. And it must be conceded that a REAGAN FOR PRESIDENT button pinned near the exposed portion of a woman's breast takes on a campy, rakish quality, making it less chilling when they flash that big smile and say they like Ronnie because he'll give us more bombs and throw the bums off welfare.

There was a contradiction here that one encountered in state after state, traveling with the Reagan campaign. On the one hand, the puritanical and aged warrior intoning a death chant against the godless Communists, permissive government, the immoral homosexuals, the welfare cheats, unrelieved and simplistic in its enmity but always self-righteous and pure. On the other hand, the people drawn to him tending to be more varied and hip than one would expect from the campaign rhetoric. It is as if they want Reagan to be something they no longer are.

That night in Augusta, the two attractive women, both divorcees in their late thirties, had imbibed a few drinks to prepare them for the meeting Reagan had planned with them and dozens of other hard workers in his local campaign. But as a result of their bar stop, they missed "the next President of the United States." They were left to the consolation of a flirting interview with a film crew sent south by TV producer Norman Lear to capture the essence of what Ronnie's campaign poster—the one with him in the cowboy hat looking twenty years younger—calls "Reagan country."

Earlier that day, in an interview with me on the plane into Augusta, Reagan had blamed the federal government for the breakup of the family by encouraging permissiveness. It therefore seemed appropriate to ask those women if they also were opposed to premarital sex. "I love it!" said one who'd worked for Reagan since her college days.

"But Ronald Reagan says the new permissiveness and the federal government are breaking up the family," I said, "and he would strongly disapprove of your engaging in sex without the blessings of marriage."

And then, with camera lights on and film presumably rolling, the aging cheerleader flashed that smile, tinged now with wisdom and cynicism, and issued her personal emancipation proclamation: "Well . . . fuck him."

Does that mean she won't support him? Hell no. She'd still like Ronnie to be President and set everyone else straight. They've always liked Reagan because he's a strong moral leader who would bring the country closer together again. And they like his attacks on permissiveness: "I think we ought to have tighter controls."

Reagan can be magical on the stump, because he can convince even a cynical observer that he is a highly moral, honest, and purposeful man who has got his act together and can do the same for the country. His appeal is the nostalgic one—as in Reagan's movie roles—that of the good boy next door who will do right by the country, as he has for his family and friends. In that role, he effectively exudes an air of simple virtue that allows the audience to ignore serious gaps in his knowledge, his lackluster eight years as Governor, and the reality that his own family life has been quite disorderly.

But people want the image more than the truth. The Reagan sermon is a throwback to the Jimmy Carter homilies of 1976—"Ah just want a country as good, honest, decent as are the American people"—and then some assurance about how wholesome everything was back home in Plains, Georgia. The people listening knew they weren't so pure, but they hoped Jimmy might be.

We rarely heard about Carter's nephew serving time in a California prison, or the widespread use of drugs by young people in the county, or the good ol' Carter boys' checking out the latest crop of divorced women at the Best Western Inn near Plains, the closest they have to a nightlife down there.

Never mind—the voters wanted to believe that someone, somewhere in America, had a better life than they were experiencing, and Jimmy's con filled the void. Virtuous, Bible-studying Jimmy could make us feel good all over again and lead us to what Reagan now calls "the shining city upon the hill"—

Reagan and Scheer on a flight during one segment of their interview

a phrase taken from the Puritans. But Jimmy's pristine image couldn't sustain him through the presidency, even though he brought the image shapers—Pat Caddell, Jerry Rafshoon, Ham Jordan, Jody Powell, and company—right into the White House. It failed because we are not always so hardworking, selfless, and lacking in greed as Carter pretended. His mind ever on the polls, he would not tell us what we didn't want to hear or lead in an unpopular direction. So the image shrivels and the man himself ends up appearing weak and vacillating.

Well, let's just try again. Now, Ronald Reagan—there's a man who rides tall in the saddle; there's a man who can solve our problems the way we used to, who can take on the Russians and anyone else who gets in our way. Let's hear it for plain-speaking, two-fisted common sense. In an interview with me for the *Los Angeles Times* of March 6, 1980, he called the President of Panama "a pip-squeak dictator who hasn't got as much gross national product as Cincinnati, Ohio." And, as an indication of his presidential negotiating style, he said, "From the minute their dictator down there told us that we had to give up the canal or there was going to be trouble—he was going to make trouble for us—that's when we should have said to him, 'Look, buster, you withdraw that threat or there's no more negotiation or sitting at a table with you, because we're not, in the eyes of the world, going to give this up in answer to a threat of violence.'"

Reagan's inherent promise is to solve our problems without additional sacrifice, without adding to our burdens—be they taxes or the draft. He is trusted the way a slicker like George H.W. Bush or John Connally wasn't—never to try any more newfangled governmental approaches or programs. Enough with change.

It is a mood well understood by Reagan's elder daughter, Maureen, who campaigns for her father but is an advocate of change and disagrees with Reagan on the E.R.A. She is an attractive and strong-willed woman who has lived a bit, been divorced, and has worked as an editor, a secretary, and an actress to pay the bills on her Los Angeles apartment. She is a delight to interview, because she keeps the Scotch coming and refuses to play the Goody Two–shoes role of a candidate's poster family. She can be brutal in her comments, as on the pro-lifers: "After dealing with those people for years, I'm convinced they are not anti-abortion, they are anti-sex." But she is also sympathetic to why people are disoriented by the changes that have occurred in this country and judges that apprehension to be the source of her father's greatest appeal: "You gotta understand that people are starting to fight change now because they're scared; they can only deal with so much; they can only handle so much that's different from the way it was supposed to be, and it isn't, and the way they were raised. Most of us are still part of a fairyland generation and, if we did it all right, Prince Charming was going to ride up on his white horse and we were going to go off into the sunset and live happily ever after. But it doesn't work that way. Maybe he's America's Prince Charming."

Maybe the Reagan phenomenon falls under what Erich Fromm called the escape from freedom. Maybe too much change, too fast, with too few good results. Then there's Iran, inflation, and the Russians, and not being able to believe in the dollar or working hard for the future. "They" just push us around and Jimmy Carter just takes it.

Traveling with the Reagan campaign, you hear it everywhere, and Reagan is the candidate best trained to play to that desperation. He has been railing against permissiveness, Big

Government, and communism for more than twenty years now and has become a creature of his one-liners. Jim Lake, his former press secretary, said in a conversation with me, "Ronnie just cannot resist throwing that red meat out to excite the audience, and he sometimes forgets whether he really means it."

Lake, who intends to vote for Reagan, was referring to the fact that in private interviews, one encounters a more reasonable Reagan, but on the campaign hustings, he gets out of control and the crowds love it.

"Just who do they think they are?" he repeats over and over to a crowd in Greensboro, North Carolina, without ever making clear just who "they" are. The sad tale that day has to do with the government bureaucrats' coming between a mother and her fifteen-year-old daughter, who is in "deep trouble." It's a story repeated in numerous other campaign stops, with the mother "hugging that child from birth on," only to suddenly lose control to the Feds. He has used it so often that in Greensboro he leaves out half the story. We never do learn the nature of the "deep trouble" and are left wondering whether she committed a crime or was knocked up by the New Deal. But the punch line—"Just who do they think they are?"—got big applause, anyway.

The best rouser is the one about the federal government's "destroying the American family." This last was even stated in the Republican primary debates, but no one had the presence of mind or the curiosity to ask Ronnie what he was talking about.

On the chartered campaign plane from Orlando, Florida into Augusta, I finally got a chance to ask the Governor to spell it out (this and all subsequent exchanges taken from the interview I did with him for the *Los Angeles Times*):

SCHEER You speak of the breakdown of the family, the federal government's intrusion into life between the parents and the children. What do you have in mind?

REAGAN There has been a constant effort on the part of government at almost every level to interfere with the family and make decisions with regard to children. For example, you've got a woman who has been appointed a judge by the President who has advocated that children should have the right to legal counsel in disputes with their parents. In California, they tried to get a bill passed that would allow underage children to go on their own, to a doctor, and get advice on contraceptives, and so forth, without the knowledge of their parents.

SCHEER But isn't that one way to avoid the need for abortions, which you oppose?

REAGAN But isn't that also government sticking its nose into the family?

SCHEER But if you have an underage child, isn't it better that he or she get a contraceptive device and then thereby avoid what you have termed murdering a fetus?

REAGAN What has ever happened to the teaching of a family . . .

SCHEER What if the family has broken down, what if the parents aren't there, what if it's a grandmother or an aunt who's raising that child, and the child needs a contraceptive device or wants one; isn't it better to allow him or her to purchase it rather than to have an abortion or an unwanted baby?

REAGAN Whatever happened to just saying no?

Is Reagan kidding? Does he not know what has been going on in this country, and does he really believe it's all due to government's "breaking up the family"?

Following that exchange with Reagan, I wandered back to my seat in the press section of the plane very much needing a drink. All I could think of was sound trucks cruising our communities, urging young people to just say no. "Hey, you, in the backseat of that car, whatever happened . . . ?" I wanted to say yes, to indulge some minor decadence. To sin in the pathetic way that one does covering a campaign, by heavy drinking. What world did Reagan live in? As in other campaigns, a number of the people around me on the plane, Reagan staff, press, off-duty Secret Service, would often spend their evenings near drunk, just hoping that some woman or man would turn up to whom they could say yes. Many of them are divorced or actively behaving in such a way as to become so. And I'd never once on any campaign trip ever heard anyone speak in other than an approving way about extramarital sex. Nor was any of this permissiveness inspired by the federal government.

But what about Reagan himself? How had he managed to avoid the pitfalls of ordinary humans? Then suddenly I realized that I had accepted the sanctimonious Reagan stance at face value. I, in fact, knew very little about Reagan's family life, and neither did others in the press corps. His family life is a closely guarded secret. The Reagan staff barely concedes that the candidate has a family and keeps the press away from the two younger children.

But since Reagan has mixed up the personal and the political, it seemed necessary to take a closer look at his family life. After interviews with family and friends, it was possible to learn that Reagan does, indeed, live in the same messed-up world that the rest of us inhabit. And it hardly seems that the federal government caused the breakdown of his own family.

Was the government responsible for his divorce from

actress Jane Wyman thirty-two years ago, or was it, as she tes-
tified in court, his attempts to subordinate her interests to his
political preoccupations?

Was the government responsible for his younger daughter, Patti's, history of teenage rebellion and later running off
to England with a member of a rock group—The Eagles—
just prior to the 1976 campaign and not letting her parents
know where she was? Or was it, as I hear it, Reagan's rigid
refusal to allow the young musician into the house because
they were living together without the blessing of marriage?
Reagan makes the point repeatedly that a wholesome family
life is the best and simplest counterweight to the ills of society spawned by a permissive government. He has also consistently led the hunt for scapegoats—hippies, radicals, lenient
judges—which obscures the complexities of raising a family
in a changing world. There is a smirking self-righteousness to
the man—"Whatever happened to just saying no?"—which
implies that he and other proper folks have been successful at
coping with family problems.

The point is not to extend gossip but, rather, to observe
that the Reagan family has experienced the same problems of
divorce, generational revolt, conflicting morality, and dilu-
tion of sense of purpose as most Americans.

The campaign does not like to mention the Reagan children, because they do not conform to the plastic normalcy
that Ronnie has been pushing all these years; but I was pleasantly surprised to find them far more interesting than the '40s
movie image of the family that he projects. True, all four
Reagan kids dropped out of college over their parents' objec-
tions, but Maureen did so to become an actress and eventually an organizer for the E.R.A. Elder son Michael races boats
and sells gasohol, and Patti, twenty-seven, is now a rock

musician. The youngest, Ronald, Jr., twenty-two, left Yale suddenly after his first year to become a ballet dancer. Maybe it doesn't fit Reagan's high-in-the-saddle image to have a son who's a ballet dancer, but his teacher's report is that he is a serious and talented student with the Joffrey Ballet who had worked extra hard to make up for his late start.

The Reagan children are an embarrassment to the campaign precisely because they are interesting. Reagan staffers cannot easily control the offsprings' comments or actions. The younger two are not currently campaigning for their father and the older two, who are, must be kept at a distance, perhaps because they are bright and funny.

Aside from being outspoken and independent, Maureen, thirty-nine, and adopted son Michael, thirty-five (children of his first marriage), who strongly support their father's candidacy, are thought to be a liability because they sabotaged Ronnie's campaign simply by growing up. They both joked to me about the campaign staff's wanting to have some little kids sent over from Central Casting to complete the campaign portrait. They support Reagan because they judge him a very good man who will effectively lead the country. But he is a good man not because, as a father, he sat them down for prayer each night—he didn't. They lived mostly in boarding schools and occasionally got a weekend with Mom or Dad. It wasn't his fault; he and his ex-wife, Jane Wyman, were actors involved with the demands of their careers in Hollywood, and, later, Ronnie was promoting General Electric and his own politics. Evidently, it is possible to be a good father even if you don't rush home from work to the suburban tract house to hug the wife and kiddies and take them to church on Sunday. But to hear Reagan's campaign speeches, you would never know that.

Wouldn't it be wild if Ronnie got up one day on the campaign trail and said, "Hey, even before *Kramer vs. Kramer,* I knew divorce wasn't the end of the world." Or, "My wife, Nancy, and I were so eagerly in love that we produced a seven-pound baby girl just seven and one half months after our wedding." Or, "I learned that kids can rebel against everything I stand for, and still be in the human race." Or, "I got divorced because I was a male-chauvinist slob who was threatened by Jane Wyman's being a much better actor. So I went off to marry a woman who lives only through me and my career." Or, "After my divorce, I drank a lot and chased women and I still managed to come out of it OK."

In his autobiography, Reagan refers to his divorce only in the last four paragraphs of a chapter detailing how he and the House Un-American Activities Committee did in the Hollywood leftists. (Perhaps the Feds *were* responsible for his divorce, after all.) As he recalls, "I arrived home from the Washington [HUAC] hearing to be told I was leaving. I suppose there had been warning signs, if only I hadn't been so busy, but small-town boys grow up thinking only other people get divorced. The plain truth was that such a thing was so far from being imagined by me that I had no resources to call upon."

The question is whether or not he has since expanded those resources. For his campaign rhetoric still reflects— indeed, celebrates—the thinking of small-town boys, at least as they were pictured in the movies of the '40s, following their father's example of hard work, pious living, and substantial success.

Reagan's real-life father, as he concedes, was something of an alcoholic who had trouble holding on to a job and was all but destroyed in the Great Depression. He and the entire Reagan family were saved from poverty only by FDR's New Deal. In fact, Reagan's father was one of those faceless bureaucrats, the "they" in the "Just who do they think they are?"—the guy who gave out the relief payments and then the jobs when they made him the head of the local WPA. The real-life elder Reagan sounds like he was terrific; and perhaps it reveals a hidden side of the son that he recalls his father's robust complexity so affectionately in his autobiography:

> *I bent over him, smelling the sharp odor of whiskey from the speak-easy. I got a fistful of his overcoat. Opening the door, I managed to drag him inside and get him to bed. In a few days, he was the bluff, hearty man I knew and loved and will always remember.*
>
> *Jack (we all called him by his nickname) was a handsome man—tall, swarthy, and muscular, filled with contradictions of character. A sentimental Democrat, who believed fervently in the rights of the working man.*

When Reagan wrote those words about his father, he had abandoned his own trade-union career with the Screen Actors Guild and gone off to preach the corporate message for General Electric.

Reagan recalls his father as "the best raconteur I ever heard, especially when it came to the smoking-car sort of stories." He claims that Jack "drew a sharp line between lusty vulgar humor and filth. To this day, I agree with his credo and join Jack and Mark Twain in asserting that one of the basic forms of American humor is the down-to-earth wit of the ordinary person, and the questionable language is justified if the point is based on real humor."

Privately, Reagan can use rough language both humorously and in occasional flashes of anger. He can also be one of the funnier candidates on the campaign trail. He likes to tell jokes, and that's why he told the ethnic joke that got him into some trouble. Perhaps if reporters didn't overreact to a politician's telling the very same joke they routinely hear and tell in the city room, we'd get more humor. Reagan seems inclined to that sort of jest, and he's even reported to have whispered an ethnic joke—about blacks and Chinese—at Jack Benny's funeral. But people who know Reagan deny that he's bigoted, and certainly not toward ethnic groups. He himself is the product of an ethnic joke—the cross of a hard-drinking Irish-Catholic father and a Bible-toting Scotch-English Protestant mother. His nickname, Dutch, derives from his father's referring to him at birth as a fat little Dutchman.

Reagan's humor may derive from his Irish father, but his puritanism bears the mark of his mother, who considered herself snatched by God from an early deathbed to stick around to convert sinners. Nelle Reagan's missionary work took her and her Bible in and out of the jails of the Midwest and later the hospitals of California. Maureen Reagan remembers her grandmother as a remarkable woman of near biblical strength and conviction, a woman of great social conscience and concern for the less fortunate. But it seems more a pie-in-the-sky missionary's vow for the sinner to be saved than, as Jack would have had it, for the poor to organize to gain their just deserts. Those are two views of poverty, and Reagan seems to have traveled from the vision of the father to that of the mother in his march from early liberalism to late conservatism.

In any event, Reagan's mother was a strong figure and he seems to have looked for similar qualities in his wives, but their strengths differ markedly. In his marriages, he went from Jane Wyman, who exhibits a mocking independence, to his current wife, Nancy, a vassal of cold public virtue. The two women represent a startling contrast and it is difficult to imagine his having been attracted to both, though each is strong-willed and possessed of a fiery temper.

I met Jane Wyman, who has shunned the press, by happenstance at a party for Ronald Reagan's daughter Maureen's dog. It was a party that was ripe for a snappy "conservative chic" dismissal, but that would have gotten it all wrong. Yes, there was a large red, white, and blue birthday cake and buttons saying, BARNAE FOR FIRST DOG (one guest offered—to considerable laughter—that it should be BARNAE FOR FIRST LADY), and the dog who received presents was one of those frisky little ones that rich people adore. But Maureen's apartment is modest and the crowd eclectic, a mix from the neighborhood including a *Los Angeles Times* pressman, who belongs to Maureen's local Lutheran church, and the local hairdresser, who doesn't. The party was an annual put-on for the little mutt who was found in the rain in Texas eight years ago, when Maureen was on tour. Brother Michael was happily telling ethnic and other jokes; he confessed he had told his father the one that got him into trouble, and he wasn't going to stop now. Actress Gretchen Wyler, who's involved in Actors and Others for Animals, talked about saving dogs, and Jane Wyman was challenging the role of multinational companies. It was L.A. at its best—an easy mix of immigrants from all over the country, featuring a variety of styles and obsessions, whose coexistence is made possible by an easygoing tolerance.

One could imagine the best part of Reagan (the one I've seen at moments in interviews and must confess to liking) enjoying this party with his two older children and his ex-wife, though Nancy would not welcome it. Nancy and Jane do not get along. And Nancy prefers socially important functions. She is a serious, no-nonsense social climber. In public, Nancy Reagan is the extreme opposite of open. She possesses the tightest smile in the land, and it can always be clicked exactly into place.

Nancy's chief mission in life appears to be to stick constantly to Ronnie's side to caution him when his momentary exuberance might lead him once again to put his foot in his mouth. I experienced her screening effect at one press conference in Sarasota in March. In New Hampshire, Reagan had called marijuana "one of the most dangerous drugs." At the Sarasota press conference, he was asked for the factual basis for that statement. Reagan referred to an HEW study showing that one marijuana cigarette had a potentially greater carcinogenic content than an ordinary tobacco cigarette. I had read the same report, which also indicated that marijuana users need far fewer joints to get high than the number of cigarettes used by the average smoker. I broke through the babble of the press conference to point that out to him and thought I had him cornered. He was, as is his custom, about to compound the error by talking even more about a subject he knew nothing about. But Nancy swiftly moved her face next to his, looked up at him with her unwavering smile, and whispered loudly enough to be heard by a few reporters near her, "You wouldn't *know*." Reagan snapped to, suddenly relaxed, cocked his head back as if to ponder his answer, and said with a smile and on camera, "I wouldn't know."

But there is still some vestige of the preconservative, pre-Nancy Ronnie who is the old actor, who won't take himself too seriously, who is aware that the world is made up of many different types. Maureen says, "How could he be thought naïve and prudish when he worked so long in Hollywood? He met *all* types."

However, on the campaign trail, Reagan frequently rails against homosexuals. As Governor, he got in a flap for his reported firing of two high-ranking staff members who were accused of being gay. Reagan's security man investigated the matter and could find no evidence, but they were fired anyway, on the basis of another staff member's accusation. The Anita Bryant people liked him in Florida; but, on the other hand, it is Reagan who, more than anyone, gets credit for sinking the Briggs initiative in California in 1978 by publicly opposing the anti-homosexual proposition. Yet his tolerance is ambivalent:

SCHEER Why do you attack homosexuals, as you did at a recent rally?

REAGAN I didn't attack them, I was asked a question. A fellow asked me if I believed that they should have the same civil rights, and I said I think they do and should but that my criticism of the gay-rights movement is that it isn't asking for civil rights, it is asking for a recognition and acceptance of an alternative lifestyle that I do not believe society can condone, nor can I.

SCHEER For religious reasons?

REAGAN Well, you could find that in the Bible it says that in the eyes of the Lord, this is an abomination.

SCHEER But should that bind the rest of the citizens, who may not believe in the Bible? Don't we have the right to separation of church and state?

REAGAN Oh, we do; yes, we do. Look, what other group of people demands the same thing? Let's say here is the total libertarian—or libertine, I should say—who wants the right to just free and open sex.

SCHEER That's the thing that's confusing me—it's the conservative who wants to keep government out of everything; why don't you keep it out of private morality? Why do you want the cops coming in, the government, the state, and telling people what their sex life should be?

REAGAN No one is advocating the invasion of the private life of any individual. I think Mrs. Patrick Campbell said it best in the trial of Oscar Wilde. She said, "I have no objection to anyone's sex life so long as they don't practice it in the street and frighten the horses."

California reporters who have long covered Reagan do not tend to judge him a mean-spirited man. He never seems the elitist and, indeed, conveys a sense of deference and concern to those who work for him or are just there to shake hands. Few people who have spent time with him dislike him, but there are far fewer people who will claim to really know him. He is a legendary loner who spends virtually all of his free time in solitary activity—mending fences on his ranch or riding his horse. Solitary except for his ever-present mate, Nancy.

The ranch house near Santa Barbara, where they spend much of their free time, was built small with little room for guests. Ronnie has few, if any, close male friends, and one aide who worked with Nancy insists that she "simply does not like other women, she is threatened by their presence, including that of her own daughter." It was also said by one family member that "he is totally and devotedly in love with her and, for that reason, suffers her not infrequent tantrums." An associate said, "She is a force, a strong woman in the pre-liberation sense of strength. Her power derives from her association with and power over a male." First there was the famous neurosurgeon father, whose name and contacts gave her entree to Hollywood and her abortive starlet career prior to marrying Ronnie. Now she manages his equilibrium and has life-and-death power over his staffing decisions. In the weeks preceding the firing of former campaign manager John Sears, both Sears and his nemesis, Ed Meese, the Governor's campaign chief of staff who won out, were compelled to make their case to the Governor through the wife. And there is little doubt that she was instrumental in this and many other final decisions. This is no Eleanor Roosevelt or even a Rosalynn Carter, smart women with their own strong social values and insights. Her life is Ronald Reagan.

Which is how Ronnie wanted it in his second marriage. His first had come to an end when his movie career foundered and Jane Wyman's flourished. (She was nominated four times for Academy Awards and won once; he was never nominated.) Wyman clearly had ideas of her own and, perhaps, was ahead of her time. At their divorce trial in 1948, according to the account offered by the *Los Angeles Times,* "Miss Wyman told the court that she and Reagan engaged in continual arguments on his political views."

Reagan was then the gung-ho president of the Screen Actors Guild. It was when he came back from being a friendly witness at HUAC, testifying against Hollywood Reds, that Wyman first asked for a divorce. According to a report of their divorce, "Despite her lack of interest in his political activities, Miss Wyman continued, Reagan insisted that she attend meetings with him and that she be present during discussions among his friends. But her own ideas, she complained, 'were never considered important.'"

Those years of HUAC and the blacklist gave Reagan not only a new wife but also a new ideological commitment. To understand his persistent obsession with the Communists, one has to view history from his point of view rather than, say, from Lillian Hellman's. Reagan still believes that there never was a blacklist against Reds in Hollywood, as he revealed to me recently: "There was no blacklist of Hollywood. The blacklist in Hollywood, if there was one, was provided by the Communists. There were blacklists by our customers and clients who said to the motion-picture industry, 'We won't go to see pictures that those people are involved in.'"

In his view, it was war, as he stated back in 1951: "The Russians sent their first team, their ace string, here to take us over . . . We were up against hard-core organizers."

Some of Reagan's critics of the time suggested that the aging actor (he was forty then) was attempting to lay out a political string to compensate for a stalled acting career. But whatever the original motivation, there can be little doubt of the passionate hatred that Reagan developed for the people he considered Hollywood's hard-core Communists and their liberal fellow travelers. And the feeling was mutual. It was a civil war within a community that pretends to familial intimacy and even attains it at times, perhaps more than in any other industry. To hear each side tell it, the other had all the guns. There is now substantial literature documenting the fact that there was a blacklist and that many artists—actors, writers, directors—had their careers destroyed because people like Reagan could reach producers and theater owners and advertisers. But as Reagan describes it, the Reds had the power of the pen and mouth—to besmirch reputations and to organize effective fronts to cloak subversion with the protection of the First Amendment. To be sure, both sides played hardball and Reagan, who was out in front for his cause, took his lumps.

It was similar to the ways in which one could view the campus disturbances at Berkeley over the Vietnam War when he was Governor more than fifteen years later. The students saw that Reagan had the regents of the university and the cops, but he must have recognized that the students had grabbed the high moral ground and would win.

It is easy for Reagan to feel the aggrieved party. But then again, that's not unusual in an activist. The problem, however, is that Reagan's basic education for the presidency—his worldview—seems to have grown rather linearly and simplistically out of the Hollywood and Berkeley skirmishes with "communism." To this date, a conversation with Reagan clearly indicates that he knows and cares less about the Sino-Soviet dispute in judging world events than he does about the battles within the Screen Actors Guild of the early '50s.

In fact, Reagan must now detest the Sino-Soviet dispute, because any such complexity, if accepted, would mitigate against the rage that still wells up in him at the memory of those Commies who first broke his liberal faith and led him on the long march toward a conservative presidency. The new faith, steeled in combat, was simple, direct: Communism is godless and its practitioners are monsters. He believed that in 1951 in Los Angeles and in 1980 in Orlando, Florida:

SCHEER You attacked "godless communism," and I'm curious about the use of the word *godless*—why is that an important element there?

REAGAN Well, because this is one of the vital precepts of communism, that we are accidents of nature.

SCHEER But is it the godlessness that makes them more violent, more aggressive, more expansionist?

REAGAN Well, it is one that gives them less regard for humanity or human beings.

SCHEER But here we have the Ayatollah in Iran, who certainly is not godless, and he seems to be—

REAGAN A fanatic and a zealot—

SCHEER But he's not godless.

REAGAN No, not in his sense—and we have had that all the way back through history. We go back to the Inquisition in Spain. So there are people who, through their fanaticism, misuse religion. But the reason for the godlessness with regard to communism—here is a direct teaching of the child from the beginning of its life that it is a human being whose only importance is its contribution to the state, that they are wards of the state, that they exist only for its purpose, and that there is no God, they are just an accident of nature that created a human being. The result is, this is why they have no respect for human life, for the dignity of an individual.

I remember one night, a long time ago, in a rally in Los Angeles, 16,000 people in the auditorium, and this was at the time when the local Communists, the American Communist Party—and this is all well documented—was actually trying, had secured domination of several unions in the picture business and was trying to take over the motion-picture industry, and with all of the rewriting of history today, and the stories that we have seen, and the screenplays and television plays, and so forth, about the persecution for political beliefs that took place in Hollywood, believe me, the persecutors were the Communists who had gotten into position where they could destroy careers, and *did* destroy them.

With Reagan, the categories get all mixed up and the Commies metamorphose into welfare socialists and the New Deal. Thus, in the appendix in his autobiography, under a section titled "Karl Marx," we find this tirade, not against the

Russian Bolsheviks but against the very Keynesians of the New Deal who kept his father from the gutter: "We are faced with the most evil enemy mankind has known in his long climb from the swamp to the stars. There can be no security anywhere in the free world if there is not fiscal and economic stability within the United States. Those who ask us to trade our freedom for the soup kitchen of the welfare state are architects of a policy of accommodation."

Is he talking about unemployment insurance and senior-citizen centers and Medicare? And why does that basic speech, now fifteen years old, still go over on the campaign trail? Because he's riding a crest of resentment toward overblown programs that don't work and bureaucrats who get paid even if they don't.

And just who do "they" think they are? If you can't afford the suburbs and must live in the inner city and get your child bused to a school with tough ghetto kids, you can get pretty pissed. Especially when they—the sociologists, the judges, the liberal scribblers, the HEW bureaucrats—send their kids to private schools.

There is pain out there among the employed taxpaying masses, and the brilliance of Reagan is that he can absolve his own politics of any responsibility while fixing blame on all past steps taken to solve any of the problems. Take tough blacks and white racists in the schools. Did the liberals invent racial hostility? Are they or their political ancestors responsible for slavery, the maiming of black culture, the persistence of segregation in the South and discrimination in the North?

Reagan's own position on civil rights is of the "some of my best friends are" variety:

SCHEER In 1966, you were quoted as saying you were opposed to the 1964 Civil Rights Act, as an example of federal intrusion.

REAGAN I was opposed at the time, I can't remember the exact details, not for the idea of doing something against prejudice, certainly. I was opposed to certain features of that law that went beyond and infringed on the individual rights of citizens that are supposedly guaranteed by the Constitution.

SCHEER Which features?

REAGAN Well, they had to do with the, let's say the person who owns property, his right to do with his property what he wants to do.

SCHEER Do you mean discriminate in renting it or discriminate in selling it?

REAGAN At that time, this was what I thought was interfering with the right, particularly, with the idea of selling. I recognize that that could lend itself to the same prejudice that we're talking about, and I'm opposed to that prejudice. I said at that time that I felt that the President had a moral responsibility to use the powers of persuasion that the office has, to help cure us of the kind of bigotry and prejudice that made those discriminations possible.

SCHEER But you would still be against the Civil Rights Act of 1964?

REAGAN No, no, I wouldn't, because I recognize now that it is institutionalized and it has, let's say, hastened the solution of a lot of problems.

SCHEER So why is that so difficult in an interview situation for a politician to say, "I was wrong in '66 and I've changed my mind and now I would have supported the Civil Rights Act"?

REAGAN One reason is because, very frankly, you of the press—and not meaning present company—you of the press have a way of seizing upon a sentence and then distorting the view and presenting a political candidate or a political official as having some beliefs or prejudices that he does not have. Now, I will weigh my fight against bigotry and prejudice against that of the most ardent civil-rights advocate, because I was doing it when there was no civil-rights fight. I, on the air as a sports announcer years and years ago, was editorializing against the gentlemen's agreement that kept blacks from playing organized baseball. I dealt with it in my personal life; I played on a college football team alongside a black who's today my best friend, when this was not commonplace.

SCHEER One thing that came up in the New Hampshire [Republican] debate was the question of the number of black people, the number of minorities on various people's staffs. I've been traveling with you for a few weeks now and I have yet to see a single minority person.

REAGAN We've been traveling with a very small segment. When we talk about staff, we're talking about not only several hundred actual staff employees but even more, literally thousands of volunteers. I know we have a committee that is totally black. I don't know their exact numbers, but we're going to do an inventory and find out. But certainly there has been no effort to exclude.

Reagan is still against the desegregation of neighborhoods and affirmative action; and, surely, having one black friend from college football days will not solve the problems. When Reagan was Governor, he said jobs created by the private sector for hard-core unemployed blacks were the answer. And the answer turned out to be fewer than 2,000 jobs in a state that has forty percent black-youth unemployment, a state of 20,000,000 people.

What Reagan added was a begrudging spirit—a contempt for those who had tried to do something. He loathed the civil-rights activists whom he termed "irresponsible militants" and was later to embrace Nixon's Southern Strategy with equanimity. He made people on welfare feel even more forlorn and weak than they were. At the time of the S.L.A./Patty Hearst kidnapping, when the Hearst family provided food to the poor as a partial ransom, Reagan said, "It's just too bad we can't have an epidemic of botulism." He challenged the patriotism of those who would stop the war in Vietnam and had his own Strangelovian solution: "We could pave the whole country, put parking strips on it, and still be home before Christmas." He derided environmentalists by saying, "A tree's a tree—how many more do we need to look at?" He delighted in humbling the great public university system with inane comments such as, "The state should not subsidize intellectual curiosity." He responded as Governor to campus demonstrations by saying, "If it's to be a blood bath, let it be now."

Ironically, as Governor, despite his vicious rhetorical stabs at programs for the poor and randomly heartless budget cuts, as in mental health, he ended up administering, indeed expanding, the liberal program of the most liberal state in the Union. He did that begrudgingly—and only in his second term, when his back was against the wall—because of the pressures from Democrats and even liberal Republicans. As the editor of *Ramparts* then, I was among those who found much to criticize. But recently, I was surprised to find Reagan more reasonable on the "social issues" than one would have expected from his public pronouncements. He also can be quite genial, as in this exchange:

SCHEER Why are you willing to talk to me? Why aren't you more uptight?

REAGAN Well, because—why does a preacher preach?

SCHEER It's an amazing encounter for me, because you seem relaxed, you don't seem like a zealot.

REAGAN No, I'm not, but I remember this also: When I was a New Deal Democrat, I remember somehow that it was easier to dislike than to like. There seemed to be something about liberalism that worked better if you were kept angry and worked up.

SCHEER And yet up on your public platforms, you convey a more hostile, nastier image than you do right now.

REAGAN Well, let me give you a few things that I haven't mentioned up there on the platform to further confuse the image. As you know, I succeeded a very liberal Governor, Pat Brown. As far as his record on minorities went, I found out that it was all talk. I appointed more blacks to executive positions than all the previous Governors in California put together. And yet I was the conservative. Our divorce rate is 29.9 percent, while nationally divorces average 40 percent."

He also went on to point out that "communism is infinitesimal in the motion-picture industry." Then, as now, Reagan was reassuring American businessmen that communism could be stopped, that the moral fiber of the country was strong, and that all would be well if we kept the old family virtues intact.

It bothered none of his listeners that two weeks after that speech, the divorced actor married his second wife. Nor that he had his statistics wrong—the national divorce rate at the time was less than that in Hollywood, not more, as he claimed it was. *Believe what I say, not what I do, and don't let's haggle over the facts.* Then, as now, people loved it.

Reagan loves the sound of his own voice, and he works hard for the applause. During the 1980 campaign, he would continue to use erroneous information that worked with crowds, even after he had been told it was wrong. For example, his claim that a government study showed that Alaska had greater potential of oil than the known reserves of Saudi Arabia. Those of us traveling with him soon discovered that he had gotten the report wrong, and press aide Jim Lake conceded it. But Reagan had grown too fond of the line to drop it and claimed to his aides that it was based on a newspaper clipping that he had picked up somewhere but could no longer find.

The sloppiness is habitual, but it is dismissed by admirers as proof that he is his own man, not the carefully programed product of advisers, as happened in the Carter phenomenon. There is a charming fumbling quality to Reagan's work habits, with his clippings stuffed into his pockets and anecdotes that he hears from those shaking his hand at receptions stuffed into his brain. The use of this "data" becomes less charming when it supports one scapegoat theory or another to explain the source of our problems. The bumbling septuagenarian then becomes the effective demagogue whipping up the passions of a public that is confused, frustrated, and ripe for the clarity of his positions, even when they are totally without foundation.

Reagan's sloppiness has caused him to be viewed with

suspicion by the elite Northeastern wing of the Republican Party, probably less for what he did as Governor than because they doubt his stability or fear that he may actually believe in some of his proposals for dismantling the federal government, which, after all, does serve the interests of big corporations. His proposal to return us to the gold standard must have been viewed as primitive by the economists at Chase Manhattan. Nor can the managers of multinational corporations, who have done quite well in a complex and changing world, be terribly sanguine about his sledgehammer nostrums for the world's problems. Those gentlemen are internationalists par excellence—world statesmen more interested in cutting deals with the Russians than in a holy crusade against them.

Unlike Carter and Nixon, Reagan has never made the journey back East to the centers of power to demonstrate his reasonableness. So the fear in those quarters persists that he may be a primitive isolationist.

Prior to the New Hampshire primary, David Rockefeller convened a secret meeting of like-minded Republicans aimed at developing a strategy for stopping Reagan by supporting Bush and, failing that, getting Gerald Ford into the race. Reagan heard about the meeting and was, according to one aide, "really hurt." This aide reports that Reagan turned to him and demanded, "What have they got against me? I support big oil, I support big business, why don't they trust me?" The aide suggested charitably that maybe it was because he was once an actor and that he attended too few important lunches in the East.

In any event, when Reagan scored his resounding triumph in New Hampshire in February, the overtures to the East began to work. New York establishment lawyer Bill

Casey, who became campaign director the day of the New Hampshire victory, began building bridges and promising that a more moderate Reagan would emerge after the Republican Convention.

The problem with the creation of a moderate Reagan after the convention will be with Reagan himself. His previous campaign manager, Sears, tried to do it during the primaries; and Reagan got so confused in the attempt to appear more restrained and reasonable that he became inarticulate. He fired Sears, went back to being his old outrageous self, and wooed them in the Southern states. William Buckley once likened Reagan to William Jennings Bryan, and there is something to that. He is far more effective as a demagogic speaker than he would be in the role of Head of State. He is happiest with right-wing rhetoric and miserably plodding in any effort to express a more complex sentiment. I saw that one day in April when he went straight from a rousing rally in North Carolina, where he had them on their feet and seemed to know what he was talking about, to a stumbling performance before the American Society of Newspaper Editors in which he might just as well have stuck his prepared speech into his ear. He was afraid of that crowd, not because they were more liberal than the electorate—they may not be—but because he feared them socially.

There is to Reagan a sense of great intellectual and social inferiority, born of the fact that he does not have the educational credentials or broad range of knowledge thought by some, including most editors, to be a prerequisite for the presidency. He mispronounces the names of world leaders and gets countries in the wrong hemispheres. He prefers to stick to the simple slogans about the welfare state and godless communism, because to venture into any greater complexity might prove acutely embarrassing, as it often has when he has tried it, be it in a discussion of his proposed blockade of Cuba or farm-price parity. He is painfully aware of the gaps in his knowledge and, for that reason, prefers to stick to his surefire one-liners. And the best ones—because he is a true believer on this—have to do with his attacks on the Russians.

The emotional high point of a Reagan campaign speech comes with his oft-repeated charge that *détente* is a failure and that we have been sandbagged by the Russians. To hear him, one would not know that our gross national product is twice that of the Soviets or that they have suffered immense reversals throughout the world, particularly with the loss of their influence in China and Egypt. Reagan's speeches about the threat of godless communism are straight out of the '50s and would have an absurdly archaic ring to them were it not for the equally absurd positions that Jimmy Carter took to increase his standing in the polls—positions that have made Reagan seem suddenly credible.

Carter's overreaction to the Soviets' Afghan intervention gave Reagan the opening he needed, and the elephant went charging through. Carter had said that Afghanistan represented the greatest crisis since World War Two, implying that it was a greater breach of international etiquette than the Berlin blockade, the Korean war, the crushing of the Hungarian revolution, and the invasion of Czechoslovakia. That's all Reagan needed to hear to dust off his rhetorical guns and go blasting away at this *détente* business, which he always thought was a trick of some sort. If the Russians were as bad as Carter now had it, how could the President have pushed for the SALT agreement? How could he have abandoned trusted anti-Communist allies like the Shah in Iran or the government of Taiwan? How could he dwell on human rights and nonproliferation of nuclear weapons when he should have been backing any anti-Communist dictator he could find as a necessary ally for the future Armageddon? Carter had managed to shift some of the rage felt over the hostages in Iran to the Soviets in Afghanistan, and as we moved through the spring primaries, it almost seemed as if we were boycotting the Olympics in an effort to free the hostages. Suddenly, the relative equanimity of *détente* was out and the old devil theories of communism were in. And that, for Reagan, is a piece of cake—he never believed they were anything other than monsters, anyway, as he states in the following exchange with me:

SCHEER The last time I talked to you, you said that no President of the United States should rule out the possibility of a preemptive nuclear strike in a potential confrontation [with the Russians] . . . Now, would that include the possibility of a preemptive nuclear strike by the United States?

REAGAN What I'm saying is that the United States should never put itself in a position, as it has many times, of guaranteeing to an enemy or a potential enemy what it won't do. For example, when President Johnson, in the Vietnam War, kept over and over again insisting, "Oh, no, no, no, we'll never use nuclear weapons in Vietnam." Now, I don't think nuclear weapons should have been used in Vietnam, I don't think they were needed; but when somebody's out there killing your young men, you should never free the enemy of the concern he might have for what you might do. See, you may feel that way in your heart, but don't say it out loud to him . . .

SCHEER Do you believe that we could survive a nuclear war?

REAGAN No, because we have let the Russians get strong and we have let them violate the agreement.

SCHEER But let's say we get stronger than them again. Do you think we could survive a nuclear war? With the right underground shelter systems, with the right defense systems, could we survive one?

REAGAN It would be a survival of some of your people and some of your facilities that you could start again. It would not be anything that I think in our society you would consider acceptable, but then, we have a different regard for human life than those monsters do.

SCHEER How did the Chinese stop being monsters? I mean, they were on a par, at least, with the Russians in treachery and monstrous deeds, supposed to have killed twenty million of their people.

REAGAN Fifty million.

SCHEER Fifty million—I don't think the Russians have killed fifty million of their own people—when did the Chinese stop being monsters?

REAGAN I don't know that they have.

SCHEER And yet we're talking about having an alliance with them.

REAGAN Because we're hoping that through time and through their animus and fear of the Soviet Union, maybe they'll become more like us. People who have gone there say there is indication—that they're trying to improve the situation and that they allow more human rights for their people.

SCHEER Why couldn't the Soviet Union change in the way the Chinese have?

REAGAN Have the Chinese changed? I don't know. The Chinese people are still the victims of tyranny.

In such private interviews, Reagan states his positions matter-of-factly, with no apparent sense that the future of civilization may hang in the balance. He comes on like a friendly but determined coach who says if we want to win in the second half, we've got to go all the way. But he does not tend to rave and rant, as he can in public appearances. This, some advisers will say, is the reassuring thing about Reagan— that he is more reasonable, even in foreign affairs, than his public rhetoric implies. And they also immediately add that his bark was worse than his bite as Governor of California— and that, anyway, he was a "nine-to-five Governor" who left running the state to a bevy of "reasonable aides."

But it was one thing to verbally shoot from the hip as Governor, attacking welfare recipients and students, and quite another to dismiss one's international adversaries (and even one's friends, as in the case of China) as monsters. It may also prove scary. He savors making important decisions by himself, albeit based on his aides' one-page memos summarizing various options, and he prides himself on acting decisively. As Nancy once said, "He doesn't make snap decisions, but he doesn't tend to overthink, either." In California, that led to pronouncements of courses of action that had to be quickly reversed. But can sudden foreign-policy decisions be reversed so easily?

Reporter Boyarsky, who wrote the incisive book *The Rise of Ronald Reagan*, says, "As Governor, Reagan used to *revel* in confrontations with dissident students. It makes me wonder now how he would act as President in any confrontation on the world scene—in the taking of hostages, for example."

After one Reagan tirade on the hustings in North Carolina, I turned to a TV reporter who had covered him extensively in Sacramento and asked, "Is this guy going to blow up the world?"

The reporter's reply was, "Only if he gets the opportunity between nine and five."

Later, I asked Reagan about it:

SCHEER What about the commonly held fear among those who distrust you—are you going to push the button? Are you going to get us blown up? Are you going to get us into a nuclear war?

REAGAN I've known four wars in my lifetime. I've been in only one of them, but, no, I don't want one. But what I've seen about all these wars is that we've gone into them every time through weakness . . . Am I a warmonger for saying, "Look, the answer is to never let an enemy believe you lack the will to defend; there is a point beyond which you will not buy peace at any price—that is slavery and humiliation"?

It's true that Nixon came in with a reputation not unlike Reagan's, as a hysterical Southern California anti-Communist, and he broadened contact with Russia and China. Perhaps Reagan would do likewise, though I just cannot imagine it. Nixon was always an opportunist, testing the winds of conventional wisdom; but Reagan has the marks of a true believer. He acts like a man who is captive of his own phrases, and it was not altogether reassuring to watch him nod solemnly when North Carolina Senator Jesse Helms introduced him one night by saying, "Perhaps God is giving us one last chance."

GEORGE H.W. BUSH'S
ENTITLEMENT COOL

THERE WAS NEVER ANY LOVE LOST BETWEEN GEORGE Herbert Walker Bush and me. How's that for presumption? As if the Skull-and-Crossbones, blue-blooded captain of the Yale baseball team, who went on to become the Director of the CIA, would give much thought to the individual reporters who covered him. Trust me, I didn't welcome the attention, certainly not after he called his good friend and my boss, Otis Chandler, the publisher of the *Los Angeles Times*, to demand that I be fired.

Before I get too far ahead of my story here, let me explain that once again, as with Jimmy Carter four years earlier, I had managed to get myself embroiled with a leading candidate for President. This time, the controversy arose over a Republican who, like Carter, was threatening to leave the pack of his party's presidential hopefuls behind.

By then I was no longer the gonzo journalist interviewing prominent people for the likes of *Playboy*; I was a national reporter for the *Los Angeles Times*, which at that point was still very staid; the very same paper that Richard Nixon always favored over the pinko mass media based on the East Coast. Those East Coast reporters were gutter snipes in Nixon's mind, whereas when he called on a scribe from this West Coast publication at a press conference, he would turn to "the gentleman from the *Los Angeles Times*."

George Bush was very much of that Nixonian school and shared the prejudice that while the *New York Times* and *Washington Post* were infected with a liberal New York virus, the *Los Angeles Times* reflected the purer Western-frontier virtues of that robber baron General Harrison Gray Otis, who had founded the paper now guided by his great-grandson, Otis Chandler. Like George, Otis was a straight-arrow, ruling-class preppie who hobnobbed with all the right people, was competitive in business and sports, and could be found popping one at just the right watering hole. Little did anyone know then that Otis was to become the family's enlightened rebel, fundamentally transforming the *Times*.

George was known as "Poppie" and married "Bar," while Otis was the issue of "Buffy" Chandler, and both families mingled at the occasional African safari, tennis match at the Longwood Cricket Club outside Boston, or cocktail party at the Huntington before Pasadena's Tournament of Roses parade. George was far more thin-skinned and exhibited a bit of the nervous twitching found often in overly inbred species, whereas Otis had a robust Western air to him but was no less primed for the power part. With his massive shoulders, thick blond hair, and chiseled features, Otis resembled a ruling-class god.

At least that's how I sometimes perceived my new boss when I went to work for the *Times*, hired in part due to the publicity from my 1976 Carter interview. The man had a presence even more overpowering than Nelson Rockefeller, another famous scion who shared Otis's physical exuberance. I mention Rockefeller because I had spent quite a few hours with him, and I thought of him often during those tempestuous spring weeks when I was trying to negotiate terrain dominated by the Bush-and-Chandler variant of the Rockefeller stock.

All three men were quite literally bred to lead, exposed to exactly the right thoughts, foods, contacts, and other stimulants of outlook and appearance geared to the carriage of ruling power. They were as painfully aware of their having been schooled for that purpose as was the mass media so studiously ignorant of the importance of elite grooming in what passed for representative democracy.

As opposed to next chapter's "po white" President—and I offer that description affectionately—who overcame unbelievably bad odds, the blue-bloods we are focusing on here were always assured enormous success as long as they played by rules designed to favor their careers. Only when they abandoned those rules did reputations crash—as was the fate of Nelson Rockefeller, when he expired during a romantic dalliance with a woman roughly one-third his age.

It was, if you will, what a future generation would come to regard as a Clintonian moment: An act that proper people knew to keep guarded was displayed for the eyes of those untutored in the legacy-lore that a sexual dalliance is one of the great perks of power, so long as it is discreet. Rockefeller did not have to fall into disgrace; this once colossal figure was rendered a nonperson to the current generation simply because his retainers weren't on hand, and because his young lover was not well trained.

"That dumb girl called the 911 number," Brooke Astor, one of Rocky's buddies, told me in exasperation one evening at socialite Lally Weymouth's Manhattan apartment. "You *never* call the 911 number!" she all but thundered, then added, "The Rockefellers had been chasing women around the table for a century, and they would stumble, but they had servants to clean up the mess."

A long digression, but not quite so, for Lady Astor's point

is highly relevant to my distressed encounters with George Bush. He, the candidate, thought that I, the reporter, was a house servant on the Chandler plantation, which he just happened to be visiting on his journey to the White House. He expected that he would be accorded all the privileges of his station, and that my servile status would ensure the cleanup of any rhetorical mess he made.

We first met in a small airplane carrying Bush to New Hampshire from his stunning victory over Ronald Reagan in the 1980 Iowa primary. An inevitable, if inconvenient, term or two in the White House represented Bush's obligation, if not his favored avocation. He was basking in the glow of victory and I was a scribe handy to document his satisfaction— but that's not what happened.

The problem with George Herbert Walker was that he had been performing splendidly for too long in high-minded activities that weren't all that much fun. After doing all of those important adult things—from fighting a war to save his country to representing it as ambassador in Red Devil China—he was getting more than a bit weary of the endless homework. You have no idea of the number of thick, boring briefing books he had to study; unlike Reagan, Bush had actually felt compelled to read the table of contents and the summaries of those damn things.

At this point in his long successful life, while not yet having reached the peak of his father Prescott, George Herbert Walker was not so much tired—the Bushes and Rockefellers never permit themselves to tire—but damn it, couldn't the country get along without him? How many decades of achievement must you rack up before you can get back to just having fun, like when he was a kid in Kennebunkport and Nelson was tooting around Seal Harbor?

But duty was calling, and Bush's mission in life was obviously not yet complete. Jimmy Carter—a peanut farmer from some redneck Georgian gulch called Plains—had managed to become President and dreadfully screw things up. Chalk that up to the loss of societal standards: George would put quite a bit of the blame on the media, which made celebrities of people with no real training or accomplishment.

So Bush hadn't had much of a choice but to enter the race, and just when things were going dashingly well, he encountered one of those media upstarts. How was he to know not to trust the fellow representing Otis Chandler's paper? The reporter just came at him with those "nasty questions," as he would later tell Otis during a meeting I attended with several other writers and editors from the *Times*. That meeting took place after candidate Bush found himself in the midst of a furor stirred up by my interview (reprinted on page 180), and Otis had invited Bush to the paper to give a fuller account of himself.

I was shocked and suddenly not quite sure why I was there. I knew that Bush had complained vehemently after publication of the interview, in which he had stated his conviction that "you can have a winner" in a nuclear war. It was an absurd and wildly irresponsible statement to make with U.S. and Soviet nuclear weapons poised for Armageddon; the whole point of the arms control regime first introduced by Nixon was to convince the Soviets that we had a common interest in preventing our "mutually assured destruction." Bush had obviously not bothered to read the details of his briefing books on this most important of subjects, and suddenly the best argument against Reagan—that he was too old or untutored or unstable to have his finger on the nuclear trigger—was wiped out. Reagan had been floundering as an outdated Cold War extremist, and now he was looking like the more reasonable of the two leading Republican candidates.

Bush's campaign was in disarray and the candidate was fast losing his entitlement cool. "I want a copy of that tape!" he had ordered me weeks earlier—after his winnable-nuclear-war statement hit the media—at Chicago's Midway Airport, where I was as one of the press covering his ailing campaign. I pointed out that he already had the tape since his press person had been sitting there during the entire interview with his very own tape recorder. His press aide nodded that it was true. Then Bush said something about his being misinterpreted and this conflict not being over.

That's how I happened to be summoned by Otis Chandler to attend the meeting with Bush that morning in the Norman Chandler Pavilion at the *Times*. At first it all seemed to be going well, with Bush talking up his credentials, and then someone asked if he was planning to raise the issue of Reagan's age in the campaign. Bush said he would not, though he expected the issue would still come up, and then he quite weirdly went off on a mini-rant against aggressive reporters that Reagan would have to contend with. Concluding his tirade, he asked, "Could Reagan deal with those nasty questions from Scheer?" There was some awkward shuffling in the room and a different line of questioning ensued. But again Bush snapped in anger and brought up my questions as a sort of unfair obstacle that might cause Reagan to stumble.

Of course, as I have confessed earlier in this book, Reagan handled me quite easily and I fell repeatedly for his Irish blarney. Bush's problem, as would later become evident, had little to do with me and much to do with his being a thin-skinned, over-protected politician who, despite his occupancy of a Texas seat in the U.S. Congress from 1966–70, had never been forced to mix it up very much. Even though he was now running for President, he was neglecting his homework and winging it.

Faced with screwing up the test of an early campaign interview, he blamed the questions. But his ruse failed later, when he had an interview scheduled with television reporter Linda Douglass at the local CBS affiliate. Douglass called me to say that since Bush was still insisting that the interview had not been transcribed properly, she would like to play the relevant portion of the tape on the air and ask him about it during her interview. I successfully convinced my *Times* editor that the only way to defend the interview's integrity in the face of this heavy-handed challenge was to make it available to the public.

I knew we were in good shape because I had listened to the interview very carefully after Bush first challenged it. I had been worried when the controversy initially arose since I had neither personally transcribed the tape nor edited the interview, as I was still on the road interviewing other candidates when it was going to press. Fortunately, the transcribers and editors at the *Times* got it perfectly right—not a word was misplaced—and when Douglass played Bush's statement back to him after he once again denied making it, the future President, in a very dramatic moment, dissembled. However, this didn't keep him from later resorting back to flat-out denial: In his vice-presidential debate with Geraldine Ferraro on October 11, 1984, NBC News correspondent Norma Quarles asked Bush if he still thought nuclear war was "winnable," to which he replied, "I was quoted wrong, obviously, 'cause I never thought that." The *Los Angeles Times* responded by reprinting the relevant portion of my original interview with him on its editorial page.

Not to make too much of this one event, but I do believe it highlighted the essential weakness of the first Bush presidency. Unlike his son, George W. Bush, George Herbert Walker was quite sharp and could master any skill or subject that interested him. But he seemed to be losing patience with matters of state. It was as if he had prepared his whole life for a role that he suddenly found so boring that it failed to engage him. Perhaps he no longer believed that the political game was one worth playing, yet felt obligated to go through the motions as a matter of training.

As for my job at the *Times*, when I walked out of the Norman Chandler Pavilion following Bush's departure, Otis put his arm around me and said, "Look, I have known George all my life and you captured the guy I've known."

❧

"Bush Assails Carter Defense Strategy" was the headline above this interview with George H.W. Bush, published on the front page of the Los Angeles Times *on January 24, 1980.*

I N THE FOLLOWING INTERVIEW WITH THE TIMES, FORMER U.N. *Ambassador George Bush, the victor in Monday's Iowa Republican caucuses, discusses the presidency and his candidacy for the GOP nomination.*

SCHEER What changes could one expect in a Bush budget?
BUSH Generally speaking, President Carter was wrong to
    knock out of the [Gerald R.] Ford budget the main things

he did, which were the MX [missile], the manned bomber, and the naval improvement—many of which he wakes up three years later and feels he now must restore.

SCHEER Don't we reach a point with these strategic weapons where we can wipe each other out so many times and no one wants to use them or is willing to use them, that it really doesn't matter whether we're ten percent or two percent lower or higher?

BUSH Yes, if you believe there is no such thing as a winner in a nuclear exchange, that argument makes a little sense. I don't believe that.

SCHEER How do you win in a nuclear exchange?

BUSH You have a survivability of command in control, survivability of industrial potential, protection of a percentage of your citizens, and you have a capability that inflicts more damage on the opposition than it can inflict upon you. That's the way you can have a winner, and the Soviets' planning is based on the ugly concept of a winner in a nuclear exchange.

SCHEER Do you mean like five percent would survive? Two percent?

BUSH More than that—if everybody fired everything he had, you'd have more than that survive.

SCHEER So have we made a mistake, then, in not thinking of nuclear war as a possible option that we could survive?

BUSH Our strategic forces should be considered a deterrent, and that is the way I'd do it, and I think I would be able to—if we did what we needed to do to be sure the trend that set in doesn't continue, the trend that makes them superior—I think what I'd be able to do would be to push away, plug away, and negotiate a reduction that can be verified.

SCHEER What is the connection between the possession of an MX missile system and being able to do something about problems like Afghanistan or Iran?

BUSH The direct linkage is rather remote, but in the overall linkage, as long as the United States is perceived to not be slipping behind the Soviets in strategic forces, the Soviets will be constrained from adventure.

SCHEER They were weaker in '68 than they are now.

BUSH Much weaker.

SCHEER In '68 they invaded Czechoslovakia. That was adventurism.

BUSH But it doesn't follow that therefore if we're weaker, that will constrain adventure. They're stronger today and they invaded Afghanistan.

SCHEER Yes, but in the late '40s, we were the only one who had nuclear weapons. Our superiority was total and awesome. It didn't stop the Soviets in Berlin, [or] from the Korean War. Aren't your ideas a throwback to the old massive-retaliation position of John Foster Dulles?

BUSH I'm going back to the fact that the United States should not be inferior to the Soviet Union in strategic balance.

SCHEER Going back to the criticism of massive retaliation, perhaps a huge MX missile system costing $55 billion would have no effect whatsoever on one's ability to intervene.

BUSH See, what the MX does is give you an ability to retaliate against hardened sites, and does not make the President have the choice of killing people. That is the key to an MX system, because without a platform of that nature you are not going to be able to retaliate against their hardened sites. And the President's choice would be at that time, if our retaliatory capacity were knocked out, his choice would be, "Sir, our retaliatory capabilities have been knocked out, but good news for you, we still have the Polaris boats, and you can destroy a third of Leningrad and a third of Moscow. Bad news, sir, is they can wipe out, because of their SS 18s, two-thirds of Washington," etc. A President shouldn't be faced with only that kind of choice.

SCHEER You were critical of the return of the canal to Panama.

BUSH Yes, I was critical of it.

SCHEER Do you still remain a critic?

BUSH Yes, I think particularly at this time. I think one of our big problems is that our foreign policy is viewed as retreating and pulling back and unwilling to keep commitments. And my concern with the Panama solution was not the desire to make a change that would take care of the so-called colonial problem—that I can understand—but rather the overall view that as we did this, as we made the deal we did, that it added to the perception that the United States was going to pull back, unwilling to keep commitments.

SCHEER But, in fact, since we've done this, the government of Panama has seemed to be a strong ally of ours, they've accepted the Shah, took him off our hands. Has it really weakened the United States?

BUSH The jury is still out.

SCHEER Right now it would be fair to say that, in fact, they've assisted us in a very major way by taking the Shah, haven't they? It got the Carter government off the hook on that one.

BUSH It was a helpful step, yes.

SCHEER One of the questions that was asked at the Iowa debate was, was there anything politically that you would take back, and I thought the answers were quite weak.

BUSH You're in a political campaign. Who wants to point out his weaknesses? I mean, I thought the question was quite dumb in terms of everybody making a confession to Mary McGrory about one's weaknesses. What kind of idiot is going to answer the question—"Wait a minute, these five things show that I've been wrong." Come on.

SCHEER Could you summarize your differences with Carter in foreign policy?

BUSH Well, I think Jimmy Carter sees the world as he wishes it were, not as it is, and thus when he came in and cut way back on many of the things that the Ford budgets had projected in terms of defense, he sent out a signal around the world that caused concern among some of our allies. I think he's—I can say this with the advantage of hindsight—that we made a mistake when we sent out a signal that we were going to pull out our troops from Korea, and then some of our allies and others begin to worry, "What commitments will the United States keep?" I think when we normalize relations with China on their terms and their terms alone, we further enhance the image of a country that was really not prepared to keep its commitments. I think when we indicated that Cubans were in Africa as a stabilizing influence, people around the world must have looked at us like we were nuts in foreign policy. Eventually, that statement was not permitted to stand, but it stood too long in my view before it was slapped down by the President. I think if we let our human rights policy appear to override everything, including our strategic interests, that the policy is wrong. Our application has often been selective, hypocritically so, in my view: Slap around Argentina and Brazil and move closer to Castro. I remember Mrs. Carter going down and meeting with the dissidents in Brazil. What would we have thought if Brazil's President's wife had come up and met with the person who bombed the laboratory in Madison, Wisconsin? I don't think we'd like that.

SCHEER Do you feel it's comparable?

BUSH I do, I do feel it's comparable.

SCHEER That dissidents in Brazil have the same avenues for peaceful protests as dissidents in the U.S.?

BUSH No, I don't, I don't think they have.

SCHEER How is it a comparable situation?

BUSH One has violated the laws of the country and so have some of the others—I don't believe that you can go out there and take the law into your own hands as guerrillas in Brazil and Argentina . . . Do they overreact? Yes, but I just wouldn't use that style of diplomacy.

SCHEER I don't understand—you don't believe it's ever—

BUSH Print it the way I've said it and you'll understand it— read it.

SCHEER Take Hungary, in 1956, the people resisted the Soviets, the freedom fighters—you would say they should not have been supported? They took the law into their own hands?

BUSH That's not what I said—I told you what I said.

SCHEER You don't think that's an example of people taking the law into their own hands?

BUSH I think that was an effort to overthrow a totalitarian regime that had violated everything in human rights. Certainly the difference between me and some others is that I see areas of gray. I don't think everything is pure and impure, and I think we have been hypocritically selective in our indignation on human rights, and have diminished our strategic interests in the process. That's what I believe.

SCHEER Let me switch to the CIA. You said in a speech that you participated [as CIA director] in President Ford's new regulations concerning the CIA. Not all of them, as you implied, were ones which would have been restrictive on the CIA.

BUSH The executive order I was talking about . . .

SCHEER Some of them, for instance, increase the penalty for someone who leaks secrets or reveals information.

BUSH We should protect sources and methods of intelligence, yes.

SCHEER And in one example you offered, you said that the alternative plans of the Defense Department ought not to be made public. Do you feel that that regulation should have applied to the Pentagon Papers case?

BUSH I believe that if you take an oath to protect classified information, you ought to protect it—yes. I think you've got remedies, you have ways to declassify—and I believe that you ought to not be the final arbiter yourself of what is properly classified.

SCHEER Do you think the *New York Times* was correct in publishing it?

BUSH I haven't thought about it, frankly. If everything the *New York Times* can get its hands on—no, I think there are some constraints, some legitimacy to the concept of national security.

SCHEER Well, do you think that should have applied in the Pentagon Papers case?

BUSH I told you, I don't have a judgment; I don't have—I don't remember all that ancient history.

SCHEER Well, it isn't so ancient.

BUSH I've told you my position and you're not going to get an answer.

SCHEER It's important because—

BUSH Well, it's important to you and it's not that important . . . I've told you my position.

SCHEER It was important to President Nixon, who you worked with, and he argued that the leak in the Pentagon Papers case was so severe that it threatened the foundations of our government, and that was the reason for the whole "Plumbers Unit" and Watergate—right?

BUSH I don't recall what he argued on that—couldn't be less interested.

SCHEER In Watergate?

BUSH Yes, in that whole area.

SCHEER Do you think there are any lessons to be learned—

BUSH Yes, some of them—don't break the law and don't lie.

SCHEER Nixon's argument is that he was protecting national security.

BUSH Interesting.

SCHEER You said you didn't want to explore Watergate again, but there's one statement I want to ask you about. You once said, "I applaud President Nixon's comprehensive statement which clearly demonstrates again that the President himself was not involved with the Watergate matter."

BUSH It came out to the contrary—oh, come on.

SCHEER What I want to ask you is—

BUSH Go back and read the whole goddamn thing that happened after this. What kind of reporting are you doing?

SCHEER You said that there are lessons to be learned. Here's a case—

BUSH Have you ever been lied to?

SCHEER That's what I'm trying to get at.

BUSH Have you ever said something and then found out the

person didn't tell the truth? I've already said that publicly—
if you'd get the rest of your file, you'd see it. I'm not going
to go back and relive this for you. And I think it's quite .
. . appropriate for you to ask that. Ask any darn thing you
want. It's a free country and I can put the answer . . . .

SCHEER No, you say there's something invalid about bringing
this up. Let me ask the question I wanted to ask.

BUSH I've dealt with many, many reporters for a year, and
you're the first guy that's going into every—trying to go
into a whole bunch of things that, obviously, others haven't
felt were particularly relevant to what I'm doing right now—
and what I see you're trying to do is a linkage to a lot of
things over which I had no control, a period where I emerged
with, hopefully, my own integrity intact, the integrity of the
institution I was heading—the Republican Party—intact.

SCHEER OK, but I think it's a legitimate question to ask a
Republican candidate. And I asked Connally and I'll ask
anyone else I interview: What are the lessons of Watergate
and what is to be learned?

BUSH And I gave you a good answer.

SCHEER When you were heading the CIA, were you aware
that the Shah was in as much trouble as he turned out to
be, his base of support was as thin as it was?

BUSH No.

SCHEER Then was the CIA malfunctioning?

BUSH It had been weakened by a lot of things, yes, and sometimes you can't accurately project or predict revolutionary
change in intelligence—the CIA or any other intelligence
service.

SCHEER It's also been said that the CIA was relying too much
for its information on Iran on people close to the Shah, his
ruling circle, Ambassador Zahedi, etc.

BUSH Yes, I've heard that said.

SCHEER But you're disinclined to believe it?

BUSH Disinclined to believe it.

SCHEER We, the American public, were told by our Administration, which presumably had the benefit of these intelligence reports, that the Shah, for better or worse, had the support of the people and was capable of continuing in that country. That's what Jimmy Carter told us when he went to Tehran.

BUSH I don't have access to the reports in the last three years, but in '76 I don't think there was any prediction that the Shah was about to be overthrown.

SCHEER What I'm asking is, how come the CIA didn't have a glimmer of understanding of the shallow basis of support for the Shah?

BUSH I can't answer your question about whether it had a glimmer of it. Sure there was. There were articles in 1973 from analysts showing up about lack of support for the Shah in some way, so—but how come one didn't read accurately revolutionary change in this country? It's because it's very hard to do.

SCHEER Do you feel there's a conflict of interest if David Rockefeller—whose bank has financial dealings with the Shah—was playing the role of a go-between between our government and the Shah in exile? Do you feel there are some serious questions raised by that?

BUSH No, no serious questions.

SCHEER Why not? You don't feel there's any problem?

BUSH He made his decisions to do what he wants to do. A government can take advice, or somebody can try to do something for a client or a friend, and the government makes it own decisions.

SCHEER But here's a situation in which the former Republican Secretary of State, Henry Kissinger, was criticizing the Administration for not coming to the aid of an ally, the Shah. And at the same time he was acting in tandem with David Rockefeller to get the Shah into this country.

BUSH I just stand by what the President said about the decision on the Shah coming into this country. I don't think he's lying to the American people.

SCHEER You have promised a $20 billion tax cut, increasing military expenditures in real dollars, and curtailing inflation. Would that mean cutting back on certain social programs?

BUSH Might be.

SCHEER What programs would you cut back in terms of real dollars?

BUSH I'll give you a list in about February.

SCHEER What about balancing the budget?

BUSH If Jimmy Carter continues on his merry way, the budget's going to be in balance between '82 and '83, doing nothing different . . . The magic is not balance, it's how you get there.

SCHEER So getting to social programs—the HEW budget, the HUD budget, the transportation budget—do you feel that there'll be any need for a cut in those budgets?

BUSH I'd like to find ways to cut them all in real dollars, if I could. Don't get me wrong—I think the budget is way too big, and I think there would be some ways in which you could have some real cuts. But the question is, when I say hold the growth, people think I'm saying cut—and that's not what we're talking about, we're talking about something very different.

SCHEER The question is, do you cut any real programs?

BUSH . . . Revenue sharing, some of CETA . . .

SCHEER Are we talking about a decline in the delivery by the government in the area of non-military services?

BUSH I think we've gone way too far—when you look at the percentage of gross national product spent on social programs and the percentage spent on defense, it has almost reversed itself in terms of which one has gotten more of the spending attention . . . I want to stimulate the private sector and I want to have less emphasis on the public sector.

SCHEER A major theme in your campaign has been the issue of over-regulation. In a speech in Alabama, you said we're over-regulated to death.

BUSH I used the example there of making everybody in the United States have an air bag, whether he wanted to or not, add $400 to the cost of the car because a handful of people in this country think that this is going to be what we need for ourselves.

SCHEER We've had a lot of regulation of auto safety—what about the things other than the air bag? We went through a period of trying to make cars safer, seat belts, moving the gas tanks, all this sort of thing. Do you feel in general we've had excessive regulation in auto safety?

BUSH Yes—the time that you couldn't turn your car on because your seat belt wasn't fastened, that went too far. And there was something we did something about, and the American people sighed a big, collective sigh of relief.

SCHEER But in your speech you didn't say there'd been some excesses; you told this audience we'd been regulated to death. Now in the area of auto safety—

BUSH And did *they* respond, because they knew exactly what I was talking about. Nobody there felt that there was no role for this, but everyone knew what I meant when I talked about the excesses of regulation. I thought that was one of my more brilliant moments, frankly.

SCHEER You didn't say excesses—you said regulated to death. But the problem when a politician says that, he doesn't say exactly in which areas we've been over-regulated, because one person's regulation may be another person's emancipation. For instance, minimum wage, occupational health and safety regulations may be welcomed by workers and thought to be over-regulation by employers. Now, for example, do you think we've been regulated to death in the area of OSHA [Occupational Safety and Health Administration]?

BUSH Yes.

SCHEER What, specifically, would you cut out?

BUSH It's gone too far: The idea that you have to put an outhouse on so many acres of land in Montana, that they tried to put in there for a while—that's too much. The idea that everybody has to have a stepladder that conforms to a design made by someone in Washington—that's too much.

SCHEER In any program, you can find the silly examples. But I'm saying, is there room for serious improvement of occupational health and safety standards? Should we go further in that direction with federal guidelines or should we move back, or should we stand still?

BUSH Right now, in terms of protecting ourselves from ourselves, we've gone about as far as we need to go. Now, if there are exceptions out there that are endangering the lives of workers, of course you should have inspection, of course the laws should be followed. But we've gone too far is my point.

SCHEER Do you think we've gone too far in protecting the environment?

BUSH I don't think you can ever go too far in the actual protection of it, but do you have some regulations that are so strong that you're shutting down the chance for a person to get a job or have any growth and help people that need it the most? Yes.

SCHEER You have said we should help the handicapped, yet one of the regulations that has come down is that you have to have a certain number of parking spaces for the handicapped, you have to have ramps. Now, someone could say that's excessive regulation . . . For the handicapped people, it's been a breakthrough. Now would you cut that out?

BUSH . . . For the overall good—is it better to make every bus kneel at the curb for the handicapped when it might be cheaper and even better for them to have some kind of transit, some kind of delivery system that would not compel the public to pay for the changes in every mode of transportation to accommodate the handicapped? Maybe it would be better to have a more specific mode of transportation to serve the handicapped. You've got to sort it out.

SCHEER What's your position on abortions?

BUSH I oppose abortion.

SCHEER What does it mean to oppose it—that it should be illegal?

BUSH . . . No federal funding except in case of rape, incest, and the life of the mother. I do not want to amend the Constitution to override the decision of the Supreme Court.

SCHEER When you say you're opposed to abortion, you're not for making it illegal?

BUSH Nope.

SCHEER So you're just opposed to making it easier for poorer women to get abortions?

BUSH I've just told you—I do not favor federal funding— there are other ways that can be done, and I don't favor federal funding for it. This is clear, concise, I can't help you by fine-tuning it any. You can ask me more questions but I don't have to answer—this is a free world, I'm protected under not having to exercise my First Amendment rights.

SCHEER So if I, as interviewer, would like to ask you whether this comes out of religious principles, what about the needs of the mother, what about economic implications—all of those questions that you're not interested in answering, I should forget them?

BUSH You know, I'm one who finds these contentious single issues to be a trend in politics that I would rather not enhance by elaborating on; I know you're fascinated by them and many of your readers are, but I've given you my position on it.

SCHEER The issue of homosexuality came up at the Iowa debate. You were asked about pornography and gay rights as an example of growing immorality. You said you were against the harassment of homosexuals but you are opposed to any codification of gay rights.

BUSH I think there's protection under the law to see people aren't abused. I don't think we need a codification, kind of putting a stamp of approval on that lifestyle. That's not what our society should be asked to do . . .

SCHEER But how do you prevent harassment unless people have rights codified in law?

BUSH I don't think American society should be asked to accept that homosexuality is a standard which should be held up for acceptance. I just don't believe that, and I'm not going to push for it.

SCHEER In the Iowa debate, you were asked about illegal

immigration. You said, "I favor return to some kind of documentation." What does that mean?

BUSH Well, you know, they used to have the green card, I don't know if you're familiar with that.

SCHEER Well, they still have the green card—a legal resident has the green card. Do you favor some sort of amnesty for the illegal immigrants that are here?

BUSH I'd take a look at that, but I don't know enough about—how many years, or how much time one would have to demonstrate he or she has been here before . . .

SCHEER What about increasing the quota for people coming from Mexico?

BUSH I don't know what the magic number is, but I certainly would be looking at relations to Mexico, and I'd know how to be sensitive to their problems if we want to get something from them, and we do.

SCHEER Connally has offered his controversial Mideast plan. What is yours?

BUSH We should improve relations with the moderate Arab countries without diminishing our commitment to Israel. My view is it should not be thrown up for negotiation—in other words, we must never have the perception as a country of being willing to trade off an ally, which is a moral and strategic alliance, for a hoped-for economic gain.

SCHEER Do you feel in your reading of the Camp David accords that there was a commitment to a Palestinian state?

BUSH Solution to the Palestinian question, yes.

SCHEER Do you have any criticisms whatsoever of either the Begin or the Sadat governments in this process?

BUSH Yeah, I've been critical of the settlements—you know,

the advance in moving forward, for example, in settlements by Begin's government and Sadat . . .

SCHEER Could you be more explicit?

BUSH No, I couldn't. I've given you that and that's all I'll give
you.

BILL CLINTON'S
RASCAL COMPONENT

BORING AS IT MAY SEEM, WHEN I THINK OF THE FAILINGS of the Clinton presidency, they are not of the man's sexual peccadilloes, but rather the welfare reform and other questionable wonkish triangulation programs that he pushed into law. The man's most potent libido ran to policy rather than to sexual affairs, and his pursuit of the former was profoundly felt by a large number of citizens, while the vastly exaggerated liaisons consisted of superficial hit-or-miss encounters that a man of his generation could easily dismiss as an expected diversion.

After all, while serving as the Governor of Arkansas, Clinton was known as a "player" to hundreds of his closest friends and political associates, and despite that, he was tapped to be his party's presidential candidate. To be fair, there was nothing in his personal life, including the much-ado-about-nothing investment in the Whitewater development, that should have ever disqualified him from holding office. The fact that those scandals dogged him throughout his presidency was less a reflection on Clinton than on the powerful obsession of his right-wing enemies, abetted by journalists—themselves obsessed with salaciousness.

As it became clear to the journalists hunkered down in Little Rock that Clinton would win his party's nomination, the sniff of scandal provided by the candidate's enemies was all they needed to distract from any serious evaluation of who the man was, which could have been revealed most significantly by an examination of how he had governed the state of Arkansas. When I showed up for an interview with Clinton for the *Los Angeles Times* back in the spring of 1992, I discovered that while the newspaper's considerable task force in Little Rock had compiled stockpiles of minutiae on any rumored Clinton scandal, they had zero information on the one program—welfare reform—that Clinton was bragging most about in his campaign.

For all of Clinton's repeated touting of his "Project Success" to "end welfare as we know it," there was no serious evaluation by the media of the actual workings of the program. The media's indifference to it has more to do with the relative affluence of national correspondents covering a campaign than with the real impact of such programs on poor people's lives. Even after Clinton pushed through his "reforms" as U.S. President several years later, there was never any recognition that children constituted seventy percent of the recipients of the main welfare program, and there was scarce concern as to how the changes in the law would impact their lives.

Ironically, Clinton's experiments in Arkansas had been fully permitted by the very federal requirements on state programs that Clinton as President later would eliminate. Before the so-called welfare reforms that President Clinton pushed through Congress, individual states had plenty of room to improve their welfare programs—forty-three different state experiments were underway—so long as they met federal guidelines designed to protect the poor. Without those federal restraints, the states tended to get into a meanness derby of benefit-cutting, often with the goal of pushing the poor across state lines.

When I interviewed Governor Clinton, he understood this issue as well as any politician in the country, and he committed to two specific principles that he would end up violating as President. In our interview (reprinted on page 209), Clinton clearly stated that federal overview of welfare programs was imperative and that more money, rather than less, must be spent on job training, child care, and educational opportunities, in order to move welfare recipients into better situations. His national welfare reform in 1996 betrayed those two points by ending the federal obligation and by failing to commit more resources to the poor.

Accountability is the key to evaluating any "reform" program, and I blame the mass media for neglecting to hold Clinton responsible for either his claims as a Governor campaigning for the presidency, or for his actions once he attained that office. The sad truth is that there was just never much interest in the subject, despite the fact that the lives of millions of people, mostly children, hung in the balance. I was to discover that harsh reality in my last year as a national reporter for the *Los Angeles Times*, when I attempted to follow up my interview with Governor Clinton by checking on his claims to have reformed welfare in his own state.

While conducting the interview, I quickly came to grips with my own inadequacies as a reporter. My goal had been to focus on this one subject that Clinton had made a signature issue and on which I felt informed because I had covered it nationally for the *Times*. But I was woefully ignorant as to the specific circumstances in Arkansas and I stupidly expected to be able to catch up in just a few days, by reading about it in the *Times'* temporary office in Little Rock.

The newspaper's team of investigative reporters had

gathered voluminous files on various aspects of Clinton's personal life, but there were only paltry references to his actual governance, and nothing at all seriously examining his assertions about successful welfare reform. For days, I frantically played catch-up, working the story in Little Rock, but I was to arrive at Clinton's office poorly prepared on the details of his state's program, and it was all too easy for him to snow me with a blizzard of details that I could not challenge.

Afterwards, I talked to my boss, Mike Miller, the *Times'* national editor, conceding the interview's weakness on that point and suggesting ways I could make amends with further reporting. Miller, who had previously worked as the Washington bureau chief of the *Wall Street Journal*, and who had won a Pulitzer Prize for investigating a salad-oil stock scandal, was more focused on the national presidential campaign and seemed disinterested in the specifics of poverty in Arkansas. He said the interview with Clinton was just fine, and that he would run it in the paper without any need for further research. The only concession—a reluctant one—that I obtained from him was permission to stay in Arkansas to do a follow-up story on the state's welfare-reform program. I spent the next weeks working up a report card on Clinton's project.

My challenge was quite straightforward: I had asked Clinton to tell me where in his state I could find the best example of the achievement of his Project Success welfare reform, and he pointed me to Forrest City, Arkansas. It was the biggest town between Memphis and Little Rock, though really not much of one, given its depressed economy at the edge of the Delta region, an American backwater. As for the cultural life of Forrest City, let me put it this way: The Holiday Inn lunch buffet was the most intellectually stimulating event of the day. That's where I got to dine on fried catfish with the Mayor, the Sheriff, and the managers of the local Sanyo plant (the white managers, that is—the Japanese guys tended to stay to themselves).

Clinton was mighty proud of that plant, and he boasted in his campaign that he had traveled to Japan to persuade the CEO of Sanyo not to close it down. It was the town's main industry and Exhibit A for the Project Success goal of moving people off welfare and into the job market. But the reality was quite different.

The Sanyo plant was a gimmick—not a real manufacturing plant at all, since the basic components of the televisions were produced in Mexico and shipped for assembly there by only a handful of workers. The value of the plant was that it permitted Sanyo to slap a *Made in U.S.A.* sticker on the sets before they were sold at Wal-Mart. When I mentioned Project Success to folks at the plant, they said it sounded like a great idea and wondered when it would be implemented. It never really was.

That was the gist of my last piece as a national reporter for the *Times*, and I left my post after the editors refused to run it; they argued that I had already written enough about welfare (the paper had recently run a series by me on the subject). I published the story in the *Economist* and the *Nation*, took a buyout from the newspaper, and worked out a deal with editor Shelby Coffey to continue a far less formal association as a contributing editor writing one column a week for the op-ed page. The humble pay and other aspects of our agreement remained in force for thirteen good years, during which the paper granted me my desire to write from my own voice. My thirty years at the *Times* ended when the newspaper's new conservative publisher killed the column in late 2005.

I wrote very critically of the Clinton Administration in my column throughout the 1990s on issues including welfare reform, the Financial Services Modernization Act, the Telecommunications Act, and other betrayals of working people for the benefit of big corporations. I only eased up when I felt Clinton had become the target of a truly vituperative campaign of character assassination by his right-wing opponents.

What confused me about the attacks on Clinton, bolstered as they were by big-business campaign contributions to Clinton's critics, is that they were taking down a true disciple of what had once been thought of as Republican economics. In one summary piece (reprinted on page 230), I predicted that Clinton would be remembered as a very effective President, but as a somewhat right-of-center figure in the tradition of Dwight Eisenhower. I meant it as a compliment, since I had thought as a kid that Eisenhower was a pretty good President, and besides, being only *slightly* right-of-center these days was a gift that should be appreciated rather than scorned.

Clinton, as indicated in his letter on the following page, appreciated my column, but was taken aback by the Eisenhower comparison. He listed for me all of what he thought were his "progressive" achievements. Even though his letter was handwritten, it never occurred to me that he expected a reply, and I stupidly did not render one. I was to be confronted with that transgression months later when I attended a White House dinner reception hosted by the President and First Lady.

The occasion was in honor of the King of Morocco, and as is typical of such events, we guests were quickly reminded that our status was akin to extras in some grand pomp-and-

THE WHITE HOUSE

WASHINGTON

4/19/00

Dear Robert,

Not surprisingly, I loved your column of Feb. 1 saying I might not be perfect but I've been a good President.

However, I disagree with the Eisenhower parallel — Our domestic agenda has been much more activist; as the attached piece, one of them very critical, demonstrate.

They don't mention Family and Medical Leave, which 15 million people have used; or the progress on guns and the NRA fights, with gun crime down 35% since 93; the doubling of educational investments, rising test scores in the poorest schools; the increase in part to the national push to set standards and the requirement to identify failing schools; opening the doors of college, with direct loans which have saved students $8 billion and the HOPE scholarship tax credit, which 5 million families have already used; tougher standards for clean air, water, drinking water, and food; setting aside more land in the lower 48 states than any administration since the two Roosevelts; and much more. Along the way we beat back the GOP Contract on America, the environmental assault, and all the rest.

Under adverse circumstances, it's a pretty progressive record. Thanks for all you've said over these last 7 years, even in disagreement!

Sincerely, Bill Clinton

circumstances ceremony. One is informed, quite sternly, by a protocol person that the handshake with the President is intended to be perfunctory, and that no conversation is in order lest it delay the receiving line and dinner to follow.

I had every intention of following those rules, especially since my wife, Narda Zacchino, kept repeating them, until I found myself in front of President Clinton. The man himself reared back as my name was announced, and he all but shouted, "You never answered my letter!" I mumbled something in shock about not thinking a reply was expected, and he restated the point. Properly chastised by the President of the United States—though he spoke with good humor—I moved on, pulled by my wife, only to have my hand grabbed by Hillary Clinton, who pronounced me her "favorite columnist." I smiled and thanked her, and she responded, but *No conversation!* was drumming in my head as I shuffled along, bumping into Moroccan royalty, totally flustered, and, according to my startled wife, I then muttered, "Sorry, King."

As a vice president and associate editor of the *Los Angeles Times*, my wife was more familiar with these occasions, and she rebuked me as something of a rube who was overly impressed with the ceremonious affair. She was usually the invited guest at such events, I along as the spouse, but this was not the case that day at the White House. Narda looked at our table numbers and realized we would not be seated together. She then scanned her table list and was pleasantly surprised to see who she would be sitting with. "What table are you at?" she asked.

Finally, my moment of marital triumph was at hand, for as it turned out, I was at the President's table. Yes, dinner with the man himself. Sorry, but despite all the independent tough-guy pretense of the journalist, we are all pushovers for that sort of status recognition, and I gloated—until I sat down and was briefly berated, very good naturedly but determinedly, for not answering the President's letter. The dinner table conversation that evening quickly moved on to other subjects, and he wrote me a gracious note shortly thereafter, printed below.

THE WHITE HOUSE

6/22/00

Dear Robert —

I was glad to see you at the dinner and sorry we didn't get a chance to talk.

Stanley sent me the attached fax — You did a real nice + well deserved piece on him + Betty —

I'm glad you took no offense at my letter — I have worked to advance a progressive agenda under less than favorable conditions —

Sincerely,

Bill Clinton

What I take from that incident—his insistence that I respond to his point-by-point defense of his own record—and my other encounters with Clinton is that he is a man of serious purpose. For all of the machinations on policy, there is his wonkish self, looking diligently for a politically acceptable compromise that actually works.

Sometimes that approach was constructive, as with Clinton's significant achievements: reasserting the value of government, calling the Republicans' bluff when Newt Gingrich's Congress shut down Washington, and demonstrating to the American people that government workers—those too-easily-dismissed "bureaucrats"—do provide important, even vital, services. Ironically, it was also during that government shutdown, with a reduced executive staff, that a White House intern was afforded access to the President that was not permitted under normal circumstances.

Narda Zacchino, President Clinton, and Scheer at the White House, April 15, 1994

The fallout from that much-celebrated Monica Lewinsky trauma, oddly enough, serves to illustrate a larger Clinton policy failure. It was amidst that scandal that Al Qaeda struck against U.S. targets in other lands, and a response from the President was required. On August 21, 1998, Clinton launched cruise missile attacks at what were presumably an Al Qaeda camp in Afghanistan and a chemical-weapons plant in the Sudan. The Republicans treated those attacks as an attempt to divert public attention away from the more important Monica scandal—and Clinton pulled back.

Clearly, the right thing to do would have been to send the Special Forces into Afghanistan for a surgical strike on Osama bin Laden. This would not have involved occupying Afghanistan and certainly not invading the totally unrelated country of Iraq. In a major shortcoming of his presidency, Clinton failed to follow up his cruise missile attacks with an attack against the Al Qaeda base in Afghanistan, and bin Laden was left to strike another day. The enemy survived intact despite Sandy Berger and the National Security Council sounding alarms of impending doom right through the transition into the new Bush Administration, which as we now know, turned a deaf ear to the warnings.

Clinton had long been alerted to the dangerous situation in Afghanistan, not only by his intelligence agencies, but most publicly and stridently by an organization called the Feminist Majority Foundation. Their main issue was the Taliban's horrid treatment of Afghan girls and women. But in the process, they, more than any others in America, were calling attention to a festering center of religious fanaticism that was the host for Al Qaeda. They wanted the President to act on this, and although their ranks included prominent contributors to the Democratic Party and social friends of the Clintons, the Feminist Majority women were not making any headway. The President was distracted by other issues.

I recall that distraction well from an encounter in April 1999 between my wife and Clinton. The setting was the American Society of Newspaper Editors meeting in San Francisco, with Clinton as the featured luncheon speaker. During the question-and-answer period, my wife, an ASNE member, challenged Clinton as to why he wasn't doing more to confront the Taliban. He shrugged off the question with some negligible remarks. But as luck would have it, Narda got to raise the question again because we were staying on the same floor as Clinton in the Fairmont Hotel, where the ASNE convention took place.

We had a small group of friends in our suite and, while made aware by the heavy Secret Service presence that Clinton was down the hall, paid it no mind. That was until one of our group, actor Edward Olmos, suddenly said, "I know Bill Clinton; I'm going to go say hello." He departed, then soon reappeared, announcing that he had just visited with "Billy" down the hall and that the man had asked to speak with me. I dutifully complied, passed through the Secret Service contingent, and was greeted by Clinton and his daughter Chelsea, who was then a student at nearby Stanford.

The President began by thanking me for my columns supporting him; I pointed out that I had also been quite critical on key issues, and he replied, "That's what makes the support all the more important—it isn't knee-jerk." Being the professional ingrate that I am, I took advantage of the good feeling to point out that he had totally ducked Narda's very important question, at which point Chelsea chimed in, "He's right, you did," and proceeded to lecture her father about the menace of the Taliban. Chelsea, like Narda, had been influenced by the Feminist Majority material when its leaders had visited the White House.

Clinton said he had to get going but that he would stop by our room on the way out to answer Narda, and I left thinking that was the end of it. But the man does like a good argument, and sure enough, he showed up at our room and instantly began a very serious discussion with my wife on the matter. In retrospect, she feels that he never did live up to the commitment he expressed that afternoon to making it easier for Afghan females to emigrate to the U.S.—but I thought it pretty impressive that Clinton fully understood the issue and cared enough to peruse it in detail. Sadly, had he gone after the Taliban and eliminated the bin Laden haven, U.S. history would have been profoundly different. The tragedy of the Clinton presidency is that the man could be so wonderfully focused on the most important issues of the day, and yet so easily distracted by the siren calls of political opportunism or some woman's dubious charms.

Clinton was far and away the smartest and best informed of all of the politicians I have interviewed, but there was a fateful rascal component in his makeup that left him at key moments oddly disconnected from the role of President that he was otherwise so superbly prepared to play.

⟨❧⟩

On May 31, 1992, the Los Angeles Times *printed this interview with Democratic presidential candidate Bill Clinton under the headline, "Clinton Sketches Scenarios for Easing Urban Problems."*

THE FOLLOWING EDITED DIALOGUE BETWEEN ARKANSAS
Governor Bill Clinton, candidate for the Democratic presidential nomination, and Times staff writer Robert Scheer was drawn from a two-hour interview with Clinton in his office in Little Rock.

SCHEER In the aftermath of the Los Angeles riots, the mayors of large cities proposed a $35-billion fund for urban areas, which they argue have been neglected. Jerry Brown has endorsed this proposal, but I gather you're not as supportive of this?

CLINTON No, that's not true. I am very supportive of it. What I'm trying to do is figure out how we're going to pay for it. You know, a panel of one hundred economists recommended a similar proposal—slightly bigger, $50 billion— that they say we should just tack onto the deficit. And I'm concerned about doing that. I think there ought to be a way to increase the infrastructure funding to the cities without doing that. I'm contacting folks in the Congress and others working on the budget to see how we could pay for it.

SCHEER The week of the riot, Representative Maxine Waters [one of Clinton's national chairpersons] gave a speech at the First AME Church in Los Angeles demanding to know why is it so difficult to find money for urban areas. She pointed out we didn't have any great difficulty finding it for the military budget. We don't seem to have a great difficulty in bailing out the Russian republics, or the savings and loans. Why is it when it comes to the cities, suddenly it's so difficult to find this money?

CLINTON Oh, I think we can find the money in the budget in

a combination of places. In the S&Ls we just added to the debt. And we did it because there was a contractual obligation to the depositors. With regards to the Russian proposal, it's a much smaller proposal in terms of money. And it's virtually all from loans. Some of it is being given through our food programs, so it's a different issue. I think the money can be found and the money should be there.

SCHEER The point Maxine Waters raised, though, was how come when it comes to the cities, when it comes to solving the problems of the poor, suddenly we get fiscally very responsible? We didn't get so responsible when it came to spending all the military money. Even with the Russian loans—there is some chance the loans won't be paid back. We are talking about tens of billions of dollars that we've committed. . . .

CLINTON On an annual basis, you're looking at a much smaller . . . I mean, what we recommended there is a couple billion bucks, as opposed to $35 billion. But I think we will find the money. But I'm not responsible for what Congress and the President have done for the last eleven years. They have always managed to find the money just by increasing the deficit. The money is there. The money is there in defense reductions, the money is there in controlling health care costs, the money is there in asking upper-income people to pay for entitlements, like Medicare, in return for a comprehensive national health program, the money is there in terms of excessive administrative costs in government, the money is there in terms of asking the very wealthy to pay their fair share again because their incomes went up and their taxes went down in the '80s. I'm not looking for an excuse not to do it.

The difference between me and other people is that I

agree with Maxine's rhetorical point. But I'm not a part of that problem, I'm coming at it from the outside. And I want to realign, dramatically, America's spending priorities. I just want to do it in a way that is responsible.

SCHEER We did once have the so-called War on Poverty, yet critics charge it with being a bureaucratic program that failed to solve the urban problem.

CLINTON Their rap on the War on Poverty is bogus. The best programs were those that emphasized one-on-one contact and had a grassroots basis. The Head Start programs, if you look at them even today, the ones that show permanent benefits are those that do the best grassroots work.

SCHEER Do you think there was a War on Poverty? Do you really think we spent a significant amount of money?

CLINTON Well, there started to be one and then it fell apart in the economic crossfire—President Johnson's domestic agenda and the Vietnam War and paying for both and the inflation that ensued. And then the reaction to both, which produced Richard Nixon's victory and later moved us even further to the right.

SCHEER But the programs tried back then, in the '60s in the aftermath of the Watts riot, sound very much like what you have proposed. Or, for that matter, what [Housing Secretary Jack] Kemp proposes: local community-based, private investment, tax credits. All of these things were tried and they failed in South-Central Los Angeles. And they have been tried by others since. The question is, what is going to happen now, in Los Angeles and elsewhere, that is going to be different? Why will it work? And one suggestion, one possibility, is maybe we weren't serious. We didn't really empower local people, didn't think through the programs, and soon the money stopped.

CLINTON That's exactly what happened. We treat these things . . . Americans are too fad-oriented. We don't want to pay the price of time. And that's a mistake. I believe very strongly that if in the late 1960s, if there had been a combination of intense public investment that was sustained, and education and job training, and a banking system that would have actually loaned money to people and made deposits in that neighborhood to start a small-business economy, there is a very good chance that these riots would not have occurred. There would have been greater domestic ownership, neighborhood ownership of the economy. And there would have been fewer empty storefronts and more thriving businesses. And the ownership would have reflected the rainbow of the community. We didn't stay after it until we figured out how to do it. What went into that community depended on shifting political winds nationally. And economic pressures . . .

SCHEER There was much talk about loans and combatting redlining, but evidently the money was insufficient. They weren't serious.

CLINTON It didn't last long enough, and it wasn't serious.

SCHEER Your welfare-reform proposals don't really seem much different than California Governor Pete Wilson's, which among other things would cut AFDC [Aid to Families With Dependent Children] payments to women and children by twenty-five percent.

CLINTON Well, on the cut . . . the across-the-board cut of the benefits, I know that California's revenues are running twenty-five percent below projections. And I don't know what else his options are. One of the things that I would want to emphasize is that all these Governors and all these legislatures are facing budget cuts because there is a national recession.

SCHEER You're saying that you are sympathetic to the idea that the first place to look is in welfare cuts?

CLINTON No. No, that's exactly what I'm *not* saying. I haven't said anything supportive of the across-the-board cut in welfare. What I am in favor of doing is breaking the chain of dependency through putting more people to work. You're going to have to provide family supports. When a person is on welfare and their youngest child reaches the age of a year, when it can be safe to put in child care, I would provide for education . . .

SCHEER Why did you decide that it would be better to get a woman who had a one-year-old child to leave the home?

CLINTON Because more than half of the non-welfare mothers with kids over a year old are in the work force.

SCHEER Well, isn't it true that the women on welfare, particularly in the ghetto communities, have a harder problem of parenting and that a little more supervision may be needed?

CLINTON I have no problem with parenting. But I think that over the long run of a child's life, a mother becomes a better parent when she has a higher level of self-confidence, develops basic learning skills, and believes that she can provide for the welfare of her children on her own. So I believe if there is quality child care available, it is not inconsistent with the duties of motherhood to ask people to be in an education and training program, and then to take a job when they can get it.

SCHEER Right, but the rub in these reform programs, whether it's yours or Wilson's, is what happens after two years of training if the woman doesn't get a job and you cut her and her children off?

CLINTON No, he wants to cut them off. What I want to do is

to give people community-service jobs in return for income.

SCHEER So you would guarantee employment?

CLINTON Yeah. Community service . . . I don't propose to cut people off of benefits.

SCHEER One important difference then between your position and Wilson's is, if I understand you correctly, that to do welfare reform properly, at least in the short run, requires spending more rather than less money. He sees it as a budget-saving—

CLINTON Yes. But you have to understand that I believe the federal government has a responsibility in that regard too. I think that the present welfare-reform act would work much better if the government funded it at an appropriate level and every state embraced it.

SCHEER But just in the last year, forty states have either cut or frozen payments to women on welfare with children. And they're doing it as a cost-cutting thing.

CLINTON Totally unrelated to welfare reform. But let me tell you how it works, and let me tell you why they did it. And I'm neither condemning nor applauding it. But we just went through a budget-cutting exercise here [in Arkansas] and bent over backward to avoid cutting AFDC.

SCHEER What is the AFDC payment in Arkansas? Isn't it $203 a month for a woman with two children?

CLINTON That's about right.

SCHEER How does one live—

CLINTON Let me finish the thing. Here's what happens. Here's the problem. A lot of this is visited on us by Congress. Congress pays for part of the welfare budget, we pay for part. It's a matching-fund deal. Real welfare benefits in America have been declining since the mid-'70s.

Half the people on welfare get on and get off in a few months. Of the ones that are left, about half of them get off in a few more months. About twenty-five percent are more or less permanently dependent. And most all of them are younger women with little children who literally do not have the capacity to earn a good living. So, most welfare reform really worthy of the name should be directed at those people, to try to empower them to support their children and to support themselves, and then to require them to move from welfare to work. To do it, you need more money than is now in the act for education, training, transportation, and child care.

I think the next step is to develop over the next few years a combination of public and private child support, a uniform child support standard in the country. And then require people who can't get private-sector jobs, after a while, to move into public-sector employment.

SCHEER What you are talking about is a very bold program saying the government is going to be the employer of last resort, you're also going to have national child-care standards maintained and financed . . . is that right?

CLINTON The child-care standards are all right now, but the program is not properly funded. And in terms of employer of last resort, I don't see what the difference is when now we're the *un*employer of last resort. Now we are paying people to be idle. I think that after a certain amount of idleness in return for the check, they ought to do community-service work.

SCHEER The proposed California welfare reform would deny extra money to support a child born to a mother on welfare. Do you approve of that particular provision?

CLINTON I have mixed feelings about it. I would permit the

states that passed the law to do it, to try it and see if it makes a difference.

SCHEER You hold up Western European countries as models of a better-functioning economy. Yet when we look at Germany and the other countries, there is a much stronger social welfare support with a much heavier tax burden than here.

CLINTON They have basic education standards nationally, basic health care systems, basic lifetime retraining for the labor market systems, and a much higher level of cooperation between the public and the private sectors. You have to fashion American solutions to American problems. But I think that when you ignore what other nations with higher productivity rates, higher growth rates, are saying or doing, I think that you do so at your peril.

SCHEER They provide more of these very same benefits that people here say is such a drag on our economy.

CLINTON They are higher. But they are in the context of a society that basically works, that has a preference for work and a tradition that is organized toward building a high-wage, high-growth country. Unemployment would drop in America and welfare would drop if we adopted an investment-oriented, partnership-oriented, high-wage, high-growth strategy. But we have to change a lot of what we are doing. I think America is very much out of step with the rest of the world in not investing more in its people.

SCHEER Some now blame the Europeans and Japanese for our problems and call for protectionism. Are you sympathetic to such calls?

CLINTON They have some protectionism. The Germans certainly. The fact is the Europeans now are closing their markets to the sixteen-percent limit on cars. And I think we are going to have to look at modulating competition. But to be fair, the biggest problems we have in maintaining the manufacturing base are our failures to work together to achieve high levels of productivity, to control health care costs, to have a tax system which is pro-manufacturing. Our tax system now is anti-manufacturing. And it was all during the Reagan/Bush years. I think, you know, it rewarded money making money and not production, not jobs, not goods, and not services.

SCHEER Well, that's what we say now. But when the last tax-reform package was passed, many Democrats supported it. It was supposed to help production.

CLINTON I never thought it would. I never thought the '86 tax act would. And the '81 tax act just fosters too much speculation. You know, the elemental principle of taxation should be [that] people should pay according to their ability to pay. And you should have incentives that do specific things. Those ought to be the two driving, in my view, principles of the tax system.

SCHEER We have these reports now that the wealthiest top one percent got sixty percent of the tax benefit of the cuts. Is it possible that this middle class has disappeared before our eyes? If the top one percent of the people in this country, according to a recent Federal Reserve report, have assets equal to the bottom ninety percent . . .

CLINTON For the first time since the '20s.

SCHEER Yeah. So what has happened?

CLINTON Well, what happened is poverty increased in the '80s. The number of people in upper-income groups increased and the middle class declined. And taxes were raised on the middle class because Social Security taxes went up seven times, more than offsetting any income tax reductions, especially when consumers lost their interest deductions. And tax rates went down for people at the upper-income levels while their incomes went up. So you had increasing unfairness, and we lost growth.

Bush's theory—and it was the Reagan theory, but Bush interestingly enough has tried to carry beyond where Reagan did—was if you kept taxes low on upper-income people and corporations, and loaded the burden off onto the middle class, and in America's case, onto the deficit, then good investment decisions would be made and jobs would bloom and the economy would grow. The problem was that the system favored money making money rather than money making products, goods, services, jobs.

That is one of the big issues in this race. That is an absolutely flawed way to run an economy. All you're going to do is make more income inequality. And you won't have real economic growth. And that is why our productivity rates have been declining and our wage rates have dropped from first to tenth in the world.

SCHEER So what would be wrong with taxing these wealthy people . . .

CLINTON We should. The *Wall Street Journal* bags me once a week for advocating taxing. You know, I think you have to raise tax rates, I like the tax bill that [Senator Lloyd] Bentsen [D-Texas] and [Representative Dan] Rostenkowski [D-Illinois] hammered out in the Congress last time. Which had . . . raised marginal rates on incomes roughly above $200,000 to thirty-five percent or so, and then had a surtax on millionaires of another ten percent. Bush vetoed it because it violated his theology of economics, which is under no circumstances should the very wealthy be asked to pay more.

SCHEER But isn't there something absurd, that we have all this rhetoric about the poor ripping off the system and so forth? When in fact the money going to the poor has steadily declined. At the same time, the top one percent have been getting enormously wealthy.

CLINTON I think so. That's why I talk about them both. I think what you want for the poor, though, is to restore the ability of them to move into the middle class. In order to do that, you have to have a growing economy. I think the most irresponsible people of all in America in the 1980s were the politicians and the executives who conspired to give us a tax system and an economic system that threw wealth way up to the top of the ladder and didn't increase growth, jobs, and incomes for middle-class and poor people.

SCHEER You have said that Democrats should concede that Bush had acted wisely in the Persian Gulf. Now we have had in the *Los Angeles Times* detailed investigative stories showing that Bush was much more involved with Saddam Hussein than anyone had thought. We have congressional testimony and so forth. Would you be interested in reevaluating that statement?

CLINTON Let's get what I really said. I said that I thought he was right to throw Saddam Hussein out of Kuwait. I did not agree with what he did beforehand nor what he did after. And I mean immediately after. I think they obviously played politics with the war. They left the Kurds and the Shiites to twist, and everything that happened after, I think was wrong. They mishandled it, by and large.

And of course we now know, thanks to the *Times*, a lot more about what happened before than we did. And I'm just appalled by it. If you look at what he did, it's easy to understand why Saddam Hussein thought he could march into Kuwait or any place else he wanted. I mean, we treated him like our last best friend, right up until we bombed him.

And it just makes you wonder what they were thinking about or whether they knew this would happen. I mean, it is a bewildering thing. And, yeah, I'm interested in reassessing what I said about what happened leading up to that. It's even worse than I ever dreamed it was. Even though I still agree that we would be worse off if Saddam Hussein had not been kicked out of Kuwait. But you realize it is almost like a monster we created.

SCHEER So as President you're going to . . .

CLINTON . . . make sure we get the facts to make the decision. You can make sure that I'm not going to be out their dancing with guys like that, then setting them up so we can go to war. I won't do that.

SCHEER The biggest problem that you're up against, and I don't think this is personal to you, is that people just don't believe politicians. You know that. You say all these things and it sounds like just words. The appeal of Jerry Brown at one point and now Ross Perot is clearly that people say, well, at least these people sound a little different.

CLINTON Yeah, but there is a big difference between me and them. I paid eleven years of my life to get up every day and come to this [Governor's] office and work on these things. And one of the things that really hacks me off is when people only evaluate politicians based on words. You know, anybody can say anything.

Now we got somebody who says, "Vote for me, I was never in office. I don't know anything about this. I'll come back in a few months and tell you what I think." And you know, there is a big difference, and by the way, I like a lot of what Ross Perot says. And he says a lot of what I say. But I'll tell you something, and the American people had better recognize this: Change is hard.

It is hard. It does not come overnight. And it does not come through words alone. I ought to have credibility because I have worked at this, I mean *worked*. Now, it doesn't count for much in this day and age because modern politics is all about images and words and positioning. But work still matters. It will matter who gets elected President and whether the President knows the first thing about any of these problems and has paid the price of time.

SCHEER Jerry Brown could make the claim that he ran a much tougher state, a much bigger state, for eight years.

CLINTON You look at the difference . . . Yeah, he sure did, he was Governor in the '70s, he had gobs of money, and he was widely criticized for not paying attention to the details of his job. The California economy was exploding and growing.

There was no place tougher to govern in America than a poor, rural Southern state in the 1980s, when rural income dropped dramatically. Let me say, I've always kind of liked Jerry Brown. He always felt he was great at figuring where the next wave was in political change. And when he came out early in the campaign, I told people he might be the last one here, because the great thing about the 800-number that is even more important than the $100 contribution, is that it empowers people to access the system which seems bureaucratic, remote, unresponsive, and broken.

SCHEER Yes, but he would claim an ideological difference that you represent an effort to take the Democratic Party back toward the Republicans, and he was going to speak to the constituencies that you were ignoring: the poor, the women, and so forth. And the people that you have defined as—

CLINTON What is the evidence of that? I have said more about the poor. You know, he was in the campaign for eight months before he had as much to say about the poor and the family income as I did. When I announced my candidacy, early on, I said the first thing we ought to do is have a refundable, earned-income tax credit, enough to lift the working poor out of poverty. I came out for a housing program that would help. I came out for health care programs that would help. I came out for preschool programs and child care and family leave. That is a bum rap.

SCHEER So you don't think there is a philosophical difference between you and Jerry Brown?

CLINTON There is a philosophical difference . . .

SCHEER I mean, in terms of where the party should be headed, in terms of its—

CLINTON He always tried to run to the right of everybody in the 1970s. The California teachers put out this statement that I had a better record on education than he did, because all he did was try to cut education. I don't know what his philosophy is. I just know he's really . . . he's bright, and he's always on the cutting edge of change. But I don't know, I can't tell you what his philosophy is. In 1990, when we were capping campaign expenditures in Arkansas, he was taking the caps off in court in California.

I also agree that Brown did some good things. But I mean, the way he's tried to sort of compare Arkansas to South Africa and call it a bush-league state, I think that was way out of line.

SCHEER He terms this race a battle for the soul of the Democratic Party, because you have defined as special interests the very groups that are most vulnerable in the economy and that he wants to support. And he lists them as workers in cities where the plants have closed—

CLINTON No, the difference between me and him is, I think if you go in and just tell people what they want to hear, then you're sounding like just another Democratic politician and you're going down the same road that we've been down. I don't acknowledge that you've got to give people the same old rhetoric to win an election.

⤏

As illustrated in the sampling below of three of my weekly Los Angeles Times columns during Bill Clinton's presidency, my opinion of his performance was not static. My own disillusionment reached its peak when he signed legislation in 1996 ending welfare as a federal entitlement, while my sympathy and support for his efforts rebounded most strongly when the Republicans tried to throw him out of office. To read more of my columns from the Clinton era, visit www.Truthdig.com.

Forget Dole; Here's the Ideal GOP Candidate
August 6, 1996

Finally, the Republicans have been presented with the perfect presidential candidate. He's more conservative than George Bush, a better salesman than Ronald Reagan, and a worthy successor to Richard Nixon in enlarging and misusing the powers of the FBI while destroying the right of habeas corpus. In the name of fighting crime and international terrorism, this guy can shred the Constitution like it was Parmesan cheese.

He was an early advocate of tough love and has recently proved that he can beat up on welfare mothers and immigrants with the best of them. True, he's pro-choice, but so are most Republicans, and anyway, their leaders want that issue to just go away.

Bob Dole should drop out and let the Republicans nominate Bill Clinton. The President will co-opt any Republican position that plays well with the electorate, no matter how shortsighted and mean-spirited. Dole doesn't have a chance, so why go through the hassle of an election?

It's hopeless. Clinton has the right stuff to win—a marriage of Nixon's ethics with Reagan's skills as a communicator. Clinton could launch a nuclear war and make it seem like a peacekeeping mission, while Dole can't order a hamburger at McDonald's without coming off like Darth Vader.

Any doubts about the depths of Clinton's chicanery were resolved with his decision to sign Newt Gingrich's welfare "reform" bill. Ending the bare-bones federal obligation to poor children is something that no Republican President dared.

And Clinton is right in claiming that he appreciated the electoral potential of welfare-bashing even before Gingrich did. Clinton knew all about welfare reform through the "Project Success" program he initiated as Arkansas' Governor. The project was not in any measurable way successful in limiting the abysmal poverty in his state. Indeed, the welfare rolls increased by twenty-seven percent during his tenure. But Clinton hyped the program in the 1992 campaign, and the media, preoccupied with Troopergate, never called him on it. This experience reinforced Clinton's confidence in promising to "end welfare as we know it" without having the foggiest notion of what would come in its place.

The Democrats are better positioned to hurt the poor and favor the rich because they have so much credibility with liberals who care. Just as it took a hawk like Nixon to embrace Mao Tse-tung and legitimize Communist rule in China as a victory for the Free World, it required a "New

Democrat" like Clinton to force millions of additional children into poverty as an act of charity. If Bush had signed a bill that targeted poor women and their children, he wouldn't be able to show his face in polite company, even in the suburbs of Houston. But Clinton and other Democratic backers of the Gingrich bill, like California Representative Jane Harman (D-Rolling Hills), are still being lionized by the liberals and feminists who run Emily's List, although not by the National Organization for Women, which led a demonstration against the welfare bill at the White House gates.

The Republicans need Clinton because he is best positioned to bring women over to the posture of heartlessness. Biologically squeamish about hurting children, women have tended to reject the Gingrich revolution. But now we have Clinton to explain the necessity for ending the dependence of poor children on food and shelter. Continuing with this reasoning, Clinton might even come to favor abortions after the third trimester.

You're being too harsh, I'm told by more pragmatic liberal friends. Just reelect this man and he will prove his commitment to the poor in a second term. To that, I will offer only Clinton's own comments on the welfare bill before he announced he would sign it: "You can put wings on a pig but you don't make it an eagle."

In a second term, Clinton will worry about the future of his successor, Al Gore, who argued vociferously for the President to sign this atrocious bill. If Clinton shows no courage now, when he's riding so high in the polls, he never will. And what does it say about the future of the Democratic Party that of seven Democratic Senators up for reelection, all—with the sole courageous exception of Paul Wellstone of Minnesota—voted against the poor and legal immigrants?

Clinton's failure to lead on this basic test of decency will long haunt him and his party. I never thought I would be sickened by the sight of a Clinton/Gore bumper sticker, but there it was on the back of a gleaming new Mercedes convertible in Republican Orange County. All I could do was mutter, "Take him, he's yours."

❧

Privacy Issue Bubbles Beneath the Photo Op
November 16, 1999

YOU CAN'T BE A SUCCESSFUL LAWYER AND NOT WORK FOR banks, Hillary Clinton once said in defense of her shenanigans as a Little Rock lawyer on behalf of the Madison Savings and Loan. Or a Senator from New York, or a President of the United States, her husband might have added.

Last Friday, the White House photo op offered a broadly smiling President Clinton surrounded by Fed Chairman Alan Greenspan and other financial movers and shakers, as Clinton signed the Financial Services Modernization Act into law. With that flourish of his pen, Clinton gave the fat cats of Wall Street everything they've long wanted, sweeping away consumer safeguards enacted at the time of the Great Depression, suddenly making it legal for banks, insurance companies, and stockbrokers to affiliate as one company.

Clinton also granted these new conglomerates the power to collectively exploit the information their varied affiliates have collected on their customers—health records, stock transactions, and credit histories, for example—shredding the basic American right to privacy.

"The White House really pulled the rug out from under consumers by agreeing to weak privacy provisions in the banking bill," said Representative Edward J. Markey (D-Massachusetts). He, along with conservative Senator Richard Shelby (R-Alabama), unsuccessfully tried to amend the financial bill by requiring consumer approval before private information was bandied about.

Clinton uttered some vague promises about backing stronger privacy protection in the future, but the broad smile on his face as he signed this giveaway to Wall Street made his priorities all too clear. The financial interests that dumped more than $300 million into the passage of this bill—the most expensive lobbying effort in history—are essential to Hillary Clinton's U.S. Senate campaign. No one gets elected from New York who doesn't play ball with Wall Street interests. That is why New York Democratic Senator Charles E. Schumer, a big Hillary backer, so strenuously lobbied Clinton to sign this law.

Also, the President has got to repay the loyalty of Robert Rubin, his former Treasury Secretary, who stood by Clinton during his time of personal troubles. Rubin has become co-chairman of Citigroup, a conglomeration between Citibank and Travelers Insurance that immediately benefits from this new legislation, which was strongly backed by Rubin and his Treasury Department and for which he lobbied in the months following his resignation.

Without this law, Citigroup would have had to divest some of its lucrative insurance business. Surely there needs to be an investigation as to whether Rubin violated federal conflict-of-interest rules by urging White House support for this bill while in negotiation for his new job. But one will not hear a call for such investigation from Republican or Democratic leaders in Congress, who have been major recipients of Wall Street funding in return for supporting this bill. Nor from the leading presidential candidates of either party, who feed at the same trough.

In signing this law, Clinton offered a pretense of concern for consumer privacy and promised his Treasury Department would come up with a new package of consumer protection to right this wrong. What rubbish! By signing the bill, this lame duck President gave away whatever leverage he had over the banking interests and their power block in Congress.

As Markey put it: "This was the perfect opportunity to protect the little guy, the average consumer, because the big boys in the financial services industry wanted the banking bill so badly. Now we have to start all over again, and it's not going to be easy. But we can't stop fighting until every American has the privacy protections they deserve."

The fight for privacy now hangs on passage of HR3320, the "Consumers' Right to Financial Privacy Act," sponsored in the House by Markey and Joe Barton, a conservative Texas Republican. Shelby and Richard Bryan (D-Nevada) introduced an identical bill, S1903, in the Senate. This legislation asserts this very clear principle: "Financial institutions would have to notify consumers before sharing their personal information, provide the consumer access to that information to confirm its validity, and most importantly, would have to gain express consent from the consumer before any personal information could be shared." Failure to comply would carry civil and criminal penalties.

This same privacy legislation also can be passed by the states and, thanks to a loophole in the Financial Services Modernization Act, would supersede the federal law. If that happens, the victory that the banks are now gloating over may prove to be somewhat pyrrhic. A candidate's support for this privacy legislation should be a voters litmus test to determine whether those who presume to represent them value consumer privacy over bank profits.

❧

Admit It; He's Not Perfect, but He's a Great President
February 1, 2000

O nce again, Bill Clinton delivered a stunning State of the Union speech, and there was much credit for him to claim. He has presided over an unprecedented period of American renewal. Inheriting a nation obsessed with an inferiority complex as to its role in a new world order, he is preparing to leave a country more confident about its economic future than it has ever been. There is no longer any talk about having to learn Japanese, ban immigration, or sacrifice our labor standards in order to survive in the emerging world economy. And there are serious prospects for an enduring peace in the tinderbox of the Mideast.

His message was bold and justified in its optimism and yet, while the public once again beams with approval, his media and political-establishment critics seem bizarrely embittered by his and the nation's obvious success which, as he laid out with impressive statistics, is impossible to deny.

The last two Republican Presidents left this nation with a debt greater than that of all Presidents in U.S. history combined. The servicing of that debt was a horrible burden preventing the federal government from supporting the research, education, social services, and infrastructure investments that a modern nation requires. In his first years,

Clinton sacrificed his party's control of Congress in order to push through a controversial tax reform needed to cut back the debt. The loud-mouthed Republican House leader who said that this couldn't be done now has left government in disgrace, and yet Clinton, who took such abuse for his economic program, still is denied the fair measure of his success.

C'mon. Clinton has been a great President. Why is it so hard for the pundits to give this man his due? His is the envy of the baby boomers toward one of their own who is simply superior at playing the power games they were raised to master. They, whose personal lives tend to be as messy as any, seem frustrated that the President's is intact, despite the slings of scandal. His wife and daughter, poised for future success, show obvious love and respect for this man. And the somber predictions of a pathetic lame duck President forced to resign or living his last days in the White House in shame now seem absurdly wrong. Last week, the President bounced from his star performance before Congress to an adoring crowd in Quincy, Illinois, and on to address a meeting of respectful international leaders in Switzerland, carrying a message of renewal and hope for the world that was eminently believable.

Except to his Republican detractors, who, like many in the media, seem inherently incapable of being fair to him. Oddly, the anger of the most reasonable in the GOP seems fueled by the fact that Clinton has co-opted the saner elements of their program. While soundly thrashing the forces of the ultra-right, which still has a death-grip on the GOP by insisting on a dangerous mixture of false moralizing and divisive politics, Clinton has emerged as the savior of the rational political center. Clinton, a moderate in what was once a bipartisan tradition, far more closely approximates the poli-

cies and stance of a Dwight D. Eisenhower than do the still
vituperative GOP congressional leadership and most of that
party's candidates for President.

Clinton is certainly a disappointment to those who
thought he might prove an inspired liberal. His domestic
agenda has been less progressively ambitious than that of
Richard Nixon who, it should be remembered, favored a fed-
erally guaranteed minimum income. Clinton, unfortunately,
leaves the legacy of his so-called welfare reform, which made
the poor, and not poverty, the enemy. We judge success in
what remains of the war on poverty by the number of people
pushed off welfare without our having the slightest concern
about their fate. That is truly shameful, given that seventy
percent of them were children. What happened to them is
anyone's guess.

So, too, has Clinton been a failure in his professed commitment to overhaul the nation's health system. More people
are without health insurance than ever before, a national disgrace. But here, as with programs to aid the poor, does anyone really think the Republicans would do better? After all,
it was the congressional GOP who gutted Hillary Clinton's
health care proposals and who continue to fight desperately
against even the most limited proposals to increase the minimum wage.

Clinton is no liberal crusader, but he is an extremely
effective, if opportunistic, man of the center who pulled the
country back from the fringes of political madness, erased the
deficit, and reasserted the U.S. role as a world peacemaker.
That is enough to justify calling him a great, if imperfect,
President.

GEORGE W. BUSH'S
PERPETUAL ADOLESCENCE

L ET ME CONFESS TO LESS CONFIDENCE IN APPRAISING
the presidency of George W. Bush than the others
discussed in this book. This is not primarily because
he is the only one that I did not spend one-on-one time with,
although that would have been helpful. But the basic problem for anyone attempting to understand Bush's motivations
is that they may not be driven by a recognizable engine.

His charm, which I take to be his most formidable asset,
lies largely in his assertion of the prerogatives of perpetual
adolescence, in his insistence that we judge him as a well-
intentioned screw-up rather than a responsible adult. While
this was not a difficult mode for Bush—a coddled offspring of
the super rich—as he made his way, heavily escorted,
through the failures of his pre-political career, what is
astounding is that the "What, me worry?" stance has continued to serve him so well as President of the United States.

As opposed to those who preceded him to the highest
office in the land, Bush affected a deliberate air of diffidence
from an early age, suggesting that he took on assignments only
reluctantly, whether as student, businessman, or politician,
interpreting each challenge in turn as more of a bother than
an obligation. Winging it, but always propped up by a considerable retinue of those more disciplined than he, has proved
an enormously effective ploy. There is an often-winning "aw,

shucks" mannerism to the man, pursued so determinedly as to hint at a genetic mutation from the model exhibited by his father (and many others driven to succeed).

In contrast with the previous Presidents chronicled in this volume, Bush the younger became an overachiever only *after* attaining the presidency. The others, and certainly the first President Bush, who more than anyone resolutely built a qualifying resume for the office, presumed that a high level of achievement was required for the world's most important job. These predecessors sweated the details required for the part, beginning with the ability to effectively deliver impromptu remarks in public. On the way up, they learned much from the elders who could take them further.

This was demonstrated most vividly by Ronald Reagan's fawning respect for the rough-hewn Warner Brothers movie moguls who launched and managed his acting career, and by his almost obsequious dependence on the "kitchen cabinet" of California millionaires who engineered his rise through the world of campaign politics. Although he was unfairly derided by critics as merely an actor, Reagan's extensive political experience both in Hollywood and in the real world forged a hard drive filled with the minutiae of past struggles and indelibly informed his outlook once in the presidency. Reagan had walked the talk. Like the others (excluding George W.), Reagan was always anxious to advance on the learning curve.

For decades, Richard Nixon served as the ever-eager apprentice to those in a position to advance his career, from Senator Joseph McCarthy to President Dwight Eisenhower, and he meticulously catalogued in his mind the details of every job he worked.

Jimmy Carter portrayed himself as an ordinary peanut

farmer, yet he was a well-educated and urbane figure, whose true mentor was the politically skillful Admiral Hyman Rickover; Carter boasted often of the career dues he paid, most notably his experiences as a Navy "nuclear engineer."

Rhodes Scholar Bill Clinton was the perpetual student who made "wonk" his middle name, and George Herbert Walker Bush gave many speeches that drew heavily from his lengthy on-the-job experience. Although Bush I's perspective on his own career may be marked by an arrogant sense of entitlement, he nonetheless had built his resume on impressive performance—an excellent college student, athlete, and soldier who survived dangerous combat experience—as opposed to grade-C yell-leading at Yale and part-time National Guard duty spent assiduously avoiding service in an ongoing war.

Yes, the others all practiced to play the part of President and were willing to mold substance to convenience to win the ultimate electoral prize, but once that desperately sought role was attained, they could rely upon their real experiences of a lifetime of hard work to guide their conduct in office. They most decidedly did not arrive at the White House, as did George W., woefully uninformed and unprepared.

Our current White House occupant seemed determined to present his pre-presidency life as a blank slate, conveniently insisting that his years before the age of forty were off-limits since he had been "reborn." But even after that moment of divine intervention, his activities—for the most part miserably unsuccessful business ventures—were portrayed as a string of sharp moves in some college MBA game, while his governorship of Texas was offered to and bought by the media as a series of vintage photo ops, with few critical references to actual achievements.

A testing of accomplishment that one would have considered a prerequisite for any mid-level management position became a consideration with Bush only after he had been elected President. Further, his felt moment of empowerment did not even accompany his inauguration to the world's highest political office. Indeed, the first nine months of his rule were marked by a sense of befuddled wonderment that he was indeed playing this role, and, not able to convince himself of his suitability, early polling data suggests he was eminently ineffective as the nation's leader.

But then 9/11 happened, and after a day of continued bewilderment, another George W. Bush surfaced. His fans and detractors alike must admit that Bush turned the tragedy of 9/11 into a grand opportunity for his presidency, and in the process recast his image from that of the untested scion of a former President to a bold, if not always wise, leader. The tragic irony in this transformation is that the attacks on the United States in September 2001 likely could have been prevented if Bush had not failed so miserably in recognizing the obvious terrorist danger documented extensively in those daily intelligence briefings during his first nine months in office.

Without any intelligence agencies reporting to me, I, like others, was able to recognize and call attention to the threat of Osama bin Laden—ignored in the Bush Administration's preoccupation with Star Wars and its Faustian antidrug coddling of the Taliban—well before September 11, in my columns of February 14, 2001 (see page 244) and May 23, 2001 (see page 246).

Until bin Laden's minions struck, the Bush presidency had all the earmarks of a failure. Bush was indecisive, lacking in vision, and a craven captive to the special interests that had very early taken full control of his presidential agenda. He was floundering as one born to the manor yet surprisingly unprepared when the family estate fell under his control.

But then the clouds parted, planes became bombs, and there can be no question that Bush quickly seized the moment of national tragedy as a conduit for a quick transformation.

In the writings that follow, I leave no doubt of my own view that Bush perverted the 9/11 attacks in ways that left the country less secure, most prominently by shifting focus from bin Laden to the totally unrelated target of Saddam Hussein. Yet as a quick-fix political tactic to save what seemed an already doomed presidency, Bush's maneuvering worked wonders.

Suddenly his presidency was reborn, not through the services of an intervention divine in its authority, but in the powerful ability to manipulate the secular political world. The new religion Bush embraced was in fact the same old reliable one of those seeking greater power in any political system: thundering against the evil of an enemy threatening our security, in the process providing the leader with an unquestionable mandate to do whatever he wants.

The war against evil provides the saving rationale for the Bush presidency, overriding any troubling matters of fact and logic. With the all-powerful enemy of the Kingdom at the gates, is the populace ever to deny the whims or judge clearly the failings of the willful ruler they suddenly discover they so desperately want?

Only later, perhaps decades afterward, will there be a time of reckoning.

᷍

Here's a representative selection of my reactions to George W. Bush's presidency in my nationally syndicated column, starting just before his so-called "victory" in November 2000 and winding hazardously up through the present day.

Dubya Offers Government Lite
October 25, 2000

WHAT A DEAL! ELECT GEORGE W. BUSH PRESIDENT AND you get government lite—eat all you want without gaining a pound. Bush promises to cut taxes for all, dramatically increase military spending, finance a trillion-dollar private Social Security system, and eliminate the national debt. And Bush claims he will put you, not some Washington bureaucrat, in charge of your life (unless, of course, it concerns your right to choose).

Just to state the main themes of Bush's campaign is to demonstrate their inherent absurdity. But there's method to the madness. Make no mistake: A Bush presidency, abetted by a Republican sweep of Congress and increasing right-wing control of the courts, portends frightening consequences for our lives.

Anyone who's been awake these past eight years should know that it's the Republicans, dominated by their right wing, who tried to block every measure to make government more responsive to the health, environmental, and educational interests of ordinary Americans. At the same time, these false prophets of smaller government were pawns of the Christian right's crusade to intrude the federal government into our most personal decisions, beginning with a woman's control of her body. At no point has Bush disowned that Republican agenda.

So why are so many otherwise reasonable people planning to vote for a candidate selling them this ludicrous bill of goods? It's because the guy comes on as a moderate with a disarming smile that could make him the impish star of a sitcom. Just when you realize he's conning you and the bleary face of Newt Gingrich hyping his "Contract with America" starts to come into focus, reminding us that we've been through this destructive drill, Bush turns on the all-inclusive charm.

The great deceit of the Bush campaign, beginning with the GOP convention last summer, has been to get voters to forget that it's been the Republican Congress that has threatened America with gridlock and political chaos unless we bend federal government to its skewed agenda—an agenda that Bush has assured the right wing he endorses.

The religious right has gone along with the charade, muting its criticisms while Bush plays to the center. Let him fake the moderate for now, they say, knowing that is what it takes to win. For example, Pat Robertson told reporters that he refrained from criticizing the Federal Drug Administration's approval of the abortion pill RU-486 for fear of costing Bush the election. Bush also avoided the issue. The payoff for the right's reserve in the campaign, as Bush has made amply clear, is that he will deliver to them on the judiciary. If the Republicans maintain control of the Senate, which now seems highly likely, a Bush victory would guarantee judicial appointees from the Supreme Court on down who are drawn from Jesse Helms's wish list.

For all of his talk of bipartisanship, Bush, in citing Antonin Scalia and Clarence Thomas as his ideal models for future Supreme Court picks, has promised to mold what should be the most independent branch of government in the ideological image of the far right. Indeed, the oft-repeated promise of the Bush campaign to the religious right is that Bush would never repeat the "disaster" that his father made in appointing moderate David Souter to the court.

With the court divided by one vote on most environmental and consumer regulatory matters as well as affirmative action, with only two votes needed to overturn *Roe vs. Wade*, and with at least three or four of its members likely to leave the court, the next President will have enormous power through his judicial appointments to shape the future of our government as we know it.

The "strict constructionists" Bush prefers are people who believe the federal government should be crippled as a regulator of big business, as an advocate for racial and economic justice, and as a protector of the environment. On the other hand, they would weaken constitutional protection of individual rights and blur the separation of church and state.

The Republican right wing is concerned about personal freedom only when it comes to indulging the National Rifle Association or corporate greed by savaging government regulation. But in matters of individual freedom, be it reproductive rights, protection from job discrimination, or hate crimes because of sexual orientation or racism, the Republican leadership, including George W. Bush, is eager to intrude a narrow religious and ideological bias into the most important decisions of our lives.

That's why this election is of crucial importance. What we're facing is the possibility of right-wing control of the presidency, Congress, and the courts. And with that will go the saving grace of our system of checks and balances.

❧

Dear George
November 22, 2000

Dear George:

You don't know me, but I did interview your father a bunch of times, and your recent behavior shows warning signs of the intemperate quirkiness that finally did him in with the public. He was always just a whine away from claiming he'd been abused by someone: Manuel Noriega, Saddam Hussein, Bill Clinton.

Those good-ol'-boy photos of you in a cowboy hat pretending to be annoyed that big-city slickers are ripping you off just don't cut it. You're too rich, coddled, and undeserving of your success to play the victim.

Not everyone gets to be President; the other guy got more votes nationally, and if that Florida fiasco had broken the other way, you and the Gore camp would now be making the opposite arguments. Heck, if Florida's Jews and blacks were Republican voters, your staff would be fervently in favor of choice for pregnant chads.

But deserving or not, it looks like you're going to be President, and I suspect that's what's put you into a dark funk. You're scared, and for good reason: More voters rejected you, the presidency will demand more than that four-hour workday you're used to, and you know painfully little about the world you're now expected to lead.

It must be more unnerving than before one of those big tests at Yale when even your tutor was hung over. This is not "gentleman's C's" time, this is being the forty-third President of the United States. Golly, there were only forty-two others in our nation's history, and now it's come down to you. You bet people will be seriously grading your performance, not like in Texas, where a Governor spends much time cutting ribbons, casually signing execution orders, and playing golf.

It doesn't help that the old advisers your daddy sent over as your minders keep nodding off, and the ones who still have something on the ball, such as Jim Baker, are getting churlish in their dotage. Dick Cheney acts like he's the boss and treats you like some kid he's keeping out of trouble. Condoleezza Rice is smart enough, but she keeps giving speeches about withdrawing troops from countries you didn't know existed. So much to know, so little time to cram. It's gotten you so anxious about being smart enough to pull this off that your severe teenage acne has returned.

I know, running for President was a lot of fun, but you're now discovering with those mock Cabinet meetings you're holding that being President is real work. The media won't let you shrug off those fuzzy numbers. There's a lot of annoying detail you have to know. Better get plenty of those three-by-five index cards Ronald Reagan carried to remind himself of important stuff.

But I didn't write this note to bum you out by dwelling on the incompetence thing. *Au contraire*, my advice is to get over it. Even if that negative assessment is true, as many appear to believe, you would hardly be the first incompetent to inhabit the White House.

You're not irredeemably inept, and anyway, there's no reason to compare yourself to that know-it-all Al Gore. He's had eight years of on-the-job training in one of the most successful Administrations in modern history, but he couldn't carry the Administration's home states of Tennessee and

Arkansas. Sure, that brainy stuff impresses people in New York, Illinois, and California, but Gore forgot to keep his intelligence hidden back home. You had no such problem.

If the voters wanted brainy leaders, Gore would've been a shoo-in instead of being left scraping for chads in Miami Beach. Clearly, almost half the voters are experiencing prosperity fatigue. They've forgotten that your father and Reagan ran up more red ink than all previous Presidents combined, and they're buying into supply-side economics once again.

My advice is to abandon the GOP economic dogma that almost gave the country to the Japanese. Forget that nutty tax cut for the super-rich that will only wipe out the surplus and prevent you from spending federal dollars on all those projects your core constituents want. Big federal bucks brought roads, airports, water, electricity, prisons, huge military contracts, and oil technology to the new capitalism of the Southwest. Attack Washington, but grab those federal tax dollars; it's the Texas way.

However, you're going to be President of the whole country, and the rest of the states want in on the federal dollar, particularly those in the rural backwater states that voted for you and that couldn't survive without congressional pork. Now, George, this is something you know a lot more about than you may think. Just use the model of how you got all that public funding to build a new stadium for your baseball team in Dallas.

The only mandate you have is to be moderate, so don't answer Pat Robertson's phone calls. And whatever happens, keep smiling, because that's what you're good at.

ᑫᔆ

Star Wars
February 14, 2001

I N THE SPRING OF 1980, PRESIDENTIAL CANDIDATE RONALD
Reagan took me into his confidence. Leaning back in his
seat as we jetted to yet another state primary, he told me he'd
been thinking about outer space. To be more precise, about
our ability to track "a glove lost by an astronaut that is still
circling the earth up there," and yet our inability to stop missiles "that are coming at us."

While he didn't actually use the words "Star Wars," this
was Reagan's first public embrace of a space-based ballistic
missile defense, as Frances FitzGerald notes in her definitive
book, *Way Out There in the Blue.*

Having always liked Reagan, since interviewing him during his first run for Governor in 1966, I didn't want to dis-
abuse him of one of his pet ideas. Reagan needed those
notions, never grounded in reality but always comforting, like
props in a child's fantasy world.

I bring it up now because the new Bush Administration
is determined to spend $60 billion on building Reagan's space
toy. While I'm as eager as anyone to create monuments to
Reagan's memory, why not finally build that training center
for high-school dropouts in South Los Angeles that he
promised as Governor? They still need one. Even carving
Reagan's image on Mt. Rushmore next to Teddy Roosevelt
and the rest would be cheaper.

One has to respect the nostalgia that grips Republicans
when they think of winning the Star Wars for the Gipper. But
despite having spent tens of billions already on Star Wars
technology, stopping a missile hidden among thousands of
cheaply deployed decoys will just not work. This kind of

ICBM defense is even sillier in an age where the only likely enemies are a few pariah nations bent not on defeating us in battle but in blackmailing us through terror.

A nuclear bomb in a suitcase smuggled in with the bales of marijuana that enter the country daily would do the job much better. Of course, a terrorist with half a brain wouldn't go nuclear—he'd poison our water or air. But let's not get too real here; we're talking Star Wars, an obsession of such enduring intensity that, in the end, proponents will not give up until something very costly is built, and I for one am tired of denying them their folly.

It's time to throw in the towel and give the defense contractors, who have been lobbying for this boondoggle long and hard, their reward for having bought the President of their choice.

Build Star Wars, big and bold. But build it not as a weapon, which frightens even the Europeans. No, build it as a game, a World Wide Web Star Wars theme park. Let's build it on a scale never before imagined, where you get to virtually shoot down objects in space, and death only comes to those who dare mention that it's just a game. But for other nations to not get nervous, I say let's build those theme parks in every land and language so that even the poorest nations lacking in indoor plumbing can have the most up-to-the-minute imitation of space-based war.

Think of it: In the most forlorn outpost of Taliban-run Afghanistan, old Osama bin Laden, long known as a computer nut, can sit on some rock outcropping pounding away on his laptop, zapping virtual heathen capitals of the world. His agents will have secured the latest Star Wars add-ons, allowing him to pretend to exterminate millions with the push of button on his wireless Palm Pilot, even when in the outhouse.

246 🍂 PLAYING PRESIDENT

Of course, no one will get killed because this will be virtual war, but there will be winners and losers depending on which side has acquired the most elaborate toys. The international arms bazaars will be bursting with the latest innovative devices; venture capitalists will invest heavily in cutting edge *Star Wars, the Game* technology. The ultimate reward, while not quite as satisfying as incinerated cities, will be much more profitable: a commanding market share in what's guaranteed to be the very newest of the new economy.

Not realistic enough? You think true fanatics will only go for blood and flesh carnage? Huh, shows just how little you know about the new world order. People and pain don't matter anymore, or we would be spending that $60 billion slated for Star Wars on vaccines and clean water in an old-fashioned terrorist abatement program.

Terrorists are no longer motivated by righting real world wrongs. What matters to them is the illusion of power while doing God's work. That's why God created violent space-based video games, so that the lunatics who speak in the Lord's name can be harmlessly diverted.

ᡠᡢ

Bush's Faustian Deal with the Taliban
May 22, 2001

E NSLAVE YOUR GIRLS AND WOMEN, HARBOR ANTI-U.S. terrorists, destroy every vestige of civilization in your homeland, and the Bush Administration will embrace you. All that matters is that you line up as an ally in the drug war, the only international cause that this nation still takes seriously.

That's the message sent with the recent gift of $43 million to the Taliban rulers of Afghanistan, the most virulent anti-American violators of human rights in the world today. The gift, announced last Thursday by Secretary of State Colin Powell, in addition to other recent aid, makes the U.S. the main sponsor of the Taliban and rewards that "rogue regime" for declaring that opium-growing is against the will of God. So, too, by the Taliban's estimation, are most human activities, but it's the ban on drugs that catches this Administration's attention.

Never mind that Osama bin Laden still operates the leading anti-American terror operation from his base in Afghanistan, from which, among other crimes, he launched two bloody attacks on American embassies in Africa in 1998.

Sadly, the Bush Administration is cozying up to the Taliban regime at a time when the United Nations, at U.S. insistence, imposes sanctions on Afghanistan because the Kabul government will not turn over bin Laden.

The war on drugs has become our own fanatics' obsession and easily trumps all other concerns. How else could we come to reward the Taliban, who has subjected the female half of the Afghan population to a continual reign of terror in a country once considered enlightened in its treatment of women?

At no point in modern history have women and girls been more systematically abused than in Afghanistan, where, in the name of madness masquerading as Islam, the government in Kabul obliterates their fundamental human rights. Women may not appear in public without being covered from head to toe with the oppressive shroud called the *burkha*, and they may not leave the house without being accompanied by a male family member. They've not been permitted to attend school or be treated by male doctors, yet women have been banned from practicing medicine, or any profession, for that matter.

The lot of males is better if they blindly accept the laws of an extreme religious theocracy that prescribes strict rules governing all behavior, from a ban on shaving to what crops may be grown. It is this last power that has captured the enthusiasm of the Bush White House.

The Taliban fanatics, economically and diplomatically isolated, are at the breaking point, and so, in return for a pittance of legitimacy and cash from the Bush Administration, they have been willing to appear to reverse themselves on the growing of opium. That a totalitarian country can effectively crack down on its farmers is not surprising. But it is grotesque for a U.S. official, James P. Callahan, director of the State Department's Asian anti-drug program, to describe the Taliban's special methods in the language of representative democracy: "The Taliban used a system of consensus-building," Callahan said after a visit with the Taliban, adding that the Taliban justified the ban on drugs "in very religious terms."

Of course, Callahan also reported, those who didn't obey the theocratic edict would be sent to prison.

In a country where those who break minor rules are simply beaten on the spot by religious police and others are stoned to death, it's understandable that the government's "religious" argument might be compelling. Even if it means, as Callahan concedes, that most of the farmers who grew the poppies will now confront starvation. That's because the Afghan economy has been ruined by the religious extremism of the Taliban, making the attraction of opium as a previously tolerated quick cash crop overwhelming.

For that reason, the opium ban will not last unless the

U.S. is willing to pour far larger amounts of money into underwriting the Afghan economy.

As the Drug Enforcement Administration's Steven Casteel admitted, "The bad side of the ban is that it's bringing their country—or certain regions of their country—to economic ruin." Nor did he hold out much hope for Afghan farmers growing other crops such as wheat, which require a vast infrastructure to supply water and fertilizer that no longer exists in that devastated country. There's little doubt that the Taliban will turn once again to the easily taxed cash crop of opium in order to stay in power.

The Taliban may suddenly be the dream regime of our own drug war zealots, but in the end this alliance will prove a costly failure. Our long sad history of signing up dictators in the war on drugs demonstrates the futility of building a foreign policy on a domestic obsession.

❧

The Fiscal Straightjacket
August 29, 2001

ARE WE ALL DIMWITS? WE JUST SIT THERE WITH GOOFY looks on our faces while the economy sputters and the President blows what remains of the budget surplus on a tax giveaway to the rich. With nary a peep as the "What, me worry?" kid has the gall to make stealing funds from Social Security and Medicare—to pay for a military buildup to fight an enemy that doesn't exist—sound like fiscal responsibility.

There is method to the President's madness, as he spelled out in his press conference Friday, proclaiming that the prospect of government red ink is "incredibly positive news" because it will produce "a fiscal straitjacket for Congress."

Get it? The plan is to bankrupt the national government so we can be reduced to life as it's lived in Texas, where the rich make out like bandits playing with public funds, as George W. did on that stadium deal, while the rest of the folks scramble. Texas politicians, including three Presidents in the past forty years, always make sure their companies are fed well at the Washington trough, even if it means going to war. Whatever the state of the federal budget, Bush is not going to be tight with the dollar when it comes to a bloated military, because big oil still needs that stick of U.S. military intervention to protect its investments abroad.

Why else do we need a military big enough to fight two wars at once, except to protect U.S. investments that stretch from the Caspian Sea to the Persian Gulf? Think of it as a Social Security program—or more accurately, welfare—for military contractors and energy companies, led by Halliburton, where Dick Cheney hustled his quick millions.

Bush never believed in a progressive federal government, including its programs for seniors, but he had to pretend otherwise to win over moderate voters. Now he blithely offers a recession he helped create and a war that he's not yet managed to find as a rationale for stealing from seniors: "I've said that the only reason we should use Social Security funds is in the case of an economic recession or war."

That was Friday, but Monday the nonpartisan Congressional Budget Office said that this year $9 billion must be taken out of Social Security, thanks to Bush's tax cut and the recession. What idiocy, to jeopardize the one domestic government program that really works. Seniors were once the poorest people around, and now they're the most secure, thanks to the guarantee of at least a minimum income and health care.

If you buy the lie that those programs just benefit seniors, consider the crushing burden on young families back in the good old days, when they struggled to provide for aging parents. Try to launch a career, raise a family, and still pay the health costs of Mom and Dad, and you'll get the picture.

Unless your family happens to be super-rich like the President's. For most Americans, Social Security and Medicare are the best family-values programs, and it's mind-boggling that we sit by while a born-rich President who has never known a second of family financial insecurity threatens to pull the safety net out from under the rest of us.

Go figure. Maybe we just find it too hard to follow the money—*our* money—particularly when all those zeros are tacked on. The federal budget is $1.9 trillion, and the $328 billion that Bush wants to give to the military must just sound like chump change. The big news, much easier to understand, is the sex life of a hick Congressman whose name the baby boomers will have forgotten ten years from now when they are informed that there is no money to cover the health and retirement payments owed them.

By then, the President who conned them will be back at his ranch in Crawford, chuckling about how he really put one over. As an ex-President, he will even get to cut ribbons at the umpteenth test of a missile defense program that will still be as far as ever from working.

Of course, wasting money on the military is a time-honored tradition, but with Bush, it's truly getting out of hand. Even Representative Jim Nussle, the Iowa Republican who heads the House Budget Committee, was perplexed by the Administration's asking for a defense hike before Defense

Secretary Donald H. Rumsfeld had even completed his review of what the military requires: "That's unacceptable if they are planning on getting more. We're not just going to throw money at defense again."

Sure he will, and so will most of his colleagues, and Bush knows it. That's why the President so smugly welcomes the shriveling of the budget surplus as good news, because it means that those nonmilitary things the government is supposed to do but which he never approved of, such as health care for the working poor, won't get done.

ᡱ

The Other World Evil
November 14, 2001

ONCE AGAIN, WE'RE BEING SOLD ON THE DEVIL THEORY OF history. Not that Osama bin Laden doesn't fit the bill as the Satan of the moment, just as Saddam Hussein did in the previous Bush Administration. But it's dangerous nonsense to suggest, as President Bush does, that we're up against an evildoer the likes of whom we've never seen.

While it's certainly necessary to eliminate bin Laden's terrorist cohort, that will hardly end the prospect of mayhem in this world. We lull ourselves into a false sense of security when we insist that madness is the exclusive province of one group of extremists, or that it inevitably finds its locus in one religion or region of the world.

When it comes to genocide, bin Laden is a minor contender. We've witnessed far worse from the good Germans— mostly well-educated, law-abiding Protestants and Catholics who killed six million Jews in the worst example of religious hatred ever. The United States caused the death of millions in Vietnam in a more recent war that never bore any reasonable connection to our security, as Lyndon Johnson's recently released tapes reveal. And what about Cheshire cat Vladimir V. Putin, a top KGB apparatchik when Soviet forces killed more than a million Afghan innocents, whose Russian troops now slaughter Chechen civilians?

By personalizing evil, Bush ignores the role of our allies and ourselves in making this such a dangerous world. That's clear when one assesses the true risks of chemical, biological, and nuclear weapons, which Bush in his U.N. speech warned bin Laden would use, saying, "No hint of conscience would prevent it." What hint of conscience prevented the United States from being the only nation in history to use nuclear weapons, killing at least 115,000 civilians in an assault that makes the World Trade Center attack pale in comparison?

Clearly, it's the leading nations that have created the world's huge arsenals of weapons of mass destruction, and if there's a danger in their use now by terrorists, it's only because those nations' stocks have been pilfered or sold and their scientists bribed.

If bin Laden possesses such weapons, it's through purchases on the black market or because he had the backing of nation-states, with Pakistan at the head of the list. He couldn't have done it alone. We've had him and his operation under constant observation, following President Clinton's orders to disable him. It's inconceivable that such an operation could have been directed undetected from the caves of Afghanistan.

However, Pakistan has been hell-bent on producing nuclear weapons, its program directed by scientists holding fanatical Islamist views who were forced to resign only after

September 11. Also forced to resign, as an additional obvious embarrassment, was the head of Pakistan's intelligence agency, which has been intimate with the Taliban and bin Laden.

The Pakistan-India nuclear arms race is the most dangerous confrontation in the world, yet we suddenly ended sanctions against those countries and will reward Pakistan's military dictator with $1 billion in high-tech military assistance for turning against his old buddies, the Taliban.

China is another nuclear-armed state that only recently was accused by the U.S. government of stealing our most valuable nuclear secrets. Indeed, the FBI all but ignored bin Laden as it kept 100 agents assigned to Los Alamos scientist Wen Ho Lee, producing a case so weak that Lee was never even charged with spying. Now that Bush has embraced China as yet another ally in the war against terrorism, the alleged theft of our rocket and nuclear technology is conveniently forgotten.

We are fickle in our anger and grief; new enemies replace the old, while the flag is waved and unity achieved. This is understandably therapeutic, as is the desire for revenge through bombing, even if it means killing children and starving the population. But it does not address the larger threat to the world's security.

Rest assured that bin Laden soon will be reduced to a violent footnote. But the danger to our civilization presented by the Cold War residue of weapons of mass destruction, which we and other civilized nations continue to produce, will haunt us long after bin Laden is a dim, if bizarre, memory.

c⟨ʒ

All the President's Businessmen
December 11, 2001

E NRON IS WHITEWATER IN SPADES. THIS ISN'T SOME CHICKEN land investment that haunted the Clinton White House, but rather the greatest presidential scandal since Teapot Dome.

The Bush Administration is up to its eyeballs in the ignominious shenanigans of a company whose much-discredited chairman, Kenneth L. Lay, was the primary financial backer of Bush's rise to the presidency. It was Lay to whom Vice President Cheney turned in devising the Administration's anti-consumer and anti-environment energy policy.

Enron provided the model for the Administration's attempt to revive an economy that's been in steep decline during its tenure in office: Give the fat-cat corporate hotshots everything they want in return for their bankrolling your political campaigns, and not to worry because this will also turn out to be good for the average American. That it didn't is now painfully clear. Enron got its way in deregulation, the Administration refused to assist California and other states, and consumers paid the steep price. So greedy was Enron that it locked its own workers into a pension plan based on inflated company stock values and suspect hidden partnerships, while the top leadership led by Lay made out like bandits. Bush should be called as a witness in the proceedings that unravel this mess.

It was then-Governor Bush in October 1997 who called then–Pennsylvania Governor Tom Ridge, at Lay's request, to help Enron crack into the tightly regulated Pennsylvania electricity market. "I called George W. to kind of tell him what was going on," Lay told the *New York Times*, "and I said that it would be very helpful to Enron, which is obviously a large company in the state of Texas, if he could just call the Governor and tell him this is a serious company, this is a professional company, a good company." Since we now know Enron lacked those virtues, it's clear Bush was used to sell a bill of goods to the unsuspecting Pennsylvania folks.

Lay was instrumental in Bush's rise to the presidency. Since 1993, Lay and top Enron executives donated nearly $2 million to George W. Bush. Lay also personally donated $326,000 in soft money to the Republican Party in the three years prior to Bush's presidential bid, and he was one of the "pioneers" who raised $100,000 in smaller contributions for Bush's presidential bid while his wife donated $100,000 for inauguration festivities.

Governor Bush did what Enron wanted, cutting taxes and large jury awards against big companies and deregulating utilities. The deregulation ideology, which both Bushes long had adopted as gospel, allowed dubious bookkeeping and other acts of chicanery that shocked Wall Street and drove a $60 billion company, seventh on the *Fortune* 500 list, into bankruptcy.

This emerging scandal makes Whitewater seem puny in comparison; clearly there ought to be at least as aggressive a congressional inquiry into the connection between the Bush Administration and the Enron debacle. Facts must be revealed, beginning with the content of Lay's secret meeting with Cheney to create the Administration's energy policy.

What was Lay's role in the sudden replacement of Curtis Hebert Jr. as Federal Energy Regulation Commission chairman? As the *New York Times* reported, Hebert "had barely settled into his new job this year when he had an unsettling telephone conversation with Kenneth L. Lay, [in which Lay] prodded him to back a faster pace in opening up access to the

electricity transmission grid to companies like Enron."
Hebert said, "I was offended" by the call and thought he
might lose his job, adding that Lay told him "he and Enron
would like to support me as chairman, but we would have to
agree on principles." Lay admits to the call, but in an unctu-
ous defense of his influence peddling said "the final decision
on [Hebert's job] was going to be the President's, certainly
not ours." Hebert was replaced by Texan Pat Wood, favored
by Lay, who'd originally pushed Governor Bush to name
Wood head of the Texas public utility commission.

Was there any conflict of interest in the roles played by
key Bush aides, including his political adviser Karl Rove, who
owned as much as $250,000 in Enron stock; economic adviser
Larry Lindsay and Trade Representative Robert B. Zoellick,
who went straight from Enron's payroll to their federal jobs?
There are other Enron alum in the Administration, including
Army Secretary Thomas White Jr., who, as an Enron executive, held stock and options totaling $50–$100 million. Were
these Enron alum tipped off in time to bail out with profit the
way Lay and the other top execs did, while their workers and
stockholders were left holding the suddenly empty bag?
Maybe there is no presidential criminal culpabality, as with
Whitewater. But let's find out.

ᑲᕒ

Build It and They Will Die
February 7, 2002

NOW WE GET TO SEE JUST HOW COWARDLY THE DEMOCRATS
in Congress can be. President Bush has proposed the
most preposterous military buildup in human history—annual

spending of $451 billion by 2007—and nary a word of criticism has been heard from the other side of the aisle. The President is drunk with the popularity that his war on terrorism has brought, and those sober Democrats and Republicans, who know better, are afraid to wrestle him for the keys to the budget before he drives off a cliff.

The red ink that Bush wants us to bleed to line the pockets of the defense industry, along with the tax cuts for the rich, will do more damage to our country than any terrorist. The result will be an economically hobbled United States, unable to solve its major domestic problems or support meaningful foreign aid, its enormous wealth sacrificed at the altar of military hardware that is largely without purpose.

Why the panic to throw billions more at the military when even the Pentagon brass have told us it is not needed? Our military forces, much maligned as inadequate by Bush during the election campaign, proved to be lacking in nothing once the Administration decided to stop playing footsie with the Taliban and eliminate those monsters of our own creation. It was obviously not a lack of hardware that made us vulnerable to the cruelty of September 11 but rather a failure of will by President Clinton, and then Bush, to brand the Taliban as terrorists and then to take out the well-marked camps of Al Qaeda with the counterinsurgency machine we have been perfecting since the Kennedy Administration.

Clinton authorized the elimination of Osama bin Laden in 1998, but the spy agencies simply failed to execute the order. Neither, apparently, were they competent enough to track Al Qaeda agents from training camps in Afghanistan to flight schools in Florida. All this, even though these agencies possess secret budgets of at least $70 billion a year, combined.

Despite the ability to read license plates from outer space

and scan the world's e-mail, our intelligence agencies lost the trail of terrorists who easily found cover with lap dancers in strip joints.

The bottom line is that we need sharper agents, not more expensive equipment. There is not an item in the Bush budget that will make us more secure from the next terrorist attack.

That being obvious, Bush is now resorting to the tried and true "evil empire" rhetorical strategy, grouping the disparate regimes of Iraq, Iran, and North Korea as an "axis of evil."

This alleged axis then becomes the rationale for a grossly expanded military budget, the idea being that the United States must be prepared to fight a conventional war on three fronts.

However, no such axis exists. North Korea is a tottering relic of a state whose nuclear operation was about to be bought off under the skilled leadership of the South Korean government when Bush jettisoned the deal. Iraq and Iran have been implacable foes for twenty-five years, and both were despised by the Taliban and Al Qaeda.

Meanwhile, a key Muslim ally of the United States, Saudi Arabia, produced fifteen of the nineteen September 11 hijackers—and bin Laden. Saudi Arabia is also where Al Qaeda does its biggest fundraising, and yet, inexplicably, it is excluded from the new enemies list.

Even if the accepted goal were the overthrow of the three brutal regimes targeted by President Bush, that would hardly require an expansion of a war machine built to humble the Soviet Union in its prime.

Is Bush the younger now telling us that his father failed to topple Saddam Hussein because he lacked sufficient fire-

power? The road to Baghdad was wide open after we obliter-
ated the vaunted Iraqi tank army in a matter of weeks. Or
does Bush the younger have even more grandiose plans in
mind?

His astonishing budget makes sense only if we are planning to use our mighty military in a pseudo-religious quest to
create a super-dominant Pax Americana.

Bizarre as that sounds, it may be the real framework for
Bush's proposed spending orgy. In any case, almost every
non-American speaker at the World Economic Forum in
New York expressed fear at this specter.

Even our own Bill Gates was alarmed at the United
States' apparent hubris: "People who feel the world is tilted
against them will spawn the kind of hatred that is very dangerous for all of us."

Is it too much to ask that these billions, *our* billions, be
spent to enhance our security rather than further erode it?

ᴂ

Hiding Behind a Veil of Executive Privilege?
May 21, 2002

A FULL-SCALE INVESTIGATION IS IN ORDER AS TO WHY THIS
nation was so poorly prepared to fend off an air piracy
attack by a terrorist group that had already killed many
Americans and attempted air hijackings and yet had total
access to our flight schools.

Unfortunately, all clues so far point to a depressingly likely
conclusion: Until September 11, the Bush Administration
was simply too distracted and/or incompetent to maintain
the American pressure on Osama bin Laden begun in 1998

under President Clinton with the missile attacks on reported Al Qaeda sites in Afghanistan.

As *Newsweek* details this week, Clinton National Security Adviser Samuel R. "Sandy" Berger was "totally preoccupied" with the prospect of a domestic terror attack. He warned his replacement, Condoleezza Rice: "You will be spending more time on this issue than on any other." Problem was, she didn't. Despite many warnings like Berger's, including the recently revealed Central Intelligence Agency briefings last summer, the new Administration treated the so-called war on drugs as more important than terrorism, and on that basis even made overtures to the Taliban leadership.

Four days before the ominous CIA briefing on August 6 that warned President Bush of the possibility of Al Qaeda hijackings, Christina B. Rocca, Assistant Secretary of State for South Asia, was sipping tea in Islamabad with the Taliban's ambassador to Pakistan, Abdul Salam Zaeef. She offered a mixed message that aptly characterized the Administration's confused priorities.

Treating the Taliban and Al Qaeda as if they were distinct entities, Rocca—in what now seems unbelievable naïvete—asked the Taliban to extradite bin Laden. Afterward, Zaeef said, "We gave Rocca our complete assurance that our soil will not be used against America and that Afghan soil will not be used for any terrorist activity." He called the meeting "very successful," adding, "The atmosphere was very cordial."

He had reason to be pleased. As Associated Press reported at the time: "In recognition of the Taliban's elimination of opium [in Afghanistan], the raw material used to make heroin, the Bush Administration is giving $1.5 million to the United Nations Drug Control Program to finance crop substitution, Rocca said."

Poppies, not terrorists, had been eliminated in Afghanistan. Five weeks later, terrorists smashed three planes into the World Trade Center and the Pentagon.

While the State Department was playing footsie with the Taliban, Attorney General Ashcroft's Justice Department was also downshifting anti-terrorism efforts to transfer focus to violent crime and drugs, reports *Newsweek*.

At the Pentagon, Defense Secretary Rumsfeld blocked an attempt to move $800 million from his pet missile defense program into counterterrorism.

The Administration simply was not focused on terrorism until it was too late. There was a blizzard of warnings leading up to September 11 that was ignored. It's a poor excuse for Rice to complain that the CIA warning was "thin." Real-time coordination of intelligence information on such a high-level problem is the responsibility of the National Security Adviser.

If Rice felt the dire CIA warning in August was incomplete, she should have demanded that the FBI and other intelligence agencies immediately brief her and the President on their full knowledge of the situation. Nor did the Administration inform the country of this lapse in security until it leaked to the media eight months later.

Indeed, Administration spokesmen have continuously misled the public from the first days after the September 11 tragedy with the claim that the President had no advance warning.

We do not yet know the full extent of those warnings, and Vice President Dick Cheney is once again circling the wagons of executive privilege around the essential data.

The Vice President insists that it would jeopardize national security for Congress to have access to the August CIA briefing.

This follows the dangerous pattern this Administration has consistently pursued of denying the public and its elected representatives potentially embarrassing information, such as notes from meetings with Enron officials before that company's spectacular implosion.

We already know enough about the intelligence failures before that grim September morning to raise strong suspicions that executive privilege is now being invoked to conceal enormous incompetence on the part of the executive branch.

It is painful, in light of the thousands of people slain in New York, Washington, and Pennsylvania—as well as later in Afghanistan in retaliation—to look back at how our security was so threatened. But as horrifying as the facts may turn out to be, we as a nation have long believed that it is the truth—full, complex, and unsanitized—that shall make us free. We should continue to act accordingly.

❧

Bush Jumps the Gun
September 25, 2002

PRESIDENT BUSH'S RECENTLY ANNOUNCED STRATEGIC GLOBAL doctrine, which for the first time justifies a preemptive U.S. strike against any regime thought to possess weapons of mass destruction, makes a mockery of the war on terrorism. A preemptive strike against Home Depot, where box cutters can be bought for a few bucks, would seem more relevant to disarming future terrorists.

After all, those tools were deadly enough when used to commandeer the four airplanes that caused the destruction of September 11. And the big-box store sells fertilizer, too, and we all know now how deadly that stuff can be.

Convenient oversights like this are all part of that sleight of hand this Administration specializes in to pursue its aims. Whether it's a giant tax cut or the dethroning of Saddam Hussein, Bush can always find a rationale in the day's headlines for what he wanted to do all along.

Just in time, Bush's formal National Security Strategy released last week attempts to justify such "anticipatory" military attacks by the United States to "forestall or prevent hostile acts by our adversaries," even if "uncertainty remains as to the time and place of the enemy's attack."

The doctrine also says we will not tolerate any nation that seeks military parity with the United States.

This posture will only encourage aggression by other nations such as India, which has every reason to be panicked about the nuclear arsenal, unstable government, and aggressive rhetoric of its neighbor Pakistan. Instead of saber-rattling, Bush should welcome the return of U.N. disarmament inspectors to Iraq.

Bush's haste to make war on Iraq is understandable only as a ploy to avoid dealing with the struggling U.S. economy, a still-shadowy Al Qaeda leadership that has not been brought to heel yet, and the alarming disintegration of the Mideast peace process.

There simply is no evidence that Iraq had anything to do with the tragedy that has so traumatized this nation. Why, then, a sudden policy shift threatening preemptive strikes against any nation producing weapons of mass destruction when advanced weaponry played no role in our troubles?

Weapons of mass destruction are certainly a threat to the

world. But for all the talk of smallpox, the apparently home-bred anthrax attacks, and Hussein's own use of nerve gas on Kurdish children, the true weapons of mass destruction that threaten human existence are nuclear.

Yet the United States is still opposed to the abolishment of nuclear weapons, and this Administration has even beefed up efforts to refine and develop our massive H-bomb arsenal. At a time when an alarming number of nations have nuclear weapons—and Iraq's wobbly nuke program is not yet on that list—it ill behooves the one nation that has dropped nuclear bombs on civilians to continue to treat them as acceptable military weapons.

The Bush Administration's ongoing emphasis on developing a Star Wars missile defense system basically endorses a nuclear war–fighting strategy.

Instead of renouncing nuclear weapons as inherently barbaric, as we have done with chemical and biological weapons, this Administration is making a shambles of the antiballistic missile and other arms control treaties so we can make better nukes.

If there is an area in which Bush is truly untutored, it is not on the subject of grammar but rather on the historical risk of moral hubris.

Consequently, his Administration's answer to all criticisms of his aggressive unilateralism is that the United States is unique, empowered to engage in "a unique American internationalism"—formerly known as imperialism.

The man seems simply incapable of countenancing the notion that this nation can ever do wrong.

This was the assumption of imperial emperors throughout history who took it for granted they were improving the lot of their colonies. We have only to look at the untenable map of the Mideast, imposed by France and Britain, to see that this was patently untrue.

Good intentions are often the most damaging. And history teaches us to beware the firepower of the angels of death, for they are never restrained by uncertainty of purpose.

In this way, the Bush doctrine is a supremely dangerous cocktail, an explosive blend of the arrogance of our uniquely powerful post–Cold War military strength laced with a mind-numbing fear of box-cutter-wielding maniacs.

‹♦›

Mr. Bush, Heed Carter and Learn
October 15, 2002

JIMMY CARTER WON THE NOBEL PEACE PRIZE FOR A CAREER OF successfully waging peace, beginning with the launching of a historic Mideast peace effort that President Bush is bent on scuttling with mindless indifference.

Oblivious to the daily slaughter of Palestinians and Israelis, whose televised mayhem fuels evil passions throughout the Islamic world, Bush focuses instead on the irrelevant sideshow of Iraq. Bush seems unaware that the Gordian knot of global terrorism pulled tightly in years past by our allies in Pakistan and Saudi Arabia—in ugly evidence again this weekend in peaceful Bali—will not be cut unless the quest for peace initiated by Carter at Camp David nearly a quarter-century ago is finally completed.

Instead, in a stunning display of willful pique more akin to a child's tantrum than to a President's policy, Bush seeks to smite Iraq as a target more accessible to his sword.

In fact, in a brief period of less than two years, an accidental President untutored in the ways of the world has surrendered the presidency to a gang of bullies in his Administration that seeks to rearrange the world to its liking, not through diplomacy and peaceful example but rather through the ravages of what Defense Secretary Rumsfeld, writing in his just-released personal cheat sheet to determine when to invade other countries that have not attacked us, politely calls a "pre-crisis" use of force.

Rumsfeld and fellow prominent Administration chicken hawks like Dick Cheney and Paul D. Wolfowitz are veterans not of combat but rather of wars they had foolishly suggested others fight. Over the protests of Secretary of State Powell, a retired general, these men have successfully installed a blatantly imperialist foreign policy.

To be sure, there are polls that show a slim majority of Americans support the overthrow of Saddam Hussein. However, setting aside the fact that ninety percent of Americans would probably support the violent overthrow of Major League Baseball Commissioner Bud Selig, these numbers are extremely misleading. If other elements are factored into the polling—should we wait for allied support, should we give the U.N. more time for diplomacy, for example—a majority of us oppose Bush's first-strike approach.

Americans don't like to concern themselves too much with what's happening in the rest of the world, and many are even content to let the CIA and the Marines dabble in international behavior modification as long as the body bags don't pile up too high. But Americans also pride themselves on common sense, and they know that Iraq had nothing to do with 9/11, the woes of the economy, or our inability to locate Osama bin Laden, the anthrax terrorist, or even the Washington-area sniper. They know that oil is black gold and

Iraq has a whole heck of a lot of it, but they also know that nation-building is a dangerous, costly, and ultimately thankless task better left to the United Nations.

Of course, Americans are concerned about nuclear, biological, and chemical weapons, especially now that our national sense of invulnerability has been so painfully damaged. Many, however, are starting to realize that the Bush Administration's claims on that front need to be treated with a grain of salt the size of the hats in Texas.

The CIA has concluded that Iraq does not have nuclear weapons and is militarily far weaker than it was ten years ago, but the response of the Administration has been to squeeze the intelligence agency to come up with reports that support its unsupportable case for invasion. And how insulting to our collective intelligence is it to have the President hold up photos of dangerous weapons sites that are found to be piles of junk by American journalists who visit the location days later? Clearly the President is eager to derail the return of U.N. weapons inspectors for fear they won't find much.

Meanwhile, Pakistan dictator Pervez Musharraf, who has a tested, deliverable nuclear arsenal, has just managed to lose an election that he unsuccessfully rigged, leaving Islamic fanatics in control of the country's most sensitive region, that which borders Afghanistan.

The religious fundamentalists exploited a slogan stating that Bush's plan to attack Iraq transforms the war on terrorism into a war on Islam. That is exactly the problem with Bush's obsession with Iraq. Whether to avenge his father or to "wag the dog" ahead of elections, Bush has undermined the lofty goal of eliminating terrorism.

While Carter has exhibited the patience of the peacemaker, a sweet Jesus for our time, willing to rebuke contemptible leaders while offering them a path for redemption, Bush has become a self-fulfilling prophet of war, delighting in the discovery of what he defines as immutable evil, thereby justifying an endless crusade against the infidels.

❧

Bush Pushes the Big Lie toward the Brink
March 4, 2003

SO THE TRUTH IS OUT: GEORGE W. BUSH LIED WHEN HE claimed to be worried about Iraq's alleged weapons of mass destruction. Otherwise, Iraq's stepped-up cooperation with the U.N. on disarmament would be stunningly good news, obviating the need to rush to war.

Instead, the U.N. weapons inspectors' verification of Iraq's destruction of missiles, private meetings with Iraqi weapons scientists, visits to locations where biological and chemical weapons were destroyed in 1991, and a series of unfettered flights by U2 spy planes have been met with a shrug and sneer in Washington. The White House line is that even if the Iraqis destroy all their slingshots, Goliath is still bringing his tanks and instituting "regime change." The arrogance is breathtaking. We have demanded that a country disarm—and even as it is doing so, we say it doesn't matter: It's too late; we're coming in. Put down your guns and await the slaughter.

Abraham Lincoln once observed that even a free people can be fooled for a time—and this, mind you, was long before Fox News existed—and in his chaotic two-year presidency, Bush has pushed the Big Lie approach so far that we are seeing dramatic signs of its cracking: an international backlash, a domestic peace movement, and whistle-blowing from inside our own intelligence and diplomatic corps.

"We have not seen such systematic distortion of intelligence, such systematic manipulation of the American people, since the war in Vietnam," wrote John Brady Kiesling, a twenty-year veteran of the U.S. Foreign Service, in his letter of resignation last week to Secretary of State Colin Powell. Kiesling, who was political counselor in U.S. embassies throughout the Mideast, added that "until this Administration, it had been possible to believe that by upholding the policies of my President, I was also upholding the interests of the American people and the world. I believe it no longer."

And this brave man is not the only one who has caught on. The entire world is astonished that our President is lying, not about a personal indiscretion, but about the most sacred duty of the leader of the most powerful nation in human history: the duty not to recklessly endanger the lives of his own or the world's people. Yet lie he has.

The first lie, claimed outright, was that Iraq aided and abetted the September 11 terrorists. There is no evidence at all for this claim. It is also interesting to note that not a single leading Al Qaeda operative has turned out to be Iraqi. The latest to be nabbed, Khalid Shaikh Mohammed, was living in Pakistan, was raised in Kuwait, and studied engineering— and presumably the physics of explosives—at a college in North Carolina.

The second lie was that Iraq's alleged weapons of mass destruction represent an imminent threat to U.S. security. Despite the most hugely expensive but secret high-tech spy operation in human history—estimated by most at well over $100 billion a year—and a vast network of defectors and spies, we have not been able to find their supposed weapons.

The third and most dangerous lie is that our mission now is to bring lasting peace to the Mideast by a devastating invasion of Iraq, which will end, as the President outlined last week, in U.S. dominance over the structure of government and politics throughout the region. After abandoning promising efforts by the previous Administration to create peace between Israel and the Palestinians, the Bush team now claims that changing Muslim governments around the world will end the downward spiral of violence there. Which leads us to another lie: that this is all good for our ally, Israel—the claim of the cabal of neoconservative ideologues running our Mideast policy. In fact, however, Israel will be placed in a terribly dangerous position, serving as a fig leaf for U.S. ambitions, further ensuring that it remain forever an isolated military garrison.

This construction of a new world order comes from a naïve and untraveled President, emboldened in his ignorance by advisers who have been plotting an aggressive Pax Americana ever since the Soviet bloc's collapse. Bush insiders Richard Perle, Elliott Abrams, Dick Cheney, Paul Wolfowitz, and Donald Rumsfeld are all members of something called the Project for a New American Century that has been pushing for a U.S. redesign of the Mideast since 1997. After September 11, they seized on our national tragedy as a way to enlist George W. in support of their grand design. Not only was this reckless scheme never mentioned by Bush during the election campaign, it was the sort of thing renounced as "nation-building," something he would never support. Yet another lie.

❦

Saving Private Lynch: Take 2
May 20, 2003

IN THE 1998 FILM *WAG THE DOG*, POLITICAL OPERATIVES
employ special editing techniques to create phony footage
that will engender public sympathy for a manufactured war.
Now we find that in 2003 the real-life Pentagon's ability and
willingness to manipulate the facts make Hollywood's story
lines look tame. After a thorough investigation, the British
Broadcasting Corporation has presented a shocking dissec-
tion of the "heroic" rescue of Private Jessica Lynch, as
reported by the U.S. military and a breathless American
press.

"Her story is one of the most stunning pieces of news
management ever conceived," the BBC concluded—the
polite British way of saying, "Liar, liar, pants on fire."

Though the Bush Administration's shamelessly trumped-
up claims about Iraq's alleged ties to Al Qaeda and 9/11 and
its weapons of mass destruction take the cake for deceitful propaganda—grand strategic lies that allow the United States'
seizure of Iraq's oil to appear as an act of liberation—the sad
case of Lynch's exploitation at the hands of military spinners
illustrates that the truth once again was a casualty of war.

Lynch, who says she has no memory of the events in
question, has suffered enough in the line of duty without
being reduced to a propaganda pawn.

Sadly, almost nothing fed to reporters about either
Lynch's original capture by Iraqi forces or her "rescue" by
U.S. forces turns out to be true. Consider the April 3
Washington Post story on her capture headlined, *"She Was*

Fighting to the Death," which reported, based on unnamed military sources, that Lynch "continued firing at the Iraqis even after she sustained multiple gunshot wounds," adding that she was also stabbed when Iraqi forces closed in.

It has since emerged that Lynch was neither shot nor stabbed, but rather suffered accident injuries when her vehicle overturned. A medical checkup by U.S. doctors confirmed the account of the Iraqi doctors, who said they had carefully tended her injuries, a broken arm and thigh and a dislocated ankle, in contrast to U.S. media reports that doctors had ignored Lynch.

Another report spread by news organizations nationwide claimed Lynch was slapped by an Iraqi security guard, and the U.S. military later insisted that an Iraqi lawyer witnessed this incident and informed them of Lynch's whereabouts. His credibility as a source, however, is difficult to verify because he and his family were whisked to the U.S., where he was immediately granted political asylum and has refused all interview requests. His future was assured with a job with a lobbying firm run by former Republican Representative Bob Livingstone that represents the defense industry and a $500,000 book contract with HarperCollins, a company owned by Rupert Murdoch, whose Fox network did much to hype Lynch's story, as it did the rest of the war.

But where the manipulation of this saga really gets ugly is in the premeditated manufacture of the rescue itself, which stains those who have performed real acts of bravery, whether in war or peacetime.

Eight days after her capture, American media trumpeted the military's story that Lynch was saved by Special Forces that stormed the hospital and, in the face of heavy hostile fire, managed to scoop her up and helicopter her out.

However, according to the BBC, which interviewed the hospital's staff, the truth appears to be that not only had Iraqi forces abandoned the area before the rescue effort but that the hospital's staff had informed the U.S. of this and made arrangements two days before the raid to turn Lynch over to the Americans. "But as the ambulance, with Private Lynch inside, approached the checkpoint, American troops opened fire, forcing it to flee back to the hospital. The Americans had almost killed their prize catch," the BBC reported.

"We were surprised," Dr. Anmar Uday told the BBC about the supposed rescue. "There was no military, there were no soldiers in the hospital. It was like a Hollywood film. [The U.S. forces] cried, 'Go, go, go,' with guns and blanks without bullets, blanks, and the sound of explosions," Uday said. "They made a show for the American attack on the hospital—[like] action movies [starring] Sylvester Stallone or Jackie Chan."

The footage from the raid, shot not by journalists but by soldiers with night-vision cameras, was fed in real time to the central command in Qatar. The video was artfully edited by the Pentagon and released as proof that a battle to free Lynch had occurred, when it had not.

This fabrication has already been celebrated by an A&E special and will soon be an NBC movie. The Lynch rescue story—a made-for-TV bit of official propaganda—will probably survive as the war's most heroic moment, despite proving as fictitious as the stated rationales for the invasion itself.

If the movies, books, and other renditions of *Saving Private Lynch* were to be honestly presented, it would expose this caper as merely one in a series of egregious lies marketed to us by the Bush Administration.

❧

A Firm Basis for Impeachment
July 15, 2003

D OES THE PRESIDENT NOT READ? DOES HIS NATIONAL security staff, led by Condoleezza Rice, keep him in the dark about the most pressing issues of the day? Or is this Administration blatantly lying to the American people to secure its ideological ends?

Those questions arise because of the White House admission that the charge that Iraq tried to buy uranium from Niger was excised from a Bush speech in October 2002 after the CIA and State Department insisted it was unfounded. Bizarrely, however, three months later—without any additional evidence emerging—that outrageous lie was inserted into the State of the Union speech to justify the President's case for bypassing the United Nations Security Council, for chasing U.N. inspectors out of Iraq, and for invading and occupying an oil-rich country.

This weekend, Administration sources disclosed that CIA Director George Tenet intervened in October to warn White House officials, including Deputy National Security Adviser Stephen Hadley, not to use the Niger information because it was based on a single source. That source proved to be a forged document with glaring inconsistencies.

Bush's top security aides, led by Hadley's boss, Rice, went along with the CIA, and Bush's October speech was edited to eliminate the false charge that Iraq was seeking to acquire uranium from Niger to create a nuclear weapon.

We now know that before Bush's January speech, Robert G. Joseph, the National Security Council individual who reports to Rice on nuclear proliferation, was fully briefed by CIA analyst Alan Foley that the Niger connection was no stronger than it had been in October. It is inconceivable that in reviewing draft after draft of the State of the Union speech, NSC staffers Hadley and Joseph failed to tell Rice that the President was about to spread a big lie to justify going to war.

On national security, the buck doesn't stop with Tenet, the current fall guy. The buck stops with Bush and his National Security Adviser, who is charged with funneling intelligence data to the President. That included cluing in the President that the CIA's concerns were backed by the State Department's conclusion that "the claims of Iraqi pursuit of natural uranium in Africa are highly dubious."

For her part, Rice has tried to fend off controversy by claiming ignorance. On *Meet the Press* in June, Rice claimed, "We did not know at the time—no one knew at the time, in our circles—maybe someone knew down in the bowels of the agency, but no one in our circles knew that there were doubts and suspicions that this might be a forgery."

On Friday, Rice admitted that she had known the State Department intelligence unit "was the one that within the overall intelligence estimate had objected to that sentence" and that Secretary of State Colin Powell had refused to use the Niger document in his presentation to the U.N. because of what she described as long-standing concerns about its credibility. But Rice also knew the case for bypassing U.N. inspections and invading Iraq required demonstrating an imminent threat. The terrifying charge that Iraq was hell-bent on developing nuclear weapons would do the trick nicely.

However, with the discrediting of the Niger buy and the equally dubious citation of a purchase of aluminum tubes (which turned out to be inappropriate for the production of enriched uranium), one can imagine the disappointment at the White House. There was no evidence for painting Saddam Hussein as a nuclear threat.

The proper reaction should have been to support the U.N. inspectors in doing their work in an efficient and timely fashion. We now know, and perhaps the White House knew then, that the inspectors eventually would come up empty-handed because no weapons of mass destruction program existed—not even a stray vial of chemical and biological weapons has been discovered. However, that would have obviated the Administration's key rationale for an invasion, so lies substituted for facts that didn't exist.

And there, dear readers, exists the firm basis for bringing a charge of impeachment against the President who employed lies to lead us into war.

ᢒ

Bush Plays Pope on Marriage Issue
August 5, 2003

I AGREE WITH THE PRESIDENT AND THE POPE: MARRIAGE IS A very serious endeavor, not to be trifled with. Just ask any of the tens of millions of divorced parents who are tied together for life in a precarious, often combative attempt to raise their kids well in separate households.

Done right, marriage—or "civil unions," if the M-word is too loaded—can be a bridge to loyalty, sexual stability, shared financial responsibility, and the more efficient rearing of children. All the more reason, then, to support anybody, gay or straight, who wants to commit to a lifelong union. Whether you are united in "holy matrimony" or simply trying to build a lasting relationship should be of no concern to the state, nor should your sexual orientation.

Where I differ from the President and the Pope is in defining marriage in religious terms. Under the U.S. Constitution, after all, church is clearly separated from state, and thus marriage is a civic institution not in any way requiring the participation of religious organizations. Government policies favor the family unit. If the state is offering special rights and benefits for those couples who marry, then to exclude gays is simply unconstitutional.

In Germany, France, Canada, and Vermont, state-sanctioned unions help gay couples clarify the legal status and rights of their partnership in everything from bank accounts to hospital visitation to child custody. For gays seeking these rights elsewhere, this is primarily a practical struggle, and it is wrong for the President to exploit it for political purposes.

The drive for gay marriage is also an affirmation of responsible love, and it is bizarre that this honorable impulse could be blocked on the basis of someone else's religious views. The desire of two people to commit to some shared order in their lives, presumably reinforcing notions of sexual monogamy, has particular relevance in the gay community, which has paid an enormous price for promiscuity. It is also a community riven by the loss of loved ones in which a partner's rights to share in managing grief have been painfully challenged when a mate faces death.

It is one thing for the Pope, a religious leader, to oppose gay marriage based on the theology that "homosexual acts go against the natural moral order." But the President of the United States, as the highest official in our secular government, is overstepping his bounds mightily when he lectures about "sin" and "the sanctity of marriage."

"I believe a marriage is between a man and a woman. And I think we ought to codify that one way or another," Bush said last week, seizing upon a question about homosexuality that didn't mention marriage. "And we've got lawyers looking at the best way to do that."

Well, lawyers can do just about anything with the law to make their case, but it is hoped that most judges will have read the Constitution and seen that it says nothing about merging church and state.

What the President didn't mention was that the U.S. high court has finally acknowledged that homosexuality is not a threat to public order, striking down discriminatory anti-sodomy laws in Texas.

If homosexual sex is legal, it doesn't matter if our born-again President believes it's a sin on the grounds that it offends his or anyone else's interpretation of Christian Scripture.

Ironically, in the same press session in which Bush acted as if our nation is a Christian theocracy, he applauded Iraq's faltering steps toward a secular society that would break with Islamic dictates. He even mentioned the prospect of an Iraqi Thomas Jefferson emerging to show those folks how to go about building a free society.

But Jefferson was an awkward choice for Bush, because he was as responsible as any of the founders for the very notion of the separation of church and state. As a public man, Jefferson even resisted identifying himself as Christian, being, as he wrote, "averse to the communication of my religious tenets to the public because it would seduce public opinion to erect itself into that inquisition over the rights of conscience, which the laws have so justly proscribed."

And, as the Supreme Court has clearly stated, being gay,

even in Bush's home state of Texas, is one of those rights of conscience.

ª

Liar and Liberator
November 11, 2003

IT TAKES STUNNING ARROGANCE FOR A PRESIDENT TO INVADE an oil-rich, politically strategic country on the basis of demonstrable lies, put his favorite companies in control of its economic future, create a puppet regime to do his bidding, and then claim, as George W. Bush did last week in a speech, that this is all a bold exercise in spreading democracy. "Iraqi democracy will succeed, and that success will send forth the news from Damascus to Tehran that freedom can be the future of every nation," the President said. "The establishment of a free Iraq at the heart of the Middle East will be a watershed event in the global democratic revolution."

Bush even invoked the blessing of a divine power, the "author of freedom," suggesting that he is not merely an overambitious imperial President but rather a modern Moses armed with smart bombs and Black Hawk helicopters come to liberate an enslaved people.

Bush presents his vision as bold and new when it is nothing of the sort.

His predecessors in the White House similarly claimed the mantle of democracy as justification for establishing American dominance in the Mideast over the last half a century. They used lies and secrecy and the lives of young Americans to create, nurture, and protect dictatorships that served narrow U.S. interests above the needs and rights of their own people.

His buddies at Bechtel, Halliburton, and the giant oil companies have been ripping off the profits of Mideast oil for decades while seeking and gaining protection from the CIA and whatever other parts of the U.S. military-industrial complex were needed to prop up "our guy"—the dictator of the moment. Despotism in the Mideast flowered on our watch, often succeeded by fundamentalist or nationalist regimes of great violence, or both. Every Mideast despot exists only because his power has proved tolerable to the economic interests that former Halliburton Chief Executive Dick Cheney and his defense-industry friendly counterparts in previous Republican and Democratic administrations have placed at the top of the American agenda.

Democracy is the most wonderful notion ever conceived, but Washington considers it a dangerous threat when the people in fledging democracies vote against U.S. interests. That's when the CIA steps in, as it did in Iran in 1953, overthrowing democratic secularist Mohammad Mossadegh and launching Iran into decades of madness.

Or how about the cynical support under Presidents Carter and Reagan of the fundamentalist mujahedeen in Afghanistan, which morphed into the Taliban and Al Qaeda? The CIA gave these "freedom fighters" shoulder-fired rockets, perfect for terrorism, and Ronald Reagan declared a day of national support for them in the U.S. Unfortunately, as the quarter of a century since has proved, we have neither the means nor the will to bring democracy to Afghanistan.

People make their own history, and though the U.S. can help, it cannot impose.

Bush is not really interested in meaningful democracy in Iraq—just as the U.S. wasn't in Afghanistan or earlier in Iran. In Iraq, the U.S. will not tolerate any opposition to the U.S.

occupation. But that excludes democracy, which will not cater to the whims of U.S. foreign policy.

Meanwhile, the chaos and bitterness of post-war Iraq continues without break, all the more tragic for its predictability. In fact, we would not be in such a mess today if the President had listened to his own father.

"Trying to eliminate Saddam, extending the ground war into an occupation of Iraq . . . would have incurred incalculable human and political costs," cowrote the senior George Bush in the 1998 book *A World Transformed*.

"Furthermore, we had been self-consciously trying to set a pattern for handling aggression in the post–Cold War world," he continued. "Going in and occupying Iraq, thus unilaterally exceeding the United Nations' mandate, would have destroyed the precedent of international response to aggression that we hoped to establish. Had we gone the invasion route, the United States could conceivably still be an occupying power in a bitterly hostile land."

Unfortunately, because of George W. Bush, it is just that.

Democracy cannot exist without truth and genuine self-determination. A liar cannot be a liberator if the flowering of democracy is truly the endgame.

⚭

The Worst Form of Exploitation
March 9, 2004

HOW PERFECT THE IRONY, HOW SORDID THE SCAM. THE President, who ignored the Al Qaeda threat before September 11, 2001, who diverted public attention in that horror's aftermath to the nonexistent threat from Iraq, and who has stonewalled the investigation of 9/11, now seeks to exploit that tragedy as a reelection gimmick.

George W. Bush avoids being photographed with the dead and injured from his folly in Iraq, but hey, those flag-draped coffins of 9/11 victims make great TV ads. What a grisly low in political exploitation.

That's why the ads were condemned by a firefighters union and many of the 9/11 victims' relatives, whose various websites contain an impressive list of the unanswered questions concerning the tragedy. As Bob McIlvaine, whose son was killed in the Twin Towers disaster, put it: "Instead of playing on people's emotions with images of that day, the President would do right to cooperate more with the independent commission investigating the 9/11 attacks so we can learn the truth about what happened on that day and why."

But uncovering the truth about 9/11 has never been Bush's intention. Instead, the President has used that tragedy for his own political ambitions—to draw attention away from his lies about Iraq, the unprecedented national debt, the disappointing jobless recovery, and the attacks on civil liberty. What's mind-boggling is the cynicism of Bush's electoral ploy when one considers that he never showed any interest in terrorism before 9/11. He had focused instead on the war on drugs and trying to one-up his father on Iraq. His abysmal failure to heed the Clinton Administration's warnings regarding the threat posed by Osama bin Laden may be one reason for Bush's extreme reluctance to permit an unimpeded, bipartisan public investigation of 9/11.

Never before in our national history has such a major event been so unexamined by the government while being so effectively hyped for political advantage. The obfuscation has been deliberate and executed with a passion that suggests Bush may have some dreadful truth to hide. Why else would he initially oppose the formation of a bipartisan commission to investigate the origins and lessons of 9/11?

Bush allowed the commission to form only after enormous public pressure led by the families of victims, who demanded an accounting of what led to the loss of their loved ones. Bush then sought to undermine an honest investigation by appointing Henry Kissinger, international grand master of mendacity, to be chairman. That gambit failed when Kissinger refused to make public his murky financial entanglements with the very regimes most likely to have links to the 9/11 terrorists.

After a more independent commission finally was allowed to form, Bush set about to systematically undermine its work by refusing to turn over documents essential to the investigation or to permit the full committee to interview the top officials in his Administration, from himself on down.

This is a President whose immediate response to 9/11 was to protect the Al Qaeda terrorists' known sponsors in Saudi Arabia and Pakistan while planning a sideshow war against bin Laden's sworn enemy in Baghdad, Saddam Hussein. In the immediate aftermath of the World Trade Center disaster, a Saudi plane was allowed to land in the United States and whisk bin Laden relatives and certain Saudis out of the country before intelligence agencies could fully question them, despite the fact that fifteen of the nineteen hijackers were Saudi nationals who had been allowed to enter the U.S. under suspicious circumstances, suggesting the connivance of the Saudi government.

Bush turned his sights on Iraq's illusory weapons of mass destruction while lifting the sanctions imposed on Pakistan, a known possessor and proliferator of nuclear weapons. Nor have any of those sanctions been restored even now, when Pakistan admits that its top scientific institute was the source of nuclear weapons technology sold to North Korea, Libya, and Iran.

Bush defends his exploitation of 9/11 with these words: "How this Administration handled that day, as well as the war on terror, is worthy of discussion." Yes indeed, but it is an Administration that delights in discussions in which it monopolizes all of the crucial information and cherry picks, fabricates, and otherwise distorts evidence, mocking the sacred notion of representative democracy.

❧

Bush Puts a "Cancer on the Presidency"
March 30, 2004

W ORSE THAN WATERGATE, THE TITLE OF A NEW BOOK BY John Dean, Richard Nixon's White House counsel, is a depressingly accurate measure of the chicanery of the Bush/Cheney cabal. According to Dean, who began his political life at the age of twenty-nine as the Republican counsel on the House Judiciary Committee before being recruited by Nixon, "This Administration is truly scary and, given the times we live in, frighteningly dangerous." And when it comes to lies and cover-up, the Bush crowd makes the Nixon Administration look like amateurs. As Dean writes, they "have created the most secretive presidency of my lifetime . . . far worse than during Watergate."

Dean knows what he's talking about. He was the one who dared tell Nixon in 1973 that the web of lies surrounding the Watergate break-in of the Democratic Party headquarters had formed "a cancer on the presidency." When Dean went public about that conversation, the Nixon White House smeared him as a liar. Fortunately, the conversation had been taped, and Dean was vindicated.

The dark side of the current White House was on full display last week when top officials of the Bush Administration took to the airwaves to destroy the credibility of a man who had honorably served Presidents Reagan, Clinton, and both Bushes.

The character assassination of Richard Clarke, the former White House anti-terrorism chief, was far more worrisome than Nixon's smears of Dean, because it concerned not petty crime in pursuit of partisan political ambition but rather the attempt to deceive the nation and the world as to the causes of the 9/11 assault upon our national security—and to justify an unnecessary war in Iraq.

First, Bush's aides suggested that Clarke had invented the meeting in which Clarke said the President pressured him to find a link between the 9/11 attack and Iraq, ignoring Clarke's insistence that intelligence agencies had concluded that no such link existed. But on Sunday, National Security Adviser Condoleezza Rice was forced to admit that Bush had pressed Clarke on an Iraq connection. This backed up earlier assertions by former Treasury Secretary Paul O'Neill as to Bush's obsession with Iraq from the very first days of his Administration, at the expense of focusing on Osama bin Laden and Al Qaeda.

That the Bush lies didn't work this time may be because too many veterans of the U.S. intelligence community are finding their voices and are willing to denounce an Administration that has seriously undermined the nation's security.

They are speaking out, as twenty-three former CIA and other defense intelligence agents did in Robert Greenwald's devastating documentary, *Uncovered*. They have stepped forward, as did David Kay, Bush's former chief weapons inspector in Iraq.

This is an Administration that has been dominated by the neoconservative ideologues who condemned the logical restraint of the first Bush Administration on foreign policy as a betrayal of the national interest.

These neocons have made a horrible mess of things, but that gives them no pause. They went to war with a nation that had no weapons of mass destruction and few connections to terrorism—but have coddled Pakistan, which sponsored the Taliban and Al Qaeda and which was recently revealed as the source of nuclear weapons technology for North Korea, Iran, and Libya.

The President's team is wrong to believe its outrageous lies can continue to lull a gullible public. Nixon's lies won him a second election, but then he lost the country.

Bush smiles better than Nixon, but when the lies are exposed, the smile turns into a character-revealing smirk. That happened last week when the White House released photos of a skit, performed for the amusement of jaded media heavyweights, in which the President pretended to look under his desk for the missing weapons of mass destruction. This may have amused his cynical audience, but to the general public, the carefully lip-synced policy pronouncements of the man who cried wolf have morphed into a sick joke.

❧

Drug War Led Bush Astray Before 9/11
April 13, 2004

WHY WON'T THEY JUST ADMIT THEY BLEW IT? IT IS LONG past time for the President and his national security team to concede that before the September 11 attacks they failed to grasp the seriousness of the Al Qaeda threat, were negligent in how they handled the terrorist group's key benefactors, and did not take the simple steps that might well have prevented the tragedy. While they are at it, they might also explain why, for more than two years, they have been trying so hard to convince us that none of the above is true.

Most recently, we learned that President Bush decided to stay on vacation for three more weeks despite receiving a briefing that told him about "patterns of suspicious activity in this country consistent with preparations for hijackings or other types of attacks" by Osama bin Laden's thugs, who were described as determined and capable enough to pull off devastating attacks on U.S. soil. We also now know that the Bush Administration coddled fundamentalist Saudi Arabia and nuclear-weapons-dealing Pakistan, the only nations that recognized the Taliban, both before and after the September 11 murders.

But what is perhaps even more astonishing is that, because the Bush Administration's attention was focused on the "war on drugs," it praised Afghanistan's Taliban regime even though it was harboring bin Laden and his terror camps. The Taliban refused to extradite the avowed terrorist even after he admitted responsibility for a series of deadly assaults against American diplomatic and military sites in Africa and the Middle East.

On May 15, 2001, I blasted the Bush Administration for rewarding the Taliban for "controlling" the opium crop with $43 million in U.S. aid to Afghanistan, to be distributed by an arm of the United Nations. Secretary of State Powell announced the gift, specifically mentioning the opium suppression as the rationale and assuring that the United States would "continue to look for ways to provide more assistance to the Afghans."

Five months before 9/11, I publicly challenged the wisdom of supporting a regime that backed Al Qaeda: "Never mind that Osama bin Laden still operates the leading anti-American terror operation from his base in Afghanistan, from which, among other crimes, he launched two bloody attacks on American embassies in Africa in 1998." I'm not clairvoyant, but I didn't need my own CIA to know that it's self-destructive to reward a regime that harbors the world's most dangerous terrorists.

After 9/11, the column was dug up by bloggers and widely distributed and debated on the Internet. Defenders of the Administration attacked it as a distortion, arguing that because the money was targeted as humanitarian aid, the United States was not actually helping the Taliban. Yet this specious distinction ignored the context of Powell's glowing remarks, and it failed to explain a similarly toned follow-up meeting on August 2, 2001, in Islamabad, Pakistan, which gave the Taliban similar kid-glove treatment. That meeting, held between Christina B. Rocca, Assistant Secretary of State for South Asia, and Abdul Salam Zaeef, the Taliban ambassador to Pakistan, took place four days before Bush received his now-infamous briefing on the imminent threat from Al Qaeda agents who were already in sleeper cells in this country, armed with explosives.

Yet Rocca said nothing to the Taliban's ambassador about Al Qaeda's continuing threat to kill Americans, ignoring the fact that the Taliban and Al Qaeda leaders were at that point inseparable, financially, militarily, and ideologically.

In her defense, Rocca did ask the Taliban representative to extradite bin Laden, for which she received nothing but bland disclaimers. "We gave Rocca our complete assurance," Zaeef told the local media, "that our soil will not be used against America, and that Afghan soil will not be used for any terrorist activity."

Zaeef was also pleased that Rocca again congratulated the Taliban for its success in eradicating the opium crop, calling the meeting "very successful" and "very cordial." And why should he not have been? As in May, the United States again was bringing not just words of encouragement but also a big cash prize.

"In recognition of the Taliban's elimination of opium, the raw material used to make heroin, the Bush Administration is giving $1.5 million to the United Nations Drug Control Program to finance crop substitution," reported the Associated Press.

Today, opium production in a tattered Afghanistan is at an all-time high, benefiting various warlords and a resurgent Taliban, while our money, troops, and attention are focused on a quagmire in Iraq, a nation that had nothing to do with 9/11, and is not known for its opium.

Go figure that out.

❧

With God on His Side
April 20, 2004

So it was a holy war, a new crusade. No wonder George W. Bush could lie to Congress and the American public with such impunity while keeping the key members of his Cabinet in the dark. He was serving a higher power, according to Bob Woodward, who interviewed the President for a new book on the months leading up to the Iraq invasion.

Of course, as a self-described "messenger" of God who was "praying for strength to do the Lord's will," Bush was not troubled about shredding a little secular document called the U.S. Constitution.

The Constitution reserves to Congress the authority to allocate funds and to declare war. Thus it would seem to be an impeachable offense to misappropriate $700 million that had been earmarked to restore order to Afghanistan and put it toward planning an invasion of Iraq—in a secret scheme hatched, according to Woodward, only seventy-two days after 9/11.

But not only has the President rejected the checks and balances installed by the nation's founders to avoid the "foreign entanglements" George Washington warned us about, he again is shown to have pursued a foreign policy that stands as a sharp rebuke to his more worldly and cautious father. During the first Gulf War, George H.W. Bush wisely heeded the concerns of Congress, as well as a broad coalition of regional and international allies, and kept to clear, limited, and sound goals.

In contrast, the younger Bush vocally disdains world opinion and international bodies like the United Nations, seeming instead to relish his role as an avenging Christian crusader who seeks—under the guiding hand of the Almighty—to cleanse the Arab world of "evildoers."

Asked by Woodward, an assistant managing editor at the *Washington Post*, if he had ever consulted the former President before ordering the invasion of Iraq, Bush replied that "he is the wrong father to appeal to in terms of strength; there is a higher father that I appeal to."

Reading the elder Bush's books and even his speeches before the latest Iraq war, one finds that the former President at least seems to understand that diplomacy, international cooperation, and patience are not just the tools of naïve do-gooders, but in fact are far more effective at advancing global stability and American aims than reckless adventures like the current quagmire in Mesopotamia. Religious crusades are often counterproductive; they tend to end up in unsustainable occupations of people who—surprise!—believe they have their own pipeline to the Almighty.

Thus, if George W. had consulted his father, he probably would have heard the message that he didn't want to hear from Secretary of State Colin Powell about the "Pottery Barn rule"—the idea that you own what you break. What Powell meant is not that you own Iraq's oil and the lucrative contracts that you parcel out to your friends at Halliburton and Bechtel. Rather, it is that if you occupy a failed state, you are stuck with the difficult, costly, and lengthy task of nation-building.

That Powell and the first President Bush did not break more forcefully with the current President over their apparent differences on Iraq is not excusable, despite their party and familial ties. As both men seem to have expected, what we have now is a deadly mess that has weakened us in the war on terror, both as a distraction and by inflaming the Muslim world's latent mistrust of the West.

After the bloodiest month of the entire war and occupation, we are told by the nation's media and political elites that we must "stay the course," "get it right," and, in the words of the President himself, "honor the fallen." How do we honor the fallen by sending more soldiers to die in a war based on lies now amply documented by insiders?

Surely the best way to honor them is to right our course and turn to the United Nations, not as a fig leaf to conceal an ongoing disaster but to admit that it was wrong to undermine the best mechanism we have for international cooperation. An honorable retreat from this calamity requires U.N. supervision of an orderly withdrawal.

The President conceded to Woodward that he had the good sense not to "justify war based upon God," but would ask for forgiveness if he took the wrong path. It is time he found God's grace in the exercise of humility rather than plunging deeper into this madness.

❧

Live with It, for Now
November 9, 2004

IT'S TIME TO GET OVER IT.

We've had our week of mourning, and there is no shame in losing a presidential election by .001 percent of the national electorate—the equivalent of 136,483 misguided Ohioans. More important, there is no room for a crippling depression on the part of Democrats while the nation remains in irresponsible hands for another four years.

The good news is that unless George W. Bush is hoping to provoke Armageddon, life will go on. In fact, there is another national election a mere two years from now. By then, some of the far right now chortling about the possibility of flat taxes, repealing *Roe vs. Wade,* and privatizing Social Security will have found that winning control of a nation on the skids isn't everything it's cracked up to be.

After all, at some point the Bush White House will have to stop blaming the Clinton Administration for its own mistakes. If the Republicans running all three branches of our government continue to pile up outrageous debt, shackle scientific progress with religious fundamentalism, erode civil liberties, and thrash about uselessly abroad, the responsibility will be all theirs.

The GOP has met its old bugaboo, incompetent Big Government, and it is them. No doubt Rush Limbaugh and friends will continue to blame us liberals for everything that goes wrong, but that old scapegoating game won't fly with the American public forever.

As we family-values folks like to tell our children when they qualify for their drivers' licenses, with power comes responsibility. "Watch where you're going" is the main advice I would offer the President, reminding him that during the last four years his steering has been erratic and his vision blurry. We don't need any more bloody wrecks like Iraq.

That John Kerry didn't make this case more clearly was the one glaring mistake of his campaign. But I don't want to get down on Kerry, an honorable and thoughtful man who eventually got around to making a strong critique of Bush's handling of Iraq. I don't think any candidate would have had a much easier time cutting through the pseudo-patriotic blather that Bush has exploited since the 9/11 tragedy.

The reality is that most Americans believe we are in an epic war that compares to those fought by generations past.

History tells us that sitting Presidents in those circumstances have something akin to political immunity. Bush also cynically put the tab for this war on the nation's credit card so he could buy votes among the wealthy with his regressive tax cuts—take voters who make more than $100,000 out of the equation and Kerry wins, according to CNN exit polls.

Seen in this light, the fact that the somewhat phlegmatic Kerry secured almost half the vote doesn't look so bad. And since when is it shocking news that an incumbent President can get away with massive lying during wartime? Or that bold strides forward for human rights, like the gay marriage initiatives, initially produce intolerant reactions?

Don't get me wrong: With an ideologically radical party in control of all three branches of government, the capacity for mischief—and misery—during the next few years is frightening. If Bush can place more ideologues like justices Antonin Scalia and Clarence Thomas on the Supreme Court, things could be very ugly. The religious hucksters who skirted the limits of federal law with partisan political proselytizing believe that they now own this President and will want changes— beginning with overturning *Roe vs. Wade*—in return.

But, as we've learned from science, for every action there is an equal and opposite reaction. Because exit polls showed that a solid majority of voters part ways with the religious right on choice and some form of legal recognition of same sex unions, victory on the social wedge issues will backfire on the Republicans. Abortion, for instance, may work as a divisive electoral strategy to energize the base, but party insiders know the GOP will suffer long-term damage if we return to the days of illegal, back-alley abortions. The same applies to attempts to wreck Social Security and other progressive programs, while driving up the deficit.

Barring another major terrorist attack of the sort that saved his first term, I would predict that in an amazingly short time Bush will be quacking like the lamest of ducks.

❧

1600 Pennsylvania Meets Madison Avenue
January 25, 2005

B Y NOW MANY COMMENTATORS, INCLUDING "REALIST" conservatives, seem to agree that President Bush's inaugural speech was radical, if not downright bizarre, in its insistence that the United States can and will deliver freedom to earth's more than six billion human residents. "If Bush means it literally, then it means we have an extremist in the White House," said Dimitri Simes, president of the Nixon Center.

What critics here and abroad are glossing over, however, is that as a political marketing device, Bush's address was absolutely brilliant. It takes a true demagogue to remorselessly cheapen the lovely word "freedom" by deploying it twenty-seven times in a twenty-one-minute speech, while never admitting that its real-life creation is more complicated than cranking out a batch of Pepsi-Cola and selling it to the natives with a catchy "Feeling Free!" jingle.

In Bush's neocon lexicon, the fight for freedom has been transmogrified from a noble, but complex and often elusive, historical struggle for human emancipation into a simplistic slogan draped over the stark contradictions and tragic failures of this Administration's foreign policy.

"America's vital interests and our deepest beliefs are now one," Bush intoned. Perhaps if we had been in a coma the last four years we could take that as a serious expression of ideal-ism in the vein of, say, Jimmy Carter.

But having seen in recent months how "America's vital interests" have sanctioned torture at Abu Ghraib and Guantanamo, war profiteering by Halliburton, and lies to the American people about the Iraqi threat, it is hard not to cyn-ically assume that "fighting for freedom" is just a new way to frame the same old hollow arguments.

It all sounds so simple coming out of Bush's mouth. In his feisty speech, two-thirds of which focused on spreading freedom abroad, there was not a single sentence that might actually tip us off as to when, where, and by what criteria our support for the international struggle for freedom will be manifested.

At her confirmation hearings last week, Secretary of State–designate Condoleezza Rice offered a little more infor-mation, naming six countries as "outposts of tyranny" that would get special attention from the U.S. in the next four years: Cuba, Myanmar, North Korea, Iran, Belarus, and Zimbabwe. But how was this unsavory sextet chosen—with a dartboard? She could just as easily have snapped off the names of six of our allies—Saudi Arabia, Pakistan, Russia, Kuwait, Uzbekistan, and Egypt—equally undemocratic, but which have arguably done more to increase the threat of global terrorism than Rice's squad of baddies.

The fact is, however, that when totalitarian nations like China and Saudi Arabia play ball with U.S. business interests, we like them just fine. But when Venezuela's freely elected President threatens powerful corporate interests, the Bush Administration treats him as an enemy.

A State Department spokesman has assured the world that the speech "doesn't mean we abandon our friends." But he added that "many of our friends realize it's time for them to change anyway." I guess that means we can expect Riyadh to allow women to drive any decade now.

Many questions remain. Because Bush said we would stand against all bullies, for example, it would follow that we should actively support the rebels in Chechnya against Bush's friend, autocrat Vladimir V. Putin. Before we do, however, we might want to recall the last time the United States overtly aided a rebellion in the Muslim world: the "freedom fighters" of Afghanistan, which included Osama bin Laden and other Islamic fanatics.

Speaking of which, what happened to the "war on terror"? Well, it appears that because he can't catch bin Laden or bring peace to Iraq or stability to Afghanistan, as repeatedly promised, the President has decided to turn his lemons into lemonade and parlay a difficult security issue into a moralistic crusade.

As the ad-men say, never confuse the thing being sold for the thing itself. Bush's passion for "freedom" extends only as far as it is useful as a political sales pitch.

❧

A New Storm on the Right
September 21, 2005

APPARENTLY, IT TOOK DIVINE INTERVENTION IN THE FORM of Hurricane Katrina to make George W. Bush, the compassionate conservative, aware of the existence of poor people in our midst.

"As we clear away the debris of a hurricane, let us also clear away the legacy of inequality," said a President who has not only overseen a nearly nine percent income decline for the poorest fifth of the nation's population, but won the job boasting of his record as Governor of a state that census figures show has the fifth-highest poverty level and highest percentage of citizens lacking medical insurance.

Unfortunately, the President still seems to believe that the severe poverty of New Orleans is an anomaly exposed by the storm, rather than a disturbing national reality he should have confronted long ago. One wishes he would take to heart the words Bishop T.D. Jakes of Dallas offered before Bush spoke at the National Cathedral on Friday: "Katrina, perhaps she has done something to this nation that we needed to have done. She has made us think, and look, and reach beyond the breach." He also noted: "We can no longer be a nation that overlooks the poor and the suffering and continues past the ghetto on our way to the Mardi Gras, or past Harlem for Manhattan, or past Compton for Rodeo Drive."

Of course, it should not have taken a devastating hurricane to reveal to our President the depth of human misery in a nation that could easily afford to have no poor people. Perhaps Bush simply hasn't fallen far enough from the tree, considering it was famously said of his father that he was a man who was born on third base and thought he hit a triple. His even more clueless mother thinks letting devastated African-American evacuees sleep in the Astrodome worked out "very well for them" because they "were underprivileged anyway."

One would have hoped that the avowedly "born again" younger Bush would have witnessed the disconnect between the teachings of the son of God, which repeatedly counsel aiding the poor and vulnerable, and his own family's "let them eat cake" approach to governance. After all, 37 million

Americans—13 million of them children—are living in poverty, 4.5 million more than when Bush was first inaugurated. This sad fact is never mentioned when the President trumpets the alleged benefits of his tax cuts for the rich.

"This is a matter of public policy," Bill Clinton said on Sunday, belatedly challenging the government's woeful response to the hurricane. "And whether it's race-based or not, if you give your tax cuts to the rich and hope everything works out all right, and poverty goes up and it disproportionately affects black and brown people, that's a consequence of the action made. That's what they did in the '80s; that's what they've done in this decade."

The man should know. After all, though he hardly solved the issue in downtrodden Arkansas or the country, poverty levels did significantly decline during his presidency (from 15.1 percent of the population in 1993 to 11.3 percent in 2000).

Bush may be getting the message that government is not the enemy. But forced by his worst political crisis to suggest that government has a major role to play in not only reconstructing the Gulf Coast, but also in confronting the reality of a patently unequal playing field, the President has angered "Reagan revolution" conservatives.

For example, conservative pundit George Will, frightened that Bush's promise to significantly assist the devastated Gulf Coast might unleash a new wave of social spending, rushed last week to assert the pervasive myth that this nation has a level playing field. Staying out of poverty is simple, he argued, if you just follow "three not-at-all recondite rules: . . . Graduate from high school, don't have a baby until you are married, don't marry while you are a teenager."

But do Will and his ilk really believe a child raised in foster homes and juvenile hall, or an eighty-five-year-old living on Social Security, can so simply pull themselves up by their bootstraps?

Sadly enough, it may be harder to get conservative journalists or politicians into the world of a junior high school kid in an impoverished neighborhood than to get a camel through the eye of a needle.

❧

The Big Lie Technique
November 16, 2005

AT A TIME WHEN APPROXIMATELY FIFTY-SEVEN PERCENT OF Americans polled believe that President Bush deceived them on the reasons for the war in Iraq, it does seem a bit redundant to deconstruct the President's recent speeches on that subject. Yet, to fail to do so would be to passively accept the Big Lie technique—which is how we as a nation got into this horrible mess in the first place.

The basic claim of the President's desperate and strident attack on the war's critics this past week is that he was acting as a consensus President when intelligence information left him no choice but to invade Iraq as a preventive action to deter a terrorist attack on America. This is flatly wrong.

His rationalization for attacking Iraq, once accepted uncritically by most in Congress and the media easily intimidated by jingoism, now is known to be false. The bipartisan 9/11 commission selected by Bush concluded unanimously that there was no link between Al Qaeda and Saddam Hussein's secular dictatorship, Al Qaeda's sworn enemy. And a recently declassified 2002 document proves that Bush's "evidence" for this, available to top Administration officials, was based on a single discredited witness.

Clearly on the defensive, Bush now sounds increasingly Nixonian, as he basically calls the majority of the country traitors for noticing he tricked us.

"Reasonable people can disagree about the conduct of the war, but it is irresponsible for Democrats to now claim that we misled them and the American people," the President said at an Air Force base in Alaska. "Leaders in my Administration and members of the United States Congress from both political parties looked at the same intelligence on Iraq, and reached the same conclusion: Saddam Hussein was a threat."

This is a manipulative distortion; saying Hussein was a threat—to somebody, somewhere, in some context—is not the same as endorsing a preemptive occupation of his country in a fantastically expensive and blatantly risky nation-building exercise. And the idea that individual Senators and members of Congress had the same access to even a fraction of the raw intelligence as the President of the United States is just a lie on its face—it is a simple matter of security clearances, which are not distributed equally.

It was enormously telling, in fact, that the only part of the Senate that did see the unsanitized National Intelligence Estimate on Iraq—the Republican-led Senate Select Intelligence Committee—shockingly voted in the fall of 2002 against the simple authorization of force demanded by a Republican President. Panicked, the warmongers in the White House and Pentagon pressured CIA Director George Tenet to rush release to the entire Hill a very short "summary" of the careful NIE, which made Hussein seem incalculably more dangerous than the whole report indicated.

The Defense Intelligence Agency finally declassified its investigative report, DITSUM No. 044-02, within recent days. This smoking-gun document proves the Bush Administration's key evidence for the apocryphal Osama bin Laden–Saddam Hussein alliance—said by Bush to involve training in the use of weapons of mass destruction—was built upon the testimony of a prisoner who, according to the DIA, was probably "intentionally misleading the debriefers."

Yet, despite the government having been informed of this by the Pentagon's intelligence agency in February 2002, Bush told the nation eight months later, on the eve of the Senate's vote to authorize the war, that "we've learned that Iraq has trained Al Qaeda members in bomb-making and poisons and gases."

The false Al Qaeda–Hussein link was the linchpin to Bush's argument that he could not delay the invasion until after the United Nations weapons inspectors completed their investigation in a matter of months. Perhaps he feared not that those weapons would fall into the wrong hands, but that they would not be found at all.

Boxed in by international sanctions, weapons inspectors, U.S. fighter jets patrolling two huge no-fly zones, and power-ful rivals on all his borders, Hussein in 2003 was decidedly not a threat to America. But the Bush White House wanted a war with Iraq, and it pulled out all the stops—references to "a mushroom cloud" and calling Hussein an "ally" of Al Qaeda—to convince the rest of us it was necessary.

The White House believed the ends (occupying Iraq) justified the means (exaggerating the threat). We know now those ends have proved disastrous.

Oblivious to the grim irony, Bush proclaims his war with-out end in Iraq the central front in a new Cold War, never acknowledging that he has handed Al Qaeda terrorists a new home base. Iran, his "axis of evil" member, now has its disciples in power in Iraq. Last week, top Bush Administration officials welcomed to Washington Iraq Deputy Prime Minister Ahmed Chalabi, who was previously denounced for having allegedly passed U.S. secrets to his old supporters in Tehran and was elected to a top post in Iraq by campaigning on anti-U.S. slogans.

Under Bush's watch, we not only suffered the September 11 terrorist attacks while he snoozed, but he has failed to capture the perpetrator of those attacks and has given Al Qaeda a powerful base in Iraq from which to terrorize. And this is the guy who dares tell his critics they are weakening our country.

෨

Terrorism's Elusive Refuge
January 18, 2006

WHAT'S UP WITH OSAMA BIN LADEN? REMEMBER WHEN capturing him "dead or alive" and eliminating his Afghanistan-based Al Qaeda, as President Bush promised, was what the war on terror was all about?

Instead, the President got distracted with his idiotic invasion of Iraq, where Al Qaeda had been effectively banned by Saddam Hussein, the secular dictator the United States deposed. Now we are left holding the bag in two desperate countries with bleak futures in which perpetrators of September 11 are reportedly thriving and guerrilla warfare and terrorist bombings have continued to increase.

"Al Qaeda is quickly changing, and we are not," Timothy

J. Roemer, a member of the bipartisan September 11 commission appointed by Bush, warned last month. "Al Qaeda is
highly dynamic, and we are not. Al Qaeda is highly imagina-
tive, and we are not."

Yet in his speeches, Bush clings to the notion that the
battle against terrorism is going well because, according to
his spin, we have been able to eliminate it in Afghanistan
and are now destroying the last vestiges of this scourge in
Iraq. On his visit to Kabul last month, Defense Secretary
Rumsfeld elaborated on this absurdity by declaring bloody,
backward Afghanistan as a "model" of progress in the war on
terrorism—even as he was admitting that "Iraq is several
years behind."

Rumsfeld's claim of progress was treated as ridiculous by
Afghan security officials interviewed by the BBC following
the Defense Secretary's visit. "We are very worried now," one
senior police official told the BBC. "The Taliban and Al
Qaeda are getting more threatening."

Last Sunday, U.S. sources claimed to have targeted
Osama's second-in-command with the bombing of a village
on the Pakistan side of the border with Afghanistan. But, as
is so often the case when applying air power to nonmilitary
targets, the corpses left in the debris of a devastated village
did not include the intended target. In the aftermath,
American flags were once again burning in the region as anti-
American protests swept Pakistan.

Meanwhile, next door in Afghanistan, a new rash of sui-
cide bombings—twenty-five in four months, according to the
Los Angeles Times—is providing evidence that Al Qaeda's old
partners in crime, the Taliban, are back with a vengeance.
Over the weekend, twenty civilians were murdered by a sui-
cide bomber, while a Canadian diplomat was killed in

another attack. This month is on pace to be the bloodiest the country has seen since the U.S. invasion.

NATO members, with troops operating out of Kabul, are balking at sending more; at least one, Holland, is considering pulling out altogether of a much-hyped occupation that seems to be accomplishing little.

"What happened to the new roads and irrigation canals, the jobs we were told about?" village elders plaintively inquired of a BBC correspondent.

Indeed, five years of "nation-building" has left Afghanistan a festering wound, with primitive warlords still dominant, an isolated capital with no control of the countryside, no national infrastructure, and a once-again booming opium trade the country's only economic bright spot.

"Of course we're growing poppy this year," one district chief told the BBC. "The government, the foreigners—they promised to help if we stopped. But where is it?"

This occupation is only the latest in centuries of cynical or, at best, ineffective meddling in Afghanistan. From the British to the Soviets to the Republicans, everybody has seen the place as useful to achieve ends that have nothing to do with making it a better place to live. As we once again draw down our economic commitment to Afghanistan's rebuilding from $1 billion to $600 million annually, it is clear the Bush team is hoping the country will once again recede from the global stage into unseen anarchy.

After our dramatic initial stab into Afghanistan following September 11, the Bush Administration has shown no willingness to do the heavy lifting required to make the country once again the functioning nation it was before Cold War games tore it apart. Rather, as with the rest of its policies, a token effort has merely been a cover for conning the

American public into believing Bush is effectively pursuing the war on terrorism.

Since most Americans could not find the country on a map, this deeply cynical approach will continue to work—at least until the next time a gang of marauders trained in the primitive badlands of Afghanistan and Pakistan and funded by our "allies" in Saudi Arabia launch another devastating attack on U.S. soil.

ROBERT SCHEER covered presidential politics for the *Los Angeles Times* for thirty years. He is the author of six books, including *With Enough Shovels: Reagan, Bush, and Nuclear War* and *America after Nixon: The Age of the Multinationals*; and coauthor of *The Five Biggest Lies Bush Told Us about Iraq.* He is a clinical professor of communications at the Annenberg School at the University of Southern California. Scheer is a nationally syndicated columnist, editor of Truthdig.com, a contributing editor of the *Nation*, and cohost of NPR-affiliate KCRW's *Left, Right, and Center.*

Tirstano, Pearl, 126, 127

Tomaszewski, Stanley, 85, 86, 89–90, 96

Tornadoes, 77
  Tri-State, of 1925, 99–118
  Waco, Texas, of 1953, 187–204

Tortorice, Sam, 129

Train wreck
  Nashville, of 1918, 53–66

Triczono, Jimmy, 8, 17

Tucker, Ben, 61

TWA Flight 266 Super Constellation or "Connie," 6

Tyler, Texas, 50

Unger, E. J., 141

United Flight 826 DC-8, crash of 1960, 1–21

United States Military commission, 172

Venice, Louisiana, 73, 75, 76, 80, 82

Virginia, 82

VOR navigation receivers, 5

Waco, Texas, 187–204

Waco News-Tribune, 187, 194

Waco Pirates, 193, 204

WACO (radio station), 190

Walter, Richard, 117

Washington (destroyer), 220

Waveland, Mississippi, 70, 76

Welansky, Barnett, 85, 97

Westbrook, Della, 41, 42, 43

Western Union, 151

West Frankfort, Illinois, 113–14

West Virginia, 82

West Virginia (ship), 174

White County, Illinois, 116

Williams, Robert, 51

Williams, Stan, 202

Wintringer, Nathan, 161, 166, 172

Wittmer, Carlos, 4

Wittmer, Olga, 4

Wollan, David, 6, 10–13

Woodvale, Pennsylvania, 144

World War I, 53, 55

World War II, 174–86

Wright, Adm. Carleton H., 185

Port Chicago, California, 174–96
Post, Patricia, 6
Powell, Dick, 210
Prewitt, R. E., 5
Princeton, Indiana, 117–18

Quinault Victory (ship), 179–82, 184

Ramierz, Beatrice, 197
Raymond, John, 123–26, 131
Redline (tanker), 183
Reems, Earl, 4
Reyes, Dimian, 8, 17
Reynolds County, Missouri, 105
Richwood, Charles, 145–46, 151
Richwood, Edith, 145–46, 151
Ringquist, Glen, 181
Roberts, Johnny, 45
Rogers, Roy, 97
Rosenthal, Leroy, 6, 12
Ruff, Benjamin, 139, 140
Ruffin, Geraldine, 44
Rusk County, Texas, 37, 38, 40–41
Russell, David, 193
Russell, Margaret, 193

St. Mary's Orphanage, 32
San Angelo, Texas, 190
Sanders, Glen, 51
Sanders, G. O., 51
Sanders, Vitra, 51
Sand Hallow, Pennsylvania, 151
San Francisco Bay, 174–86
Sarno, Joannie, 131
Sarno, Ronnie, 131
Sawyer, Capt. R. J., 5
Scheidt, Richard, 119
Schools
    Chicago fire, 119–36
    New London, Texas, explosion,
        37–52
Seraphica, Sister, 129–30, 135
Shaffer, Josiah L., 57, 64

Shafter, Benjamin, 211
Shafter, John, 211
Shafter, Neil D., 211
Shaw, Superintendent, 41–43
Sheffield, Wilbur, 84–85, 92–93
Sheridan Station, Pennsylvania, 151
Simpson, Dr. Robert, 82
Sinclair, 48
Skinner, George, 149
Skylark (escort ship), 214–7, 219
Smith, Henry, 145, 146
Smith, Isaac, 182
Smith, J. L., 148
Sokolsky, Alvin, 2, 4
Sokolsky, Ruth, 2, 10, 18
South Fork, Pennsylvania, 143
South Fork Dam, 138–43, 154–56
South Fork Fishing Club, 139–41,
        154–56
Speed, Capt. Frederic, 162, 172
Spikes, Dewitt, 170
Squalus (submarine), 213–14, 219–20
Stonycreek River, 138, 147
Stround, Helen, 51
Stround, Lama, 51
Styles, Stan, 192–93
Sullivan, Bobby, 86
Sultana (riverboat) explosion,
        157–73
Swenson, A. B., 6

Tate, Tracy, 50
Taylor, R. G., 161, 162
Texas, 68, 69
    Galveston hurricane of 1900,
        22–36, 68
    New London school explosion,
        37–52
    Waco tornado, 187–204
Texas Rangers, 48
Therese, Sister, 130
Thompson, J. D., 61
Thresher (submarine), 205–21

Lowenstien, Milton, 57, 64
Lucenay, Ted, 202

McCaddin, Henry, 7–8, 17–18
McClure, Luther, 51
McCord, Donald, 210
McEschern, Robert, 6
McLain, Willie, 198
McTerre, Rickel, 185
Madison County, Missouri, 105, 106
Magnuson, Richard, 6
Mahoney, Mary, 5
Marsden, Lee, 51
Marshall, Barbara, 210
Martinez family, 187–88
Mason, J. C., 161–68, 171–72
Matkin, Lillie, 197, 203
Meadows, Luther, 60
Mellon, 139
Memphis, Tennessee, 171
Miahelo (boat), 183
Miller, Doris, 174–75
Mineral Point, Pennsylvania, 143–44, 154
Mississippi, 68–82, 107
Mississippi Bridge, 72
Mississippi City, 80
Mississippi River, 73, 75, 157–73
Missouri, 100–104
Moals, Wayne, 191, 192
Mobile, Alabama, 80
Morgan's Raiders, 57
Morrelville, Pennsylvania, 151
Morris, Bernice, 44
Mullins, Cecil, 6
Murphysboro, Illinois, 109–11
Myers, Denny, 86

Nashville, Tennessee, 53–66, 157
Nashville Banner, 63
National Guard, 81
National Hurricane Center, 82

National Weather Service, 68, 81–82, 100, 190
Natural gas, raw or "green," 40–41
Nettles, Willie, 182
New London, Texas, 37–52
New Orleans, Louisiana, 72–73
Newsweek, 80
New York City, 119
    airplane collision of 1960, 1–21
New York Sun, 147
Norris, Robert, 51

Ogle, Harriet, 151
Ognibene, Father Joseph, 129
O'Neil, John, 89, 95
Operisano, John, 7, 16
Our Lady of the Angels (OLA) Elementary School, 119–36
Overton, Texas, 48, 50

Parke, John, 140–42, 154
Parks, Beverly, 4
Parrish, Illinois, 115–16
Pascagoula, 81
Pass Christian, Mississippi, 71, 72, 75–80, 82
Paul, Gerard, 9, 14
Paul, Peter, 9, 14
Pauline Caroll (riverboat), 162
Paulson, Jennie, 145
Payne, Billy, 84, 85–86, 93, 95
Pearl Harbor attack, 174
Pennsylvania, 137–56
Pennsylvania Railroad, 139, 145
Pensacola, Florida, 80
Peralta, Jerry, 72
Permit (submarine), 214
Perry County, Missouri, 105–7
Peters, Evelyn, 44
Petersen, Maude, 9, 13
Phillips, C. D., 59
Piecing, R. W., 5
Plunger (submarine), 214

Goss, Capt. Nelson, 175–77, 181, 185

Gray, Mrs. Homer, 42, 50

Griffin, Indiana, 116

Guerra, Simon, 195–96

Gulfport, Mississippi, 80

Hall, George, 57

Hamilton County, Illinois, 116

Hardy, George, 46

Harper, 139

Harris, Milton, 44

Harrisburg Telegraph, 155

Harvey, Lt. Comm. John W., 208–9, 211–12, 214, 220

Harvey, Manning, 209, 220

Haskins, John, 185

Hecker, Commander, 216, 217, 219

Henderson, Texas, 48, 50

Hess, John, 143, 144–45

Hill, Cluster, 182

Hillary, Sir Edmund, 1–2, 20

Hitler, Adolf, 51

Holy Cross Crusaders, 83, 84, 86, 89

Honeycutt, Truman, 51

Huacos Indians, 188

Hudkins, Evelyn, 45

Hughes, Leroy, 182

Humble Oil Company, 43, 47, 48

Hund, Father, 131

Hurricane Audrey, 68

Hurricanes, 99
  Betsy, 68
  Camille, 67–82
  Galveston, of 1900, 22–36

Hurst, Illinois, 112–13

Illinois, 107–16

Indiana, 116–18

International-Great Northern Railroad, 48

Interstate Commerce Commission, 65

Iron County, Missouri, 105

Isaac's Storm (Larson), 31

Jackson, Lawrence, 182

James River, 82

Johnson, Barbara, 200

Johnson, Gabe, 182

Johnson, J. S., 59

Johnstown, Pennsylvania, 137–56

Joiner, C. J., 37, 38

Jones, Buck, 85–89, 93, 94, 96, 97

Jordan, Jerry, 195

Kamin, Charlie, 133, 134

Karnes family, 115

Kayton, George, 167, 168

Keller, Pat, 5, 15

Kelley, John, 54, 55, 58

Kennedy, David "Uncle Dave," 54–56, 58–62, 64–65

Kennedy, John F., 7, 219, 220

Kilgore, Texas, 48

King, Walter, 117

King, William, 117

Kirsk (submarine), 206

Klier, Billy, 210

Klier, Billy, Jr., 210

Knoch, William, 57

Knox, 139

Kock, Henry, 149

Lake Pontchartrain, 70, 72–73

Lane, Susie, 201–2

La Riviere, Milton, 2, 10, 18

La Riviere, Peggy, 2, 4

Larson, Erik, 31

Leadanna, Missouri, 104, 105

Lee, Robert E., 157

Lewis, Wallace E., 8, 16

Lincoln, Abraham, 160, 173

Long Beach, Mississippi, 80

Louisiana, 69–72